DEFYING THE ODDS

DEFYING THE ODDS

Banking for the Poor

Eugene Versluysen

KUMARIAN PRESS

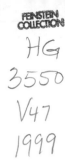
Defying the Odds: Banking for the Poor

Published 1999 in the United States of America by Kumarian Press, Inc.,
14 Oakwood Avenue, West Hartford, Connecticut 06119-2127 USA.

Production and design by The Sarov Press, Stratford, Connecticut.
Index by Linda Webster.
The text of this book is set in Adobe Sabon.

Printed in Canada on acid-free paper by
Transcontinental Printing and Graphics, Inc.
Text printed with vegetable oil-based ink.

∞ The paper used in this publication meets the minimum requirements
of the American National Standard for Information Sciences—Permanence of
Paper for Printed Library Materials, ANSI Z39.48–1984.

Library of Congress Cataloging-in-Publication Data
Versluysen, Eugene.
    Defying the odds : banking for the poor / Eugene Versluysen.
      p.   cm.
    Includes bibliographical references and index.
    ISBN 1–56549–094–0 (cloth : alk. paper). — ISBN 1–56549–093–2
(pbk. : alk. paper)
    1. Banks and banking—Developing countries. 2. Credit—Developing
countries. 3. Small business—Developing countries—Finance. 4. Poor—
Developing countries.   5. Economic development. I. Title. II. Title:
Banking for the poor.
HG3550.V47 1999
332.1'09172'4—dc21   98–55379

03 02 01 00 99   5 4 3 2 1   First Printing 1999

CONTENTS

For my son, Philippe

ACKNOWLEDGMENTS

I would like to express my thanks to the women and men, in villages and small towns in far-flung places, who inspired me to write this book. They were generous with their time and made every effort to make me feel welcome, sharing their lives with me, even if only briefly. I particularly remember Nelida Palomino, Irma Manrique and their friends in the Santa Teresita and Santa Angela "mothers' clubs" in the slums of Lima, who are dedicating their lives to help their neighbors defy hardship and regain their dignity. From them I have learnt that poverty need not be debasing and that self-reliance brings self-esteem. They, and countless others, have made me look at life differently and be more humble

I am also indebted to many people in microfinance institutions who made my research possible. Thus I wish to express my appreciation to: Tazemul Haque, Provash Das and Shek Abusayeed of the Grameen Bank for their exceptional hospitality, and for their unfailing dedication to working with "the poorest of the poor"; Pancho Otero, Ximena Schmidt and many others in BancoSol for telling me that lending to microentrepreneurs and making profits need not be mutually exclusive; Fatchudin and the members of the International Visitor Program of Bank Rakyat Indonesia for their generous welcome in Java and Sumatra, and for demonstrating that it is often wiser to save than to pile up debts; Paul Rippey of PRIDE in Conakry for his ebullient optimism, and for his commitment to microfinance in Africa; Lynn Paterson of Pro Mujer for introducing me to the women of "El Alto" in La Paz; and the managers and staff of the Municipal Savings Banks in Piura, Sullana, and Paita for their hospitality, and for the time they spent taking me to visit their clients in northern Peru.

Last but not least, I owe a big thank you to two people. To my wife, Jane Cave, for her insightful comments on early drafts of the most difficult chapters, and for being so patient during the many evenings when I spent far too much time at my laptop. To Linda Beyus of Kumarian Press, whose unfailing enthusiasm for this project boosted my morale when it was sagging, encouraging me to go the last mile. Without them this book would most likely not have seen the light of day.

INTRODUCTION

This book is about the poor and the specialized financial institutions that work with people who have no access to commercial banks. It is based on what I have learned during the time I spent with the clients and staff of selected microfinance institutions in South and East Asia, West Africa, and Latin America.

In writing this book I have four objectives in mind. The first, which is also the unifying theme of the book, is to draw the linkages between the rise of self-employment and informal activities, and the budget cuts and structural reforms which developing countries had to adopt to deal with the aftermath of external shocks and misguided economic policies. What makes this theme pivotal is that, in country after country, free-market policies, fiscal austerity, and cuts in programs for the needy have widened income inequality, and caused massive job losses and poverty. These are "the odds."

My second objective is to show how, by financing income-generating activities, "banking for the poor" can stave off some of the effects of economic programs and policies that push or trap people in destitution, at the margin of society. Instead of handouts that perpetuate passivity and dependency, small loans for self-employment can help fight poverty and marginalization. They make people self-reliant, build their confidence, and empower those who are excluded from the mainstream of society. Encouraging self-reliance is also more cost-effective and equitable than the anti-poverty programs of international development agencies that take charge of people (and countries), tell them what is best for them, and usually bypass the neediest. Banking for the poor has become one of the central tenets of a new paradigm of socially oriented development. Much of its focus is on women and indigenous communities, whose needs are mostly ignored by conventional poverty-reduction strategies.

My third objective is to stress the importance of blending savings with credit. If impoverished households have sufficient incentives to save, even if only a few cents at a time, they can begin accumulating working capital and build up a safety cushion for emergencies. The truth is that saving is *always* better than having debts. But for the majority of people in the informal sector that is a moot point, since they can only begin to save after receiving a loan to start a small business.

My fourth objective is to do a comparative analysis of microfinance programs that are leaders in their field, and illustrate their successes, as well as their shortcomings. I have chosen the five country case studies that are presented in the book on the basis of the role and place of microfinance in those countries, and to illustrate the contrasts between institutions that already have several million clients, and others that are shoe-string operations. In selecting institutions for these case studies, inevitable time constraints and a finite research budget forced me to make difficult choices. Thus, my all too limited coverage of the Bangladesh Rural Advancement Committee (BRAC) and Thailand's Bank for Agriculture and Agricultural Cooperatives (BAAC), to name but two, does not, in any way, imply that they are less worthy than microfinance institutions to which I have given more ample coverage.

As the case studies will show, microfinance is shaped by the geographic, economic, social, and cultural environment in which it operates, and its success and social impact depend on adapting financial services to people's needs. Between them, the four largest programs, all in Asia, already have more than nine million clients. They and others have created and expanded opportunities for income-generating activities by people who did not have jobs or access to credit. They have shown that the "unbankable" poor are credit worthy and that most of them use small loans productively. A landless woman who borrows a few dollars to buy chickens or a couple of goats can usually earn enough from selling eggs or milk to supplement her family's income, clothe her children, and still have enough money left over to repay her loan and save a little. In Bangladesh I even met "landless" women who had managed to save enough to buy small parcels of land.

But the benefits of self-reliance go deeper. Nutrition and hygiene standards usually improve in the households of women who belong to microfinance programs, and women who are given the opportunity to work independently gain a greater say in family affairs, are less likely to be abused, have fewer children, and become examples for others. This is particularly important in societies where the status of women is defined in terms of their reproductive role, and where they are treated as inferiors.

The book is divided into five parts.

Part I sketches the *political economy of microfinance*. It consists of three chapters. *Chapter 1* develops the central theme of the book. The argument follows two lines. The first is that poverty is not created by the poor. It is the product of social, economic, and cultural factors that reinforce class and ethnic divisions, and gender discrimination. The second is that the intervention of multilateral agencies, to restore economic order in developing countries and make them adjust to the demands of the global economy, has had perverse distributional effects—job losses, widening income disparities, and, quite often, mass impoverishment. The result is that, instead of "trickle down," there has been growth without development, and that the most vulnerable people—women, children, and indigenous communities—have made great sacrifices, to no avail.

Chapter 2 documents the emergence of informal, family-run businesses in countries where there are too few jobs for the unemployed, let alone for the new entrants in the labor market. Small, unregulated businesses, which were among the earliest forms of organized economic activity, make up a huge, unregulated, parallel economy in cities, townships, and villages in Africa, Asia, and Latin America. In some countries the parallel economy is the sole source of work and income for two out of every three economically active people, and the informal sector is expanding faster than the rest of the economy. But, even though self-employment raises income and improves living conditions in poor households, and can lift some people out of poverty, it is not a panacea. Self-employment cannot eradicate poverty by itself, or become a catalyst for sustained economic growth and development. One of the reasons for this is the inherent limitation of small-scale production by artisans, which generates no economies of scale, uses rudimentary technology, and cannot compete with machine-made goods.

Chapter 3 offers an overview of the evolution of microenterprise financing, from small self-help groups and moneylenders, to specialized microfinance institutions that can accommodate the financing needs of urban and rural microentrepreneurs. As the discussion points out, microfinance on a large scale is still a relatively new phenomenon, especially in rural areas. To be accepted and overcome the reticence of farmers and villagers who are inherently reluctant to experiment with new ideas, microfinance must blend into village culture and adapt its services to local needs and customs.

Parts II through IV are the core of the book. They review the activities, successes, failures, and impact of microfinance programs in selected countries in Asia, Africa, and Latin America. Each country chapter begins with a survey of the economy and society, and revisits the central theme of the book in reviewing the extent (and causes) of poverty, and the size of the informal sector in each country.

Part II is devoted to microfinance in two Asian countries: Bangladesh, one of the world's poorest and most densely populated countries, and Indonesia, a (former) "tiger economy." The contrasting social and economic conditions in these two countries are reflected in the activities of their leading microfinance programs. But there is also a common thread that sets microfinance programs in these countries apart from those in other regions: they work in densely populated areas, have large numbers of borrowers, and they are financially sustainable.

Bangladesh is the birthplace of the Grameen Bank. Its founder and managing director, Muhammad Yunus, is one of the pioneers of modern microfinance. Among Grameen's many achievements, the one that stands out most is that its small loans to landless women are catalysts for change in a country where religious conformism and cultural norms exclude women from the public domain. BRAC, which also lends to some of the poorest women, takes women's empowerment even further, by giving them the tools to defend their constitutional rights, and by financing education and health programs.

The Indonesia chapter documents the rise and fall of economic prosperity in this country where, until the middle of 1997, there was sustained growth and a decline in absolute poverty. Now, amidst a deep financial crisis that is still engulfing East Asia, joblessness and informality are rising rapidly, and it is estimated that eighty million Indonesians are living in poverty. The increasing militancy of the poor has unleashed a groundswell of protest against the effects of globalization. The rest of the chapter is devoted to the activities of Bank Rakyat Indonesia (BRI), which has a nationwide network of village banking units, and is, by far, the world's largest microfinance program.

Part III is devoted to microfinance in Latin America, a region where many countries amassed huge loans from foreign banks during the 1970s. They were trapped in a protracted debt crisis after Mexico declared a moratorium on the service of its external debt in 1982. Cut off from external funding, they sought financial support from the International Monetary Fund (IMF) and the World Bank. The ensuing fiscal retrenchment and adjustment process was so severe that the 1980s became Latin America's "lost decade" during which informal activities grew exponentially. The resulting demand for credit explains why microfinance is highly developed in this region.

The two country chapters of Part III trace the evolution of microfinance in Bolivia and Peru, two countries where informality and poverty rose sharply after 1982. BancoSol in Bolivia, and the Municipal Savings and Credit Banks in Peru, dominate microfinance in Latin America. Of the two, BancoSol is, by far, the more interesting. Until 1997, it was the only private commercial bank working solely with microentrepreneurs, and it has more clients than all the other banks in Bolivia combined.

Both countries also have NGOs that lend to indigenous women. The two that stand out are Pro Mujer in Bolivia, and CARE Peru. They are examples of what grassroots organization and participation can achieve in even the most deprived communities. In Lima, for instance, with the support of CARE, women from the city's worst slums have organized "mothers' clubs" and communal kitchens that sell cheap, nourishing meals to women and children in their neighborhoods. What makes these self-help clubs special is that they pool their small profits in rotating loan funds, from which members can borrow to start their own businesses.

Part IV reviews recent trends in microfinance in West Africa. It highlights the challenges of working in countries where extreme rural poverty, high rates of illiteracy, and the dismal state of rural infrastructure make it extremely difficult to reach a critical mass of clients. Programs with more than 10,000 clients are rarities in this part of the world.

There is only one country chapter in Part IV. It deals with Guinea, whose leading microfinance institution, PRIDE, was launched with a grant from USAID. PRIDE has adopted Grameen's group lending and puts a strong emphasis on client training and institutional capacity building.

Part V consist of a single chapter that concludes the book. It describes how the success of microfinance in developing countries has helped reorient the lending philosophies and poverty focus of multilateral and bilateral agencies. It also shows how self-reliance as a way out of aid dependency is already being used to fight poverty and unemployment in the inner cities of North America, at a time when welfare reform is eliminating many social benefits. The chapter goes on to draw the broader lessons from this multi-country comparative study of microfinance.

Eugene Versluysen
Washington, D.C.

Part 1

The Political Economy
of Microfinance

On the eve of the third millennium the world has more accumulated wealth, resources, and know-how than ever before. Yet more than one billion women, children, and men live in absolute poverty. They are trapped in "a condition of life so degraded by disease, illiteracy, malnutrition, and squalor, as to deny its victims basic human necessities." [1]

This does not mean that poverty is created by the poor. On the contrary, a combination of social, cultural, and economic factors traps them in an unbreakable vicious circle. These include overpopulation, gender and ethnic bias, corruption, and bad governance. The level of poverty in different countries is also influenced by changes and upheavals in the global economy, and by the unprecedented mobility of capital.

Since the causes of poverty are so complex and intractable, there is an innate belief that the economically and socially disenfranchised can do nothing about their destinies. The prevailing orthodoxy is that the task of alleviating their plight should be delegated to omniscient development agencies, and that the "invisible hand" of free markets serves the common good by guiding economic decisions that bring benefits to all. The results are disheartening, to say the least. Despite countless billions of dollars in development aid, many countries do not even have basic safety nets for the sick and the elderly. Meanwhile, the gap between rich and poor countries—and people—continues to widen and destitution and unemployment remain widespread, even in countries that have achieved strong growth. The shameful truth is that today, in 1998, 80 percent of the world's inhabitants earn less than 20 percent of the world's income.[2]

For lack of other means, the poor and those who cannot find jobs are increasingly resorting to self-employment in order to survive. Their small businesses have grown into a huge parallel economy that is altering the social geography of cities, towns, and villages in developing countries. The growing role of self-employment and the fact that the poor are considered "unbankable" has also given rise to a new generation of financial intermediaries that are willing to work with the poor and self-employed. Their activities are premised on the intrinsic belief that small loans for income-generating activities can help pave the way out of poverty, and that lending to the poor can be self-sustaining and profitable. The advocacy of self-help as a way out of poverty differs radically from the approach of conventional welfare programs, which do things *for* people and frequently engender passivity and dependence. It also challenges the doctrine of the multilateral development agencies that see themselves as agents of change, and take charge of people—and countries— and tell them what they need.[3]

To see how self-employment and special credit programs can offset *some* aspects of poverty, one must estimate the odds of succeeding in this way, and assess how people in developing countries are affected by free-market policies and the integration of their countries into the global economy. These themes are developed in Chapter 1 and are revisited in later chapters, in the context of individual country studies. Chapter 2 analyzes the dynamic of self-employment and discusses the social, legal, and economic obstacles people face when working in the informal sector. Chapter 3 shows how people who have no access to loans from commercial banks finance their businesses. The central theme of this chapter is that microfinance is shaped by the social, economic, political, and physical environment in which it functions. While virtually all microfinance programs focus on self-help, there are fundamental differences in their business philosophies. The most focused programs lend only to the poorest who have no experience of independent work. They do poverty lending, and work mostly with women. Other programs have no specific target groups, do not aim to reduce absolute poverty, and lend primarily to the middle tier of the poor—people whose income puts them above the level of absolute poverty and who are already self-employed.

1

Poverty Is Not Created by the Poor[4]

Everyone has a right to a standard of living adequate for the health and well-being of himself and his family, including food, clothing, housing and medical care and necessary social services.[5]

Being poor means having no assets, no job, and too few means to support oneself and one's family. The easiest way to measure poverty is to relate people's income to a baseline: the subsistence level, or poverty line. People whose income is below the baseline are poor. Among the poor, the absolutely poor are those who earn less than one US dollar a day. They generally suffer from calorie deficiency. Economists use income and consumption data from household surveys and interviews to determine who is poor. To make international comparisons possible and relevant, estimates of subsistence-level income are corrected for purchasing-power parity. An easier, but less reliable, way to measure living standards is to use the quality of a household's housing as a proxy for income, or to ask village or community leaders which are the people they consider to be poor. For example, Crédit Rural de Guinée relies on the judgment of village chiefs to identify the poorest villagers and select its clients.

The Vicious Circle of Poverty

The face of poverty and hunger is the same the world over. In poor countries people often greet each other by asking, "Have you already eaten?" More often than not the answer is "Not yet, how about you?" The World Food Summit of the Food and Agricultural Organization (FAO), which met in Rome in November 1996, considered it "Intolerable that more than 800 million people throughout the world, and particularly in developing countries, do not have enough food to meet their basic nutritional needs." Delegates at the summit unanimously resolved to *halve the number of hungry people to 400 million* by the year 2015.[6] By any reckoning, accepting that 400 million people will still be suffering from hunger in the next millennium is an admission of defeat.

Moreover, judging by past experience, the actual number of people who will go hungry in 2015 is likely to be much larger.

Being malnourished means bearing children who are underweight at birth and who, if they manage to live past their first birthday, will remain prone to sickness and infection—even moderately undernourished children are more likely to fall ill and die than well-fed children.[7] In poor families bad health, chronic vitamin deficiency, frequent illnesses, high infant mortality, and birthing-related injuries are inescapable facts of life. There is also a high incidence of pregnancy-related deaths among the poorest—every year more than a half million women in developing countries die from causes related to childbirth or pregnancy.[8] But, if the poor fall ill, access to doctors and health posts is scarce. In Guinea and Senegal, for instance, fewer than 50 percent of the people have access to formal health care.

Rural poverty is as debilitating as urban poverty, but less stigmatizing. In most villages in developing countries all but a few landowning families are poor, and differences in social status are minimal. In cities social distinctions are greater, the contrast between the living conditions of the rich and the poor is brutal, and people who have money have become adept at shutting out the world around them. Beggars, the disabled, and the street children who dart barefoot through traffic, washing windshields with squeegee bottles, or performing acrobatic tricks in the hope of receiving a few pennies, are ignored. If the poor become too "pushy" the non-poor sometimes take extreme precautions. The richest people have bodyguards. Those who cannot afford personal guards use cruder methods. A few years ago, while riding in a taxi in Lima, I was aghast when I noticed that the driver was holding a high-voltage stun-gun at the ready whenever we stopped in traffic, just in case.

Most of the world's poor live in the least-developed countries of sub-Saharan Africa, South and East Asia, parts of Latin America, and the Pacific islands.[9] They are trapped in a vicious circle that was first conceptualized by the Norwegian economist, Ragnar Nurske: low income means too little savings, and low investment and capital accumulation. The ensuing lack of technology and low productivity causes low income and results in chronic, self-perpetuating underdevelopment.[10]

The vicious circle starts with class and caste divisions, gender bias, and discrimination against indigenous people and minorities. In many a country patriarchal social systems and religious conservatism stress women's reproductive role and exclude them from the public sphere. Almost everywhere women and children, especially girls, are more likely to be deprived than men: more than two-thirds of the people who live in absolute poverty are women.[11] One of the reasons for this is that women's multiple responsibilities, as mothers, homemakers, and breadwinners, expose them to greater hardship than men. In villages in poor countries, women's customary domestic duties and responsibilities include gathering firewood for cooking and fetching water from distant wells, often several times a day, yet they have unequal access to education—in India, for instance, villagers believe that educating girls is wasteful and as rash as watering a neighbor's garden. Women also become the sole breadwinners when men lose their jobs. In subsistence farms they have the added burdens of raising small livestock and chickens, and processing and selling surplus farm products.

People are poor because they have no productive assets, especially land. Peasant farmers and sharecroppers rarely have land or title to their homesteads, and land ownership becomes increasingly concentrated when smallholders cannot pay their debts and lose their land to creditors. In households headed by women, women's limited property and inheritance rights make ownership and access to land even more unlikely. Uncertainty over property and tenancy rights means that big landowners can treat peasant farmers as squatters. The risk of eviction, the lack of education, and primitive tools and farming techniques thus result in low crop yields that perpetuate rural poverty. Such conditions encourage able-bodied young men and women to migrate to cities, in search of jobs and a better life. Rural migration often leaves villages virtually devoid of men of working age, destroys communities, and leaves women behind, as heads of households that consist mostly of elderly people and children.

Land reform and redistribution can be powerful tools to reduce rural poverty and slow down rural migration. But, because they threaten the power and endowment of elites and landowners who control political and economic power, these measures invariably face strong opposition. The elites—be they landowners, members of higher castes, businessmen, high-ranking government officials, or army officers—are always loath to accept changes that undermine their social and economic status. Equity and poverty reduction seldom feature among their preoccupations, unless social discontent threatens to cause political upheaval.

The "Cancer of Corruption"

Corruption is the use of public office and political power for private gain. It is endemic in many countries, particularly—but not only—in the developing world (one only needs to look at Italy and Japan to realize that developing countries have no monopoly on corruption).

In the lower ranks of the public sector in low-income countries, pitifully low wages that are barely at the subsistence level are strong incentives to extract bribes at any opportunity. Customs officials, police officers, and other petty officials routinely use their positions to extort money from people who need their services. For instance, in many parts of Africa the police routinely set up roadblocks on highways, stopping all vehicles to demand baksheesh from divers and passengers. People grudgingly do so because refusal to pay usually has unpleasant consequences.

On the whole, small payoffs that grease the wheels of petty officialdom are little more than an inconvenience. They raise the cost of doing business, but their overall effect on the economy is fairly minimal. Corruption by high-ranking officials is on a much larger scale, and much more damaging. This happens in countries where venal dictators use nepotism and political patronage to enrich themselves, and their relatives and cronies. When corruption amounts to outright theft of state funds, it becomes a drag on development, and the greed of dishonest officials perpetuates hardship and poverty for the masses. In extreme cases, such as the kleptocracies of the late presidents Duvalier, Mobutu, and Marcos, and Suharto's crony capitalism, "corruption disintegrates the social fabric, perverts culture and strengthens illegality and clientelism."[12] Corruption at the top also engenders a collective mentality that gives some legitimacy to the shady behavior of petty officials. This is the case, for instance, in Latin American countries where drug money is suborning the entire political apparatus. Put more generally, venality on a large scale not only diverts resources from the poor to the rich, it distorts public expenditures, deters foreign investors, and becomes an obstacle to fair and sound development.[13]

One of the factors that creates opportunities for corruption is that the first point of contact of foreign aid and development lending is with government officials, local businessmen, foreign contractors, suppliers, and consultants. When contract awards involve large payoffs to corrupt government officials, projects that should have been earmarked for infrastructure development and poverty reduction serve instead to "fatten the elite."[14] The lack of accountability of government bureaucracies, bad governance, and the inefficient use of public resources compound the harmful effects of venality. They are barriers to economic development which perpetuate poverty.

Development Lending and Structural Adjustment

A 1996 study on poverty by the World Bank states that "The primary responsibility for fighting poverty lies with the governments and people of the developing countries themselves. Institutions such as the World Bank have an important supporting role to play in providing information, analysis, and finance, and by working in partnership with others to coordinate international action to reduce poverty."[15] But despite their public commitment to reduce poverty, multilateral and bilateral development agencies have done too little to promote good governance and force governments to eradicate corruption and pursue equitable development. In fact, development lending frequently has the opposite effect, making the rich richer, and the poor poorer. Inequality of income is also accentuated by spatial inequality of access to services between low-income and high-income areas, which hinders the development potential of inner cities and shantytowns.

Commenting on the plight of sub-Saharan Africa—where more than half of the population lives in absolute poverty, and where poverty is projected to go on increasing into the next millennium—the World Bank's president stated (in March 1996) that "Money has not historically been the problem (in foreign aid to Africa), the issue is how we spend the money."[16]

What is at issue for this discussion is that the way in which the World Bank spends its money underwent a sea change in the early 1980s, with the introduction of structural-adjustment lending. Until then its main activity had been project lending, which financed investment in industry, agriculture, and infrastructure. To ensure that the funds are spent as stipulated, project loans are disbursed to the suppliers and contractors who are executing a project, not to the government of the country that is borrowing and in which the project is located. For major projects—such as airports, highways, and dams—that take a long time to complete, disbursements are spread over several years.

Structural-adjustment lending is different. It evolved in response to up-heavals in the world economy during the 1970s and 80s. Its purpose was to help countries adopt structural reforms and adjust to the changing economic environment, by providing financing during the adjustment period. This meant that adjustment loans had to be fast-disbursing, and that the funds had to go directly to governments—not to contractors—as soon as they implemented the policy changes and reforms that were part of the loans' conditions. A critical factor is that adjustment lending involves a loss of sovereignty: in return for structural-adjustment finance a government effectively surrenders control over its monetary and fiscal policies to a multilateral agency.

The Roots of Structural Adjustment

The roots of adjustment lending lay in the early 1970s, when OPEC qua-drupled the price of crude oil. OPEC's move left the world's major banks awash with dollar deposits from cash-rich Saudi Arabia and other Middle Eastern oil exporters. This influx of liquidity was a mixed blessing at a time when the investment and credit needs of the banks' corporate clients in Eu-rope and America were plummeting during the recession that followed the oil-price shock. To put their excess funds to productive use, the banks had to find new clients in other parts of the world, and they began offering loans to developing countries. As soon as some countries showed interest, the banks began recycling huge amounts of "petrodollars" in loans to them. The banks also pooled their resources, forming large "syndicates" to leverage their lend-ing power, share risks, and make bigger loans. Because the banks assumed that countries, as sovereign entities, could not and would not go bankrupt, lending to them was regarded as risk-free business. It did not matter how or for what purposes the money was used, as long as the loans had uncondi-tional government guarantees.

In the topsy-turvy environment of the late 1970s, when the real, inflation-adjusted cost of borrowing abroad became absurdly low—it fell to as little as *minus* 5 percent[17]—the lure of what looked like free money made countries amass hundreds of billions of US dollars in foreign loans. Mexico, Venezuela, Nigeria, and other oil exporters began mortgaging their future oil revenues, while oil importers used cheap funds to defer making the necessary changes to adapt their economies to higher energy costs. Access to large amounts of cheap money also made it possible for the economies of the borrowing countries to continue growing at a time when the United States, Europe, and Japan were caught in a deep recession.

Even so, accepting large loans was fraught with dangers. The influx of US dollars made the currencies of the borrowing countries appreciate. This resulted in price distortions that made their exports uncompetitive and encouraged import-oriented policies. By the end of the 1970s, trade deficits had reached unsustainable levels in all but a few oil-exporting countries. What made matters worse still was that, instead of using foreign loans to build new industries, create jobs, and invest in social infrastructure—schools, low-income housing, health centers, and sewage systems—most governments had used the loans to shore up their budgets. Many squandered the rest of the money on extravagant projects of limited economic value—grandiose palaces, monuments, and expensive weapons among them—and to line the pockets of corrupt officials.

As the 1970s drew to a close, abrupt changes in the international economy put an end to cheap money and free-wheeling lending, and caused severe problems for the countries that had borrowed beyond their means and for the wrong reasons. The watershed was OPEC's decision, in 1979-80, to raise the price of crude oil again. Although the initial effects were positive for oil exporters, for the rest of the world the second oil-price shock was even more damaging than the first one. Higher oil prices further eroded the terms of trade of already weakened oil-importing countries and precipitated a new recession in industrial countries. In countries that produce and export primary commodities, trade imbalances deepened when export revenues dropped in the early 1980s, as a result of falling commodity prices and lower demand by the recession-plagued industrial countries. These effects were compounded by a sharp rise in US dollar interest rates, when the US Federal Reserve Board raised interest rates in 1981 to counteract the inflationary impact of higher oil prices. In a matter of weeks what had been negative interest rates on foreign loans rose to 20 percent and more in real, inflation-adjusted terms, and remained at that level for several years.

What is astonishing is that the borrowing countries' mounting debts and widening trade and fiscal imbalances went unheeded for so long. Syndicated lending was so lucrative that it caused generalized "danger myopia" among banks and multilateral institutions. To wit: in June 1982, less than two months before the outbreak of the debt crisis, a multinational task force, chaired by the central bank of Mexico and hosted by the World Bank, considered it "most essential" that the volume of non-concessional flows to oil-importing countries should increase. The members of the task force also believed that the multilateral institutions should increase their own lending, or improve the international environment to induce others to increase theirs.[18]

What the task force had overlooked was that the total external public debt of the seventeen most highly indebted countries had risen to $391 billion, or $110 billion more than two years earlier, and that close to one-third of the countries' debt was short-term, maturing in less than one year.[19*] This, and high interest rates that were adding billions of dollars to the cost of servicing foreign loans, made debt problems inevitable: in August 1992, Mexico declared a moratorium on all debt service to foreign commercial banks. This triggered a chain reaction among the banks. Maturing short-term loans were not renewed and they stopped lending, even to countries that were not about to default on their obligations. With the suspension of lending, what had begun as a liquidity crisis became a self-fulfilling solvency crisis that engulfed all the highly indebted countries.

The World Bank and IMF managed to contain the initial fallout of the debt crisis by imposing fiscal restraint on debtor countries and giving them financing for macroeconomic stabilization and structural adjustment. Their intervention gradually restored order in financial markets and narrowly averted a full-blown banking crisis that would have caused catastrophic bank failures around the world. The way out of the impasse was that the banks were willing to reschedule overdue loans and to capitalize unpaid interest as long as they had the assurance that the debtor countries would undertake stabilization under an IMF Stand-by Agreement.[20]

Deferring debt service was far from ideal for the banks. But stretching out payments was better than forcing countries to default. It meant that the banks did not have to write off hundreds of billions of dollars of non-performing loans. As long as the debtor countries complied with the IMF's conditionality and maintained a modicum of debt service, the banks could pretend that their loans to developing countries were still "performing assets," thereby keeping loan-loss reserves within manageable limits. Had the situation been different, large loan losses would have pushed all but the largest banks into bankruptcy.

For the debtor countries, however, the situation was bleak. Even though lending had stopped, their external public debt almost doubled between 1981 and 1986 as a result of capitalizing interest arrears on rescheduled loans.[21] Moreover, after years of import-led growth and heedless spending, 1982 marked the beginning of a prolonged period of economic retrenchment and decline for the debtor countries. To meet the IMF's balance-of-payment and fiscal targets (see below), and continue making partial interest payments on rescheduled loans, the debtors' trade balances, which had been negative until 1982, had to move into surplus. This meant that the debtor countries had to boost exports and cut all non-essential imports as fast as possible. They did. Whereas the current-account deficits of the highly indebted countries averaged 6 percent of GDP in 1982, they were in surplus two years later.[22]

Cutting imports, and moving resources from internal consumption to exports, involved considerable sacrifices. During each of the six years following the outbreak of the debt crisis in 1982, imports, investment, and personal consumption dropped sharply in virtually all the highly indebted countries. In

---

* All dollar amounts are in United States currency, unless otherwise noted.

the most extreme cases—Bolivia, Nigeria, Peru, and the Philippines—investment in new plant and equipment declined at annual rates ranging form 10 percent to 17 percent from 1982 to 1986. The negative rates of growth in investment meant that the countries' capital stocks were being depleted, and that their productive potential and future growth were severely impaired. Thus, whereas boosting exports normally creates jobs and growth, after 1982 the pressure to generate export revenue was so great that resources had to be diverted from the domestic to the external market. Instead of creating growth, higher exports were accompanied by a decline in investment, growth, and income.

These negative effects were compounded by the allocation of scarce budgetary resources to debt service, and by unchecked capital flight. The highly indebted countries, which had close to $30 billion in net *in*flows between 1980 and 1982, suffered a net *out*flow of nearly $100 billion during the following five years.[23] In Latin America, where the largest debtors made $66 billion in net payments to their commercial creditors between 1982 and 1987—which represented an annual average of 6 percent of their GDP—capital flight during the same period added $34 billion to the outflow.[24] Debtor countries had become capital exporters, and the shift out of domestic consumption to the export sector was dramatic and extraordinarily fast. To add insult to injury, the commercial and investment banks that had been lending developing countries had switched roles after 1982, and began competing for the deposits of the well-to-do in the debtor countries. In doing so, they helped the fortunes of the rich find safe havens abroad, but deepened the countries' solvency problems.

As is discussed later here and in Chapter 6, after 1982 there was a marked increase in poverty and employment in debtor countries. Stabilization and structural adjustment were nevertheless applauded as successes because they had managed to avoid a global banking crisis. Capitalizing on this success, the World Bank made adjustment lending a staple of its activities. By 1984 sixteen countries had undertaken structural-adjustment programs, and structural-adjustment lending represented 7 percent of World Bank lending. More than a decade later, in 1996 and 1997, that percentage had risen to respectively 21 and 25 percent, and in 1997 forty countries were undertaking various forms of adjustment.[25]

The Social Impact of Stabilization and Adjustment

While the policy content and conditionality of the World Bank's and IMF's intervention vary over time and between countries—even countries that do not have excessive external debts can have high inflation and unsustainable deficits, and may need stabilization—their intervention is a two-stage process. In the first stage, the IMF takes the lead with stabilization programs that consist of deflationary measures to restore macroeconomic stability and fiscal discipline, purge inflation, and curb budget deficits. The second, in which the

World Bank acts alone, involves structural adjustment, which intervenes at the microeconomic level by imposing sectoral and policy changes, including financial and trade deregulation. The World bank's programs are designed to revive growth and increase a country's competitiveness in the global market. Because it is difficult to implement sectoral reforms in an unstable macroeconomic environment, IMF-led stabilization always precedes the World Bank's structural adjustment. The agencies' intervention is considered successful if countries "turn their economies around by fostering internal competition, implementing sensible fiscal and monetary policies, and maintaining an incentive structure that is conducive to investment."[26]

To draw up a social and economic balance sheet of stabilization and structural-adjustment lending, and see how different social strata have been affected by it, one must look at individual policy components.

Macroeconomic Stabilization, Fiscal Austerity, and Income Distribution

Restoring stability in countries that have excessive current-account imbalances, large fiscal deficits, and high inflation is done by inducing (that is, provoking) a recession in order to slow down the pace of economic activity by reducing aggregate demand—namely public expenditure, private consumption, and investment. To that end, the IMF always imposes fiscal restraint, including the elimination of food subsidies for the needy, and sets specific public-expenditure targets (defined as percentages of GNP) to reduce budget deficits. In most cases the IMF also prescribes currency devaluations to curb current-account deficits and make their exports more competitive. Only countries that comply fully with these conditions and implement the macroeconomic measures prescribed by the IMF receive funding in support of stabilization. These loans are disbursed in installments ("tranches"), and noncompliance with the IMF's conditionality invariably results in suspension or deferral of disbursements. Working in tandem with the IMF, the World Bank only grants structural-adjustment loans to countries that are in full compliance with the IMF.

On the positive side, in countries that do comply, the IMF's intervention usually restores macroeconomic stability and fiscal discipline, shrinks fiscal and external deficits, and reduces inflation. Because inflation is a tax on the poor, restoring (relative) price stability has an immediate (positive) income effect for wage earners and people on fixed incomes, for whom uncontrollable inflation wipes out the purchasing power of wages and pensions. In countries such as Argentina, Bolivia, Brazil, and Peru, where hyperinflation was in the thousands of percent per year—it reached 24,000 percent in Bolivia in 1985—money had lost its role as a medium of exchange and store of value, and wages were worth almost nothing when merchants had to raise the price of goods several times a day. When this happens, people try to do all their shopping as soon as they get paid, because their paychecks become worthless in a matter of days, or even hours. In fact, with persisting hyperinflation, US dollars became the de facto legal tender, and Latin America's high-inflation economies became "dollarized" during the 1980s. Hyperinflation can also cause hoarding and food shortages. Because hyperinflation also disrupts investment and long-term contracts, price stability is also necessary to renew business confidence.

Predictably, macroeconomic stability was restored more rapidly in fast-adjusting countries (Bolivia, Indonesia, and Mexico, among others) than in slow-adjusting countries (Peru, Brazil, and Argentina). In Bolivia inflation dropped in a matter of months from 24,000 percent to a benign 10 percent, whereas inflation was still at 7,600 percent per year in Peru in 1990.

This being said, stabilization always comes at a price: rising unemployment, higher prices for basic foods and necessities (as a result of the elimination of subsidies and currency devaluations), and the elimination of social programs for the needy. The outcome is invariably more poverty and marginalization, with a disproportional effect on women and children. In the aftermath of 1982, the deflationary impact of stabilization was magnified by the allocation of scarce budgetary resources to debt service, tight credit, currency devaluations, and higher prices on imported goods.

Eliminating subsidies for staples, such as rice, wheat, cooking oil, and heating oil, hurts the poor who spend most of their income on basics. When the price of food rises, the poorest cannot afford to buy staples and often go hungry. As many governments have found out, this can cause social unrest. In Indonesia and Thailand, for instance, the elimination of subsidies for rice and cooking oil caused riots and looting in early 1998. To restore order, the governments of both countries reinstated the subsidies, in defiance of IMF conditions.

For its part, lower investment in social infrastructure (schools, health services, welfare programs) hurts children, women, and ethnic minorities—for instance, spending cuts in public health force women to stay at home with sick children and parents, which gives them less time to work and earn money and causes more hardship for their families.

Besides eliminating subsidies, the quickest way to meet fiscal targets and reduce public spending is to cut payrolls and shed workers in government agencies and state-owned enterprises, starting with unskilled and semi-skilled workers. The income effects of redundancies in the public sector are all the greater during recessions, when the private sector is also laying off workers. Once again, in developing countries, where the lower rungs of the public sector are one of the few sectors in which women can find formal employment, job cuts in the public sector hurt women more than men because women are usually the first to be let go. Jobless, women have few options, other than working as domestic servants, or becoming self-employed.

Yet another way to bring fiscal deficits under control is to generate income by privatizing viable state-owned enterprises and liquidating unprofitable ones. This too pushes up unemployment when, as tends to be the case, the new owners of these enterprises also cut their payrolls in order to make the companies more profitable. For example, after it was privatized, Argentina's state-owned oil company (YPF) made 50,000 workers redundant. Elsewhere, in Bolivia and Peru, the combined job cuts in the public sector and newly privatized enterprises during the 1980s were so large that wage employment in the formal economy shrank to less than half of the active labor force.

Structural Adjustment and the Myth of Trickle Down

Structural adjustment complements stabilization. It intervenes at the sectoral level through market-friendly supply-side reforms that are designed to restore conditions for resumed growth and offset the deflationary impact of budget cuts and fiscal austerity. Sectoral reforms aim to cut waste and inefficiency, and make resource allocation more efficient. Typical World Bank policy prescriptions include liberalizing the financial sector, replacing government regulation with voluntary private regulation, opening markets to foreign competition, and making labor and investment codes "more flexible." This means that environmental codes become less stringent, workers lose protection against arbitrary firing, and the rights to strike, join unions, and engage in collective wage bargaining are curtailed or abolished.

The underlying assumption of the free-market policies that are embedded in structural adjustment is that deregulation creates an "enabling environment" for private initiative and investment. Politicians and policy makers try to justify the social cost of stabilization and adjustment on the grounds that "sacrifices" are needed to restore stability, investor confidence, and growth before the benefits of growth—new jobs and higher incomes—can "trickle down" to the rest of society, and reduce poverty. In other words, there is an assertion that a rising tide of income and prosperity will lift all boats, meaning that, when the conditions for resumed growth are in place, the poor and the unemployed who had sought refuge in the informal sector will find new jobs in industry and commerce.

Trickle down is an ideological construct of the prevailing neo-liberal paradigm in development economics, which is itself a throwback to nineteenth-century laissez-faire capitalism. It puts faith in the guiding force of the "invisible hand" of efficient and self-regulating markets, which ensures that individual pursuits and decisions add up to the greatest common good, provided that markets are left free of "interference" in the form of excessive regulation. This framework leaves no place for the state as an engine of economic growth, or even as a defender of social equity, and social objectives are replaced with incentives for the private sector. The role of the state in the economy is then reduced to creating a favorable environment for private enterprise, and public safeguards against the excesses of private initiative are minimized. "Inflation is (then) to be feared more than unemployment, because the self-regulating economy will tend to eliminate unemployment automatically, but one must be vigilant against the inflation-producing errors of governments."[27]

While it is true that deregulation did restore growth in many countries, the question is "what kind of growth?" It is beyond dispute that excessive regulation and red tape stifle initiative and slow down the pace of economic activity, and that fiscal and monetary policies that distort the allocation of resources are obstacles to job creation and cause economic rigidities. But it is equally true that there *is* a role for the state as an arbiter of market relations and defender of equity. More to the point, in developing countries, where neither governments nor markets function well, the purpose of structural adjustment should not be to replace one with the other, but to make markets *and* governments more efficient.[28] There are good reasons for this. The first is that without efficient and accountable governments, corruption becomes endemic and good governance is impossible. The second is that market forces, unchecked by state regulations, allocate *all* the benefits to those who hold the greatest power in the market place. Finally, governments and state agencies are the principal interlocutors and counterparts of foreign donors and multilateral development agencies, and proper project implementation and structural adjustment require adequate institutional capacity.

In reality, the problem with free-market policies is that "the trickle-down effects of even fairly high rates of growth have been so slow that without remedial pro-poor actions it will take an *unconscionably long time* before a sizable dent is made in the backlog of poverty."[29] The reason this is so is that, during the initial stages of growth, instead of creating jobs, private corporations frequently shed workers and downsize in the name of efficiency. In other cases, employers take advantage of flexible labor codes to replace their employees with lower-wage workers. What this means is that labor suffers during the initial period of adjustment, and that wage workers who lose their jobs or suffer steep cuts in real wages become poor as a result of policy changes that are part of the adjustment process. In countries where unemployment rose significantly after 1982, countless non-poor households were driven below the poverty line. Again, in such cases women are more vulnerable than men. Because they are disproportionately concentrated in low-wage sectors or occupations and are often segregated into the informal sector, their position deteriorates during periods of structural adjustment.

A further effect of structural adjustments is that opening developing-country markets to foreign competition creates opportunities for multinational companies but often harms local small enterprises and traditional crafts and industries, which cannot compete with mass-produced goods.

The point is that, in countries that underwent stabilization and adjustment, prolonged sacrifices only yielded benefits for the rich. But for the majority of people, the regressive distributional effects of fiscal austerity and the abolition of subsidies were compounded by the absence of trickle down. After bearing a disproportionate burden during externally induced recessions, the urban and rural poor are forced to wait an "unconscionably long time" before they are able to become stakeholders in the post-adjustment recoveries.

Most of them are still waiting.

Despite expectations that trickle down would eliminate some poverty, the fact that there was none was apparently no surprise for the World Bank. Discussing the impact of growth on poverty, in 1980 one of the earliest *World Development Reports* already stated that "There is general agreement that growth, in the very long term, eliminates most absolute poverty; but also that some people may (at least temporarily) be impoverished by development—as when a tenant farmer is displaced by his landlord's tractor or a shoemaker by mass-produced shoes."[30]

The clearest evidence of the absence of trickle down is in Latin America, where the adjustment process was most rigorous, growth was gradually restored, and countries such as Mexico and Peru enjoyed spurts of rapid growth during the 1990s. Yet the number of Latin Americans living in poverty increased by more than one-third, from 120 million in 1980, to over 160 million in 1995, and continued to rise during the period of rapid growth. Moreover, the percentage of people living in poverty remained constant at roughly 33 percent of the total population, from 1980 to 1995, after rising to close to 40 percent between 1985 and 1990.[31] Not surprisingly, the lack of trickle down caused a backlash against free-market reforms in many parts of Latin America. Mass demonstrations and food riots, which reached a peak in 1995 and 1996, were clear signs that sacrificing social objectives in the pursuit of market efficiency was no longer acceptable.

The only part of the developing world that had trickle down was East Asia, where a decade of sustained growth created a relatively affluent middle class in a handful of "tiger economies." But the effect was limited. There is still much urban and rural poverty, and the urban-rural income gap continued to widen during the growth period. Besides, the tiger economies achieved their record-breaking growth with mercantilist policies that are the antithesis of free markets, and they all experienced a sharp reversal of fortunes in 1997 and 1998, that wiped out the gains of the previous decade.

The Global Economy: A Challenge for Developing Countries

To complete the social and economic balance sheet of stabilization and structural adjustment one must look at the effects of the broader purpose of financial deregulation and trade liberalization, namely integrating developing countries into the global economy.

Globalization means interdependence. In the global economy commerce, investment, and production take place as if the world consisted of a single market and production area, with regional and national sub-sectors, rather than of a set of national economies that are linked by trade and investment flows.[32] For the first time in history, competition in trade and services is increasingly taking place on a global scale. While claims of a border-free global economy are still exaggerations, interdependency has already reached a point where events and decisions in one country can, and do, have almost immediate repercussions in other parts of the globe. Such are the perils of globalization that bad news travels even faster than good tidings: the massive sell-off in the Hong Kong stock market in October 1997 instantly sent stock prices tumbling on Wall Street, and in Europe and Latin America.

The Mobility of Capital

Globalization is premised on the mobility of the factors of production: capital and labor. The degree of mobility is greatest in financial capital, somewhat less in capital that is invested in plant and equipment, and least in labor. This explains why financial institutions and investors in capital markets are reaping the greatest benefits from globalization, and labor the fewest.

Globalization also adds a great deal of complexity to economic decisions, and the fact that large corporations must cut production costs in order to remain competitive in the global economy is a source of unexpected challenges and problems for developing countries. Competition on a global scale creates opportunities for low-wage economies, if they can attract foreign investments and create jobs in labor-intensive industries such as textiles, footwear, and low-cost consumer goods. To do so, countries must compete against each other, and in this race beggars cannot be choosers: countries must offer substantial tax and financial incentives to foreign corporations, and have adequate infrastructure, educated labor forces, technological potential, flexible environmental and labor codes, and political stability. By implication, poor countries that primarily produce and export raw materials, have limited infrastructure and largely illiterate populations, and are politically unstable—which is the case in much of sub-Saharan Africa—cannot attract foreign capital. Thus, the gap between them and the rest of the world is widening. Furthermore, the "benefits" of globalization have still not trickled down to the urban and rural poor, even in the countries that have managed to attract large amounts of foreign direct investment.

Globalization and the international mobility of financial capital have also changed the magnitude and composition of capital flows to developing countries. Lured by the prospect of rapid capital gains on investments in the shares of newly privatized enterprises, individual and institutional investors from the United States and Europe began making forays in the fledgling stock markets of developing countries during the late 1980s. Being rational, these investors place their funds in markets where the risk/reward trade off is most favorable, and countries are pulled into the global capital market to a degree that is in direct relation to their level of economic development and political stability. Whereas the poorest low-income countries are shunned by investors, and must rely on bilateral and multilateral development aid, in middle-income countries official creditors and commercial banks have been replaced by private capital flows from foreign investors.

Fickle Finance Capital—Mexico's Peso Crisis of December 1994

The problem is that the cross-border mobility of finance capital is such that it can rapidly destabilize countries that follow "imprudent" economic policies and undermine investor confidence. A good example of this is Mexico's brush with disaster in 1994 and 1995.

Having stabilized and liberalized its economy after the 1982 debacle, Mexico gradually regained access to foreign private capital and the government began repeating past mistakes—using short-term foreign capital to finance imports. Foreign capital continued to flow in as long as the policy distortions were not too blatant. When economic stress reached a breaking point in December 1994, and a devaluation of the peso could no longer be avoided, foreign investors lost confidence in Mexico, and the situation rapidly turned into financial mayhem when they pulled out their funds.

The crisis of 1994–95 raises serious questions about the social consequences and balance-of-payments effects of unchecked inflows of short-term speculative capital. The events of December 1994 are also an interesting case of collective amnesia in financial markets and multilateral agencies. Indeed, the crisis could have been avoided, but for the naiveté and lack of foresight of foreign investors who had been misled by a premature vote of confidence by the World Bank, which had given its imprimatur to the economic program of the (utterly corrupt) Salinas administration. Anxious to demonstrate the success of its policies, the World Bank had presented Mexico as a model of successful stabilization and structural reform, whose fiscal discipline, privatization programs, and financial deregulation should be followed by other countries. Confident that Mexico's economy was solid, foreign investors began buying massive amounts of short-term, dollar-denominated Mexican treasury bills (*tesobonos*), and also bought shares of Mexico's newly privatized utilities and industries.[33] This created a speculative bubble, and the resulting appreciation of the peso led to a growing current-account deficit.

As in the late 1970s before the debt crisis, danger signals were ignored until it was too late. In November 1994, Mexico's central bank had to intervene by raising domestic interest rates to shore up the peso and avoid panic sales of *tesobonos*. It could only support the peso as long as it had enough foreign currency reserves to do so. After spending more than $20 billion in a desperate but unsuccessful attempt to shore up its currency and reassure foreign investors, the central bank was forced to devalue the peso in December, when the country's external reserves had dwindled to less than $6 billion.[34] The peso's slide could only be halted after the central bank raised interest rates to 60 percent in late December, and the IMF and US Treasury intervened with a $50 billion bailout in January 1995.[35]

This marked a new departure for the IMF, making it a global lender of last resort, and was a precursor and model for its role as global arbiter in East Asia in 1997 and 1998. As during the debt crisis of 1982, the IMF's intervention in Mexico in 1995 gradually restored calm to financial markets, but, as is discussed in greater detail in Chapter 6, it did little to attenuate the domestic impact of the crisis. As in 1982, after Mexico's debt moratorium, there was also a contagious loss of confidence, this time among private and institutional investors who began withdrawing their funds from capital markets throughout the region. This band-wagon effect became known as the "tequila effect."[36] Its fallout was most severe in Argentina, where unemployment climbed to 16 percent in Buenos Aires, and more than 12 percent in the interior in the wake of the peso crisis.[37]

Unbeknownst at the time, Mexico's peso crisis of 1994 was a harbinger of other, even more severe, financial crises to come. It was also a classical case of uncontrollable shifts of funds and speculative bubbles in capital markets that are driven by fear and greed.[38] As shown by events in East Asia in 1997 and 1998, when speculative bubbles burst, the social and economic consequences can be brutal. The financial and banking crisis that engulfed Indonesia, Malaysia, Thailand, the Philippines, and South Korea in 1997 was precipitated by massive withdrawals of capital by foreign investors. These countries, which had a net inflow of $93 billion in foreign capital in 1996, suffered a net *outflow* of $12 billion in 1997, or a total reversal of $105 billion.[39] As discussed in Chapter 5, the stabilization measures which these countries had to undertake in 1997 and 1998 as part of IMF bailouts, were repetitions on a much larger scale of what happened in Latin America during the debt crisis: extreme fiscal retrenchment, unemployment, rising poverty, social upheaval, and a backlash against globalization.

Foreign Direct Investment and Economic Progress

Capital that crosses frontiers to be invested in plant and equipment becomes foreign direct investment. Because investment capital loses its liquidity as soon as it becomes bricks and mortar and machines, it is far less mobile than financial capital. This is why most savings stay in their home countries, and there is a close correlation between domestic savings and investment.[40]

Foreign direct investment is the purest expression of economic globalization. It is the domain of multinational corporations, whose factories and offices are scattered around the globe. The globalization of investment is driven by technological innovation and the increasing shift towards a knowledge- and information-based economy. Globalization and the corporate profits it is generating have, in their turn, become the main driving forces for more cost-saving technology, and more free trade. Of the world's one hundred largest economies, fifty-one are *companies*, and the two hundred largest corporations account for more than one quarter of global economic activity (but employ less than 1 percent of the world's labor force).[41] The competition between industrial giants is driven by trade liberalization: Ford Motor Company competes not only with General Motors for a share of the US market, but also with Volkswagen, Fiat, Nissan, and Toyota for a share of the global car and truck market. In this race each company tries to gain a competitive edge over its rivals by reducing labor costs. Similar pressures also exist in lesser industries, such as sportswear and clothing. Nike and Reebok vie for supremacy in the global sneaker market, and must also strive to lower production costs.

The quickest way to bring down costs is to locate factories and assembly lines in countries that offer tax concessions, cheap and skilled labor, and flexible labor and environmental codes. Locating factories abroad is not a new phenomenon. What *is* new is that technological breakthroughs have made it possible to automate even quite complex production and planning processes, and that economies of scale are gradually being replaced with economies of process. Indeed, one of the unexpected windfalls of innovation in communication and information technology is that instant communications around the globe makes it comparatively easy to break up complex production processes into discrete components that can be located any place in the world where labor is cheap, non-unionized, and productive. This, and the fact that labor is far less mobile than capital, gives companies unprecedented flexibility in deciding where to locate their factories and offices. In the automobile, aviation, defense, and electronics industries, the large integrated factories of yore are being replaced with smaller, computerized, and automated plants. These small factories, which produce or assemble all or part of motor cars, computers, or shoes, are scattered around the globe—for example, the fine print on the packing box of my "Japanese" Toshiba laptop states that it was "assembled in the United States, from parts made in the USA and other countries."

The ability to locate factories almost anywhere makes it possible to circumvent the taxes, environmental regulations, and high wages that make production costs in Europe, the United States, and Japan too onerous. The smaller scale of the new production units also makes it comparatively easy to close down small plants if wages in a particular country become too high, and to relocate production in another country where labor is cheaper. Nike is an example of a company whose sneaker production lines have tracked cheap labor across the Far East.

For blue- and white-collar workers in high-wage labor markets in industrialized countries the mobility of productive capital creates a "race to the bottom." It undermines job security and the power to resist the export of jobs to low-wage environments, where workers' rights have little protection. Admittedly, in low-wage countries foreign investment does create jobs in high-unemployment environments, but at wages that are rarely commensurate with the work involved, and in working conditions where workers' have few rights and are often crudely exploited. NAFTA is a prime example of this: in the *maquilladoras* of northern Mexico workers often endure long hours, low wages, and unhealthy working conditions. Workers in the developing world's modern sweatshops seldom have the right to organize, protest, strike, and bargain wages collectively through unions.[42] An example: Taiwan's Bao Yuan Company, which makes Nike, Reebok, and Adidas sneakers for the US market, has three shoe factories in Donguan, in mainland China. These factories employ 40,000 workers, more than two-thirds of them women, who work and live at a single enclosed site. Shifts begin at 6:30 in the morning, workers are only allowed fifteen-minute lunch breaks, and management imposes military discipline. Workers who do eighty hours overtime work per month—a violation of Chinese labor laws—earn around $80 per month.[43] One could argue that Boa Yuan has created 40,000 new jobs, and that it pay its workers more than the average wage in China. But the fact remains that they earn less than 30 US cents per hour, and work in conditions that are close to those of a labor camp.

Instant, worldwide communication via the Internet and electronic mail even mean that goods and services which used to be non-tradables have become tradables. For example, the transcripts of patients' medical records for some hospitals in the United States are being processed on computers in offices in Bangalore, and transmitted back and forth half-way around the world over high-speed data lines. Because transcriptors in India are highly skilled but earn a pittance by US standards, it is cheaper—and faster—for a hospital in, say, Chicago, to have its patients' records processed in India, than to give the job to a local medical transcription service.[44]

Few Winners Among Developing Countries

While corporations try to gain a competitive edge by lowering labor costs, countries with excess labor but too little capital must compete against each other to entice the corporations. This gives corporations a strategic advantage, threatening to locate factories elsewhere to extract tax concessions and other benefits from potential host countries. To oblige foreign companies, many countries even allow them to repatriate profits to their home country, which actually hinders the process of capital accumulation in the host country.

The competition for foreign investment is intense and leaves many losers in its wake. Until 1997, Thailand and Indonesia were among the relatively few countries that had adapted successfully to the global economy, and benefited from it. Some poor countries, India and Bangladesh among them, have also managed to attract foreign investment with cheap labor in order to build export-oriented textile industries. For example, most T-shirts that are sold in Europe are made in Bangladesh. The losers are the countries that have a weak legal and institutional environment, and too little skilled labor and infrastructure to be magnets for foreign capital. That, and the dominant role of technology as an agent of globalization, makes those countries increasingly marginalized. They cannot attract foreign investors, build up their own export industries, or secure a place in world markets. Sometimes their only option is to export their most valuable commodity: labor. Hence the large numbers of African, Asian, and Latin American immigrants, working in minimum-wage jobs in the United States and parts of Europe.

Sub-Saharan Africa faces the toughest handicaps. Its pitifully inadequate infrastructure, harsh climates, lack of skilled workers, commodity dependency, weak and corrupt institutional and judiciary systems, and political volatility, virtually exclude it from competing in the global economy, except by offering lucrative concessions for the exploitation of its vast mineral resources. But concessions seldom do more than create modern "enclaves" in otherwise backward economies. The foreign companies—and embassies, banks, foreign NGOs, aid agencies, and hotels—one finds in these enclaves pay wages that are substantially above local levels, but the backward linkages to the rest of the economy are minimal.

More generally, countries that are predominantly agrarian, and only export a few cash crops or other raw materials, have been affected by the secular decline in the price of commodities, relative to that of manufactured goods, which has created unfavorable terms of trade.[45] The unfavorable position of the least-developed countries can be judged from the fact that their share of trade in world markets continues to decline—from 7.47 percent in 1983, to 6.17 in 1993.[46] In contrast, the world's five hundred largest corporations account for 70 percent of global trade.[47] Although there are some export opportunities for high-value agricultural products, only a handful of the least-developed countries have managed to develop non-traditional exports.[48] For commodity-exporting countries Nurske's vicious circle of poverty remains largely unbroken. In exports they face a continued erosion of their share of world trade, domestic producers are driven out of business by imports, and replacing food crops with cash crops for export makes them net importers of staple foods.

In discussing the consequences of globalization for developing countries, one must also look at how different social strata are faring *within countries*. Those who benefit the most are the well-to-do and the rich who can afford imported luxury goods. Less well-off consumers also benefit to some extent from trade liberalization. In street markets in Mexico and Central America people eagerly buy low-priced, mass-produced shoes, consumer electronics, music cassettes, toys, razors, textiles, and footwear, most of which are imported from China and other low-wage countries in Asia. What tends to be overlooked when lauding the benefits consumers derive from free trade, is that free trade does more harm than good when low-priced imports displace traditional domestic crafts and industries, destroy local culture, and cause unemployment in countries where job creation is already far too low to absorb new entrants in the labor market. Trade liberalization should, therefore, be seen in the overall context of a consistent and sustainable development strategy, not as a policy change imposed from above by multilateral agencies. Besides, unless importing countries can build up their own export capacity, whether by mass-producing consumer goods or expanding their existing export industries, current-account deficits inevitably widen and become crippling.

Growth Without Development

The bold intervention of the World Bank and IMF during the last decade and a half has yielded many benefits. It helped resolve the debt crisis, has purged hyperinflation, and, by restoring macroeconomic stability, set the stage for resumed growth and private investment in former problem debtor countries. The global economy is also becoming the main determinant of national trade and financial policies, and some countries have benefited, at least temporarily, from the tremendous increase in the flows of foreign portfolio and direct investment. Some countries have also benefited from trade liberalization, while others managed to achieve spectacular growth rates after undergoing adjustment—for a short while, in the mid-1990s, Peru had one of the highest growth rates in the world. On the other hand, the financial crises of Mexico in 1994–95, and Asia in 1997–98, are examples of the perils of the balance-of-payments effects of capital flows, which become lethal weapons when foreign investors pull out short-term speculative funds.

But, most of all, the multilateral agencies squandered a unique opportunity to lift all boats and create a better world for the coming millennium. Inequalities of income and wealth have risen, and continue to widen within and between countries. The rich are becoming richer, and the poor poorer, and little has been done to rid the world of the triple curse of hunger, poverty, and unemployment. Despite costly stabilization and adjustment, unemployment is still rising in much of the developing world, and more than one billion people are still living in conditions that are so appalling that do they not belong in a civilized world. Only local elites, urban middle classes, and skilled workers who make up a relatively small labor aristocracy, have benefited from the improved economic climate that followed the economic reforms of the 1980s and 90s, and are reaping the fruits of the inflow of foreign capital. Those who found jobs in new factories, built with foreign capital, are undeniably better off. But, in a sense, they too are losers: they compete fiercely for jobs in modern sweatshops, where they have few rights, and work long hours for low wages.

The cost of stabilization and adjustment was socialized among the poor and workers, in the form of job losses and the elimination of subsidies for the needy, while the benefits—to investors and commercial banks—were private. What this amounts to is growth without development. Structural adjustment and the introduction of market-based policies have also strengthened class divisions within developing countries, while economic globalization is maintaining the relations of dominance between advanced and developing countries.

The Outcome Could Have Been Different

The social and economic consequences of stabilization and deflation would have been less harsh and shorter-lived, if the initial economic problems and the resulting externally induced recession had been less pronounced. The fact is that the initial problems *were* severe, which became an excuse for the fact that the implementation of adjustment programs was less successful than anticipated, and that many countries had to endure prolonged periods of economic stagnation and worsening social conditions.

The outcome of forced deflation and induced recessions would neverthe-less have been different, regardless of the initial severity of problems, if, instead of asking governments to shed public-sector jobs and social infrastructure and eliminating subsidies and programs for the needy, the World Bank and IMF had forced governments to cut arms purchases, or eliminate subsidies for large landowners and agribusinesses, and privileges for the elites. The Brandt Commission of 1980 had already noted that the cost of one tank was equiva-lent to the money needed to provide classrooms for 30,000 children, and that, for the price of one jet fighter, one could build 40,000 village pharmacies.[49] The fact that many developing countries still spend more on weapons than on schools and village pharmacies, and more on subsidies for large commercial farmers and industrial plantations than for small farmers, is irrational and damaging. That irrationality is a result of vested class interests and patronage. Few government officials are willing to take risks, and sacrifice the interests and political support of the elites and the military by directing public expendi-ture towards basic services from which the wealthy do not benefit. It would also have harmed the lucrative business of arms traders. One refreshing de-parture from this trend is that Thailand, which was forced to undertake drastic fiscal contraction as part of the 1997 IMF bailout, asked the US government to cancel the Thai Air Force contract to purchase $500 million worth of F18 fighter jets.[50]

There are also enough easy, transparent, and cost-effective measures that could have been used to mitigate the regressive distributional effects of defla-tion and expenditure cuts—subsidies for the poor through targeting and social safety nets for the most vulnerable in society. Bilateral and multilateral devel-opment agencies could also increase the availability of funds for social programs in the least-developed countries by rescheduling or canceling all or part of their loans to those countries. But too little has been done to use these mea-sures to offset the regressive impact of macroeconomic stabilization. As a result, the only alternative for the poor and the tens of millions of "new poor" who became unemployed in the 1980s is to work in the informal economy. Self-help and self-employment are their only means of survival.

Notes

1. Robert McNamara, the former President of the World Bank, quoted in Catherine Caufield, *Masters of Illusion* (New York: Henry Holt and Com-pany, 1996), 99.
2. Akash Kapur, "Poor but Prosperous," *Atlantic Monthly*, September 1998.
3. See also David Bornstein, *The Price of a Dream* (New York: Simon & Schuster, 1996), ch. 31.
4. This is a frequent statement by Muhammad Yunus, the founder and manag-ing director of the Grameen Bank.
5. *Universal Declaration of Human Rights*, Article 25, para. 1.
6. *Rome Declaration on World Food Security*, November 17, 1996. Note that this was a comparatively modest target, in comparison with that of the 1974

World Food Conference, which had resolved to eliminate hunger by the year 1984.

7. A 1990 UNICEF survey found that in developing countries one-third of all children under the age of five are malnourished (*World Resources 1992–93*, Oxford University Press, 84).

8. *World Development Report (WDR) 1996*, The World Bank, 198. *Note*: unless mentioned otherwise, all socioeconomic data presented in this book are drawn from various issues of the *WDR*.

9. *UNCTAD's 1996 Report of the Least-Developed Countries* places forty-nine countries in this category (see p. 9 of the report).

10. Donald Curran, *Tiers-Monde: Evolution et Stratégies de Développement* (Paris: Editions Eyrolles, 1990), 96.

11. *Human Development Report, 1995*, United Nations Development Program, Foreword.

12. Paul Constance, *IDBAMERICA* (Washington, D.C.: Inter-American Development Bank, November 1997), 10.

13 James Wolfensohn, President of the World Bank, speaking at the Bank's 1996 Annual Meeting in Hong Kong.

14. Howard French, *The New York Times*, April 7, 1996.

15. *Poverty Reduction and the World Bank—Progress and Challenges in the 1990s* (Washington, D.C.: The World Bank, 1996), vii.

16. Comments made in March 1996, when announcing a joint UN, World Bank, and IMF initiative to provide $25 billion in development aid to Africa over the next decade. Cited in Barbara Crosette, *The New York Times*, March 17, 1996.

17. Leopoldo Solís and Ernesto Zedillo, "The Foreign Debt of Mexico" in *International Debt and the Developing Countries* (The World Bank, 1985), 261.

18. "Nonconcessional Capital Flows to Developing Countries" in *Finance and Development* (Washington, D.C.: The World Bank, December 1992), 19 (4).

19. *World Debt Tables 1888–89*, 30.

20. Under a Stand-by Agreement the IMF "stands by" a country with short-term financing for macroeconomic stabilization, provided that the country agrees to undertake the stabilization measures which the IMF prescribes (and makes a condition of disbursement).

21. *WDR 83*, 178–179, *WDR 88*, 252–253.

22. *World Debt Tables 1988–89*, xviii.

23. *WDR 88*, Figure 1.10, 30.

24. *World Debt Tables 1988–89*, 31.

25. The World Bank, *Annual Report 1996*, 22 and 37; *Annual Report 1997*, 8 and 199; and *WDR 85*, Box 4.8, 66.

26. *World Debt Tables 1988–89*, xii.

27. John Weeks, *A Critique of Neoclassical Macroeconomics* (MacMillan, 1989), 235.

28. Robert Klitgaart, *Adjusting to Reality*, (International Center for Economic Growth, 1991), 85.

29. Pradnab Bardhan in *Annual Bank Conference on Development Economics 1995* (Washington, D.C.: The World Bank), 63 (emphasis added).

30. *WDR 80*, 35.

31. *The Economist*, November 30, 1996.

32. *Globalization and Liberalization: Development in the face of Two Powerful Currents* (Geneva: UNCTAD, 1996), 6.

33. *Tesobonos* are Mexican treasury notes whose value is linked to the US dollar.

34. In February 1994 Mexico had $29 billion in foreign-exchange reserves (UNCTAD 1996, 75).
35. *World Debt Tables 1996* I, 11.
36. Silvia Pisani, *LA NACION* (Buenos Aires), May 22, 1995.
37. *CLARIN* (Buenos Aires), June 7, 1995.
38. Between 1990 and 1994, private and institutional investment in middle-income countries amounted to close to $660 billion, *The Economist*, June 24, 1995, 65.
39. *Financial Times*, February 16, 1998, editorial page.
40. *The Economist*, June 24, 1995, 72.
41. Robert D. Kaplan, "The Future of Democracy," *Atlantic Monthly*, December 1997, 1.
42. Mark Levinson, "Economists and Sweatshops," *Dissent*, Fall 1997, 12.
43. See Anita Chan, Outlook Section, *The Washington Post*, November 3, 1996.
44. See Mike Mills, *The Washington Post*, September 17, 1996.
45. The FAO has also pointed out that low-income countries that import food would suffer from the latest round of trade negotiations, leading up to the establishment of the World Trade Organization (WTO). See *Impact of the Uruguay Round on Agriculture*, FAO, Rome, paras. 60–63.
46. *The Least Developed Countries, 1996 Report*, (Geneva: UNCTAD), 51.
47. Kaplan, *Atlantic Monthly*.
48. UNCTAD 1996, 47.
49. *North-South, a Programme for Survival* (London: Pan Books, 1980), 14.
50. Fred Bardacke, *Financial Times*, March 8, 1998.

2

Self-Employment: A Cure for Poverty?

Defining Self-Employment

Self-employed people own and operate microenterprises. They are microentrepreneurs. In many developing countries microenterprises are often the sole sources of income for the majority of people, either because they lack the skills and education to find jobs in commerce and industry, or, as is mostly the case, because there are too few jobs in the wage economy. Microenterprises engage in informal activities, and the informal sector encompasses the universe of microenterprises.

Definitions of the informal sector sometimes exclude on-farm work—land preparation (plowing, fertilizing, and seeding), harvesting, and animal husbandry—but include off-farm activities such as processing and packaging produce, and drying, husking, and milling rice and other grains. This exclusion is based on the (false) assumption that small farmers have privileged access to farm credit, and do not need microfinance. This has no foundation in reality. While it is true that there are specialized banks that only serve farmers, it is usually only large farmers and landowners who have access to "farm credit." Even in predominantly agrarian economies in Africa and Asia, where the vast majority of farmers are landless sharecroppers and peasant farmers, for whom working the land is the sole source of income, subsistence farmers do not receive farm loans. Hence the fact that subsistence farming and sharecropping are recognized as bona fide informal work, and eligible for credit by leading microfinance institutions such as the Grameen Bank and Thailand's BAAC.

Informal businesses are part of a long tradition. Making handicrafts, selling goods in local markets, and moneylending are among the earliest forms of organized economic activities. Small-scale manufacture was already commonplace in Babylon, more than 4,000 years ago. There were blacksmiths, potters, weavers, tanners, tailors, jewelers, and dye makers. In ancient Greece and Rome, some slaves were allowed to work as craftsmen and borrow money for their trades, and female slaves worked as seamstresses, laundresses, child minders, and potters. They also sold salt, fruit, bread, and hemp, worked in the fields, and looked after farm animals.

In Europe, small informal businesses remained the principal forms of economic activity in commerce and crafts until the late Middle Ages. In the thirteenth century saddlers, spurriers, tanners, weavers, tailors, masons, thatchers, and other craftsmen began forming craft guilds. The guilds' master craftsmen became proprietor-producers who owned the raw materials and tools of their trades, employed apprentices and journeymen, and sold their goods for profit. By setting quality standards and prices, and training craftsmen, the guilds paved the way for "formalization" and production on a larger scale.

The Informal Sector: A Mirror of Socioeconomic Conditions

In high-income economies, where the unemployed have social safety nets, informal work is the exception. There, the informal sector consists mainly of unlicensed child minders, domestic staff, peddlers, tradesmen who do work "on the side," and migrant farm workers who follow seasonal crops. In the developing world the situation is the opposite, and informal work is frequently the norm, not the exception.

In the poorest countries and regions, where there are far too few jobs in the modern wage economy, self-employment is the main source of income in cities, and often the only one in small towns and villages. This is the case in sub-Saharan Africa, small island economies, and large parts of Asia, which are still mostly agrarian and where the level of urbanization is low. There, the wage economy is small and predominantly urban. It consists of banks, the public sector, port facilities, embassies, hotels, and airports. Job openings are few, and much sought after, and employers can be selective, to the point that, for white-collar jobs, applicants must be university graduates. (In the Grameen Bank, for example, branch managers and specialized technical staff have postgraduate degrees.)

The rest of the economically active urban population is in the informal economy. People are self-employed artisans, or engage in service activities, ranging from peddling goods in street markets, to cooking food, and operating informal taxis and minibuses. There is a constant inflow of rural migrants who flee their villages to escape poverty, violence, and natural calamities. In rural areas, extractive industries, textile mills, and food-processing plants tend to be the sole sources of wage employment. The rest of the rural economy consists of basic survival microenterprises—subsistence farms and sharecropping. Able-bodied men are often away, looking for work in cities or on plantations that produce export cash crops, and women are the main breadwinners. They grow vegetables, raise small farm animals, husk rice, and sell farm produce in markets. For many rural households in Africa and South Asia, selling farm products in local markets and obtaining small loans are the only contacts with the cash economy. In Bangladesh, for example, women only venture outside their villages to collect their loans from the Grameen Bank or BRAC.

In the large middle-income countries of Latin America—Argentina, Brazil, Colombia, Mexico, and Venezuela—the situation is different. There the informal sector shrank during the long spell of post-war economic growth. For more than two decades, corporatist states expanded the public sector and provided steady employment in state-owned enterprises, protected by trade barriers. During the 1970s, at a time when industrial economies were in a deep recession, Latin America used loans from foreign banks to expand and grow. Civil servants, and workers in state-owned factories, public utilities, development banks, mines, and oil companies, became a labor aristocracy, sheltered by labor laws that virtually assured job tenure. The expanding wage economy became a magnet for rural migration. This changed the region's social geography, making Latin America one of the most highly urbanized parts of the world.

Unemployment among white-collar workers, and skilled and semi-skilled workers in industry, remained a rarity until the outbreak of the debt crisis. Informal work was mostly rural, in plantations, cattle ranches, and small farms, and in indigenous communities. The situation changed dramatically after 1982, when millions lost their jobs and had to seek refuge in the informal sector. They fueled a huge parallel economy that stretched from the Rio Grande to Cape Horn. Because of the high level of urbanization, poverty and informality became predominantly urban. A case in point is Lima's historic downtown. In the aftermath of the debt crisis it became a gigantic street bazaar, where tens of thousands of hawkers (the *ambulantes*) were vying for space on roads and sidewalks. In many parts of Central and South America the informal sector still accounts for a substantial part of the urban work force and for a major share of trade and small-scale industrial production.

In East Asia, the role and place of the informal sector differ from the situations one encounters in sub-Saharan Africa, South Asia, and Latin America. During the 1980s, when debt-ridden Latin America was mired in a deep recession, and living standards continued to decline in sub-Saharan Africa, growth took off and accelerated in East Asia, unfettered by external debt. In Thailand, new industries could tap a huge reserve pool of rural under-employed. There, and in Indonesia, Korea, and Malaysia, growth was fueled by foreign direct investment and large capital inflows. But, even though living standards improved in the tiger economies, informality remained extensive in countries such as in Thailand and Indonesia, even at the height of economic growth. Beneath their facades of growing urban affluence, with large middle classes, booming tourist industries, and urban glamour zones, Indonesia and, to a lesser extent Thailand, are still poor, and population growth was too high to absorb all new entrants in the labor force into the wage economy.

Thailand's economic boom also offered a rare example of informality piggy-backing on industrialization. In the industrial belt around Bangkok the informal sector actually *expanded* as a direct result of rapid industrialization, when factories in the fast-growing garment and footwear industries began subcontracting some of their work to informal workshops and self-employed home-based workers. In these highly cyclical industries subcontracting became common practice, as it was more economical, and less risky, to contract out than to build new factories, and hire and train workers. Predictably, with the outbreak of the financial crisis in 1997, a more traditional pattern of unemployment-driven informal work emerged, and the unlicensed workshops were among the first to shed workers.

Cultural factors also have a profound influence on the nature and types of activities in the informal sector. For obvious reasons there are no shoeshines in villages where people go barefoot, one sees no sidewalk acupuncturists in Dakar, and there are no snake charmers in La Paz. Moreover, some cultures encourage collective activities, while others favor individual work.

Another common observation is that, because women are more likely than men to lose their jobs in periods of economic decline, and always have greater difficulties finding work in the wage economy, the informal sector is highly feminized. In fact, there is a "glass ceiling," even in the informal sector. Much like in ancient Greece and Rome, women still mostly engage in what are regarded as traditionally "feminine" activities: sewing, dressmaking, doing laundry, and working in food-vending stands.

The Multi-tiered Universe of Informality

The informal sector is far from homogeneous, and microenterprises come in many shapes and sizes. In countries where self-employment and microfinance are already firmly anchored, the informal sector is highly stratified. While the types of informal work vary from country to country, one can classify these activities into generic groups and income strata.

The *lowest tier* consists of the survival businesses of the poorest, whom one might call "proto microentrepreneurs." They are the peddlers who roam streets and markets with baskets of fruit, or sell trinkets, chewing gum, candy, cigarettes, and tourist souvenirs. Others are the women in open-air markets and city streets, who sit in the same spot every day, with small piles of vegetables, and rice cakes or tortillas they made before dawn. There are also fortune tellers and the ubiquitous shoeshines who ply their trade in streets, cafés, and markets all over Latin America, and the millions of men who rent pedicabs, rickshaws, wheelbarrows, or rowboats by the day, trying to make a living by carting or ferrying people and freight to and from markets.

The poorest of the poor often do degrading work, such as collecting sewage and night soils in neighborhoods that have no sewers. In Dhaka I saw men bearing dripping baskets of night soils on their heads. Theirs is gruesome, unhealthy work, but it is often the only option for people of the lowest castes. For them, and others on the bottom rung of society, emptying latrines, carrying sewage, and recycling garbage is the only way they can make a living. In El Salvador I came across groups of families who were living and working on top of festering landfills, sifting through garbage to find scrap metal and other "recyclables" which they would sell to dealers.

One also encounters degrading activities among the poor in comparatively affluent societies. In Belo Horizonte, in the state of Minas Gerais, one of Brazil's richest, hundreds of street people are paid a few cents a day to shred and bag old newspapers. Their "houses" are cardboard boxes, perched on sidewalks in front of the printing plants of the city's newspapers. Others live on the sidewalks in the business district, and spend their nights shredding waste paper from office garbage cans.

The more established *middle-tier microentrepreneurs* are merchants who own cubicle-like shops and market stalls. The goods they sell range from pirated audio tapes, to cosmetics, household goods, and groceries. In this tier one also finds village barbers and moneylenders, the workshops of seamstresses, carpenters, blacksmiths, and leather workers. It also includes mechanics who repair cars and household appliances, and the owners of the bicycle rickshaws and wheelbarrows that others rent by the day. Others still are public scribes who write letters for the illiterate, and the unemployed plumbers, painters, electricians, and carpenters who congregate in town squares in Latin America, advertising their trades on small boards, in the hope of finding a day's work.

In Mexico and parts of Central America, this middle tier even includes small bands of modern troubadours, the *marriachis*. In Mexico City every evening dozens of *marriachi* bands assemble on the same square in the city center, awaiting customers. Each time a car pulls up, the bands jostle for attention and give impromptu auditions, trying to get a night's work, serenading people in their homes and at parties.

The *top tier* consists of businesses that are on the borderline between the informal and formal sectors. Many of them began quite small and prospered over time. Some of these business are mini-factories, whose owners are managers and supervisors, but no longer work themselves. In Yogyakarta, on the island of Java, I visited a small furniture factory. The owner did the bookkeeping, stock keeping, and marketing for her two workshops, and supervised the work of her twelve employees. There are similar examples in other countries, such as a metal workshop in Dakar that makes aluminum window frames and doors. This business has three workshops in different districts of the city and employs thirty workers. The owner uses a small truck and a car to ferry workers and material between his workshops. In most countries a business of that size would belong to the wage economy and have access to bank loans. Yet, in Senegal that business is a client of a microfinance institution.

The Costs and Benefits of Informality

Once they become established, microentrepreneurs must weigh up the benefits and costs of remaining in the informal sector.

Low Entry and Exit Costs, and Overheads

By definition, informal businesses fall outside the scope of official regulations and work codes, and the costs of entry and exit are negligible. A microentrepreneur needs no licenses or permits, does not need proven skills or qualifications to start a business, and neither pays, nor charges sales and purchase taxes. Low entry costs make certain segments of the informal sector highly transient, with a high turnover of business start-ups and closings. This is especially the case in the lowest tier, where hawkers and shoeshines drift in and out of work, resorting to begging (and sometimes petty crime) when they cannot make enough money polishing shoes or peddling trinkets.

Although they fall outside the purview of laws and regulations, most informal businesses are legal and legitimate—the parallel market is not a black market. But there are exceptions. Some people specialize in selling contraband, ranging from stolen television sets and cassette players, to smuggled cigarettes and liquor. Their businesses are usually controlled by gangs. In Bolivia and Peru the rural informal sector also includes numerous smallholders who grow coca leaf which they sell to the middlemen of Colombian drug cartels.

Capital outlay and overhead costs are also low, especially at the entry level, where working capital is minimal. A shoeshine needs only a few boxes of shoe polish, some rags, a rickety stool, and strong hands. Rickshaw drivers who pay the rental for their conveyances at the end of each day can start a working day without money. All they need is strong legs, and enough stamina to work long hours on an empty stomach.

People's dwellings normally double up as their workplaces. Even the smallest adobe hut or dingiest shack can be a workshop. These workplaces are invariably cramped, and beds, tables, and other furniture customarily double up as work surfaces. In a small printing shop I visited in Indonesia, stools and chairs served as printing tables, and fresh prints were left to dry on a bed. Because electricity is scarce and costly, many workshops are lit by candles and kerosene lamps. Others tap overhead power lines for electricity. That is dangerous. Many a workshop catches fire from poorly insulated high-voltage wires or tipped-over candles.

There is an active informal labor market, where workers are always near at hand. If a microentrepreneur needs help, it is customary to employ children and relatives, friends and neighbors. If the family is the basic production unit, no wages are paid. Even when microenterprises try to keep accounts, business and household expenses are intermingled. What is left over after buying food and shelter, repaying loans, and covering other business expenses, belongs to the household. It is either saved or used as working capital.

Hidden Costs for Microentrepreneurs and Their Workers

The advantage of low entry and exit costs is largely offset by substantial hidden costs that limit the economic potential of informal activities.

First of all, microentrepreneurs seldom have property rights, or title to their homesteads-workshops, and own few, if any, assets of value. Leaving aside that commercial banks are unwilling to finance their businesses, the self-employed are not protected by laws, cannot take out insurance, and have no legal recourse to enforce contracts. This means that, in their business dealings with one another, microentrepreneurs spend a lot of time investigating and monitoring each other to make sure they won't be cheated.[1]

There are other hidden costs. Unlike people in wage employment, workers in the informal sector can never "retire." Because they do not pay taxes or make social-security contributions they do not qualify for old-age benefits. To survive they must work into old age.

One aspect of informality that tends to be overlooked is exposure to harassment. Hawkers and street merchants who work in public view face constant risks of being penalized for working without permits, or failing to pay taxes. They go to great lengths to avoid punishment by the authorities.[2] Even so, they are frequently hassled by police and petty officials who give them fines for imaginary offenses. Another annoyance is harassment by criminal gangs who use threats to extort money. For instance, in Moscow, the small private kiosks that flourished during Gorbachev's *perestroika* were constantly hassled by thugs who vandalized the kiosks of merchants who refused to pay "protection money."

For its part, the absence of regulations creates risks for workers in microenterprises. They have no employment contracts, no recourse to labor laws and codes, and are not protected by health and safety regulations. There is no workers' compensation for the all too frequent accidents and injuries of workers who rarely have protective clothing or safety equipment, even when they do hazardous work. In lumber yards and furniture workshops in Bangladesh and Indonesia, I saw men using high-speed electrical saws that had no hand safety guards. More than once I saw workers standing in puddles, while using electrical tools. This can be lethal. The owner of the small furniture factory in Yogyakarta told me in a matter-of-fact way that one of her workers had recently been electrocuted, while cutting wood with an electrical saw that was not insulated.

Even people who work by themselves often do so in hazardous and unhealthy conditions. In Mymensingh District, in northern Bangladesh, I met a young couple who were making a living by filling and assembling ball-point pens, which they sold to wholesalers. The couple and their two-year-old son lived and worked in a single room, on the second floor of a dingy building. At night they kept the tools of their trade—ball-point parts, a bucket of ink, and an ink pump—under their bed. By day, the man spent most of his waking hours squatting on the floor beside the bed, spooning ink into the pump, and filling the tiny plastic tubes of hundreds of ball-point pens. There was ink everywhere, on the floor, on the walls, and on the man's face, hands, and clothes. His wife's job was to assemble and package the pens, while trying to keep her child as far away as possible from the beckoning ink bucket. She worked squatting on the bed. There was no other free space in the room.

One major problem is that child labor is commonplace in the informal sector. The are about 250 million child laborers in the world today. Most of them are in developing countries. In Bangladesh, where child labor was widespread in the garment industry, the Garment Manufacturers' and Exporters' Association has been cooperating with the ILO, the US embassy in Dhaka, and UNICEF to draw up a plan to remove younger children from the labor force, and to provide them and their parents with alternative sources of income. The association also agreed to set up a health clinic for garment workers, and establish a school for child workers. The ILO's Dhaka office monitors compliance with the agreements. Unfortunately, child labor remains widespread in the urban informal sector, doing dirty, unhealthy work. For instance, because Bangladesh has no rocks or quarries, and no natural sources of gravel, young boys and girls spend their days making gravel by smashing bricks with hammers.

Even in the poorest families, the working conditions of children who are employed by their parents tend to be better than those of the children who work in factories and sweatshops. Parents may need the extra cash brought in by their children's labor, but are likely to treat them well. The problem is that child labor keeps children out of school, perpetuating the vicious circle of illiteracy and poverty.

A Source of Unbounded Initiative

Low entry and start-up costs mean that microenterprises can be highly responsive to market conditions, and that they can easily switch from one activity to another, to take advantage of new business opportunities. There is a perfect example of this in Peru. Shortly after he was elected in 1990, President Fujimori liberalized imports and reduced all import duties, except on new cars. This created a niche for imports of used vehicles. As it happens, in Japan people rarely buy second-hand cars and there is always a large surplus of perfectly serviceable cars. Some of these were exported to Peru. The problem is that the Japanese drive on the left, so that the imported vehicles were all right-hand drives. In Peru it is illegal to drive such cars, and a new cottage industry sprang up within a matter of weeks. As soon as car mechanics had figured out how to turn a right-hand drive car into a left-hand drive, scores of "conversion" workshops opened for business. They set to work on the Japanese automobiles with hacksaws and acetylene torches, moving steering wheels and pedals from right to left, cutting a hole here, patching one up there. These conversions are accident prone—a ride in a "converted" taxi is an interesting experience, but it should not be repeated too often. The point is that resourceful mechanics saw a market opportunity and seized it, which is the quintessence of market responsiveness.

There are countless examples of similar ingenuity. I found a most remarkable one in an ancient Toyota taxi, on my way to the airport in San Salvador. To my amazement, the car had not one, but two gear levers—one for automatic, and one for manual transmission—but no hand brake. Somewhat perplexed I asked the driver what he had done to his car. He explained that, because mechanics in El Salvador do not have the tools—or skills—to repair automatic transmissions, he had removed the automatic gearbox and replaced it with a manual one. To cut costs he had left the old automatic gear lever in its original position, and had put the manual shift in the place where the handbrake had been!

Informal businesses are often the sole providers of public services in poor areas and urban slums. West Africa's bush taxis, Kenya's *matatus* (informal minibuses), and the thousands of "microbuses" in cities and towns in Latin America are the only forms of public transport the poor can afford, and the only way they can reach city centers from outlying areas. Elsewhere, in urban slum and shantytowns, such as Rio's hill-top *favellas* and the *pueblos jovenes* (young townships) on the outskirts of Lima, there is no running water and people purchase drinking water from tanker trucks. The water trade has few health controls and regulations, and unscrupulous freelance truckers sometimes sell contaminated water that is unsafe to drink. On the outskirts of Lima I once saw a water truck that was filling its tanks by pumping water from a garbage-strewn stream.

Organizing the Informal Sector

Because they are vulnerable to harassment and interference, self-employed traders and craftsmen sometimes form support groups, such as neighborhood committees, and street vendors' organizations that provide safety through numbers.[3] These initiatives are transforming parts of the informal economy into structured, quasi-formal activities. This is the case in Lima, where groups of street vendors have formed trade associations, with elected officials.

Competition in the informal sector also follows structured patterns. In the bazaars of Bangladesh, the street markets of Africa, and the souks of the Middle East, merchants and craftsmen are grouped by trade. There are particular sections for scribes, cloth merchants, blacksmiths, cobblers, fishmongers, butchers, and sellers of fruit, spices, and rice. Bargain hunting is easy in these "shopping centers of the poor." Concentration by trade makes it easier for customers to comparison shop—and for lenders to assess the creditworthiness of prospective borrowers.

The same pattern of concentration by type of activity can be found among craftsmen in urban informal sectors. Lima's downtown, for instance, has a garment district that consists of converted warehouses and office buildings, abandoned by companies that moved to safer areas. Similarly, in Bangkok, a stone's throw away from five-star luxury hotels along the river front, there are dozens of mechanical workshops that recycle the engines, transmissions, and rear axles of old trucks and buses. In each shop, vehicle parts are stacked up in huge, oily piles, waiting to be reused, to give trucks, taxis, and riverboats a new lease on life.

Self-Employment and the Labor Market

One of the reasons self-employment and informality are receiving so much attention from development agencies is it that informality acts a safety valve for the labor market. The fact that people who lose their jobs in the wage economy can usually find some of type of work in the informal sector is an important feature of labor-market adjustment. This happens during periods of structural adjustment, when workers are laid off, or when there are too few jobs in the wage economy for all the new entrants in the labor market. In such situations, young people, including college graduates, frequently bypass the formal labor market altogether, and move directly into the informal sector.

Mature informal sectors that have their own rules and codes of conduct are potent social safety valves, and can even cushion the effects of low wages: in developing countries it is not uncommon for underpaid civil servants to supplement their meager salaries by moonlighting with informal work.

There is also an interesting twist in the relationship between the informal sector and the business cycle. As already noted, in Latin America informal activities grew exponentially during the 1980s, sometimes to the point of becoming the largest, most dynamic part of the economy, and numerous informal businesses became self-sustaining with loans from microcredit programs. This gradually institutionalized informal work, and desynchronized it from underlying trends in the economy. That, and the high cost of "re-entering" the mainstream economy, creates a ratchet effect, as a result of which the level of informality remains high and barely falls, if at all, during economic upswings.

The cost of re-entry can indeed be prohibitive. To take but one example, in Peru, in the 1980s, obtaining the necessary permits to open a business in the formal economy usually took forty-three days, and cost $590, fifteen times the minimum monthly wage at that time. Furthermore, once a business is formal, remaining formal involves recurring costs: taxes, utilities, and the costs of renewing permits.[4]

Other factors also contribute to the ratchet effect. One of them is that people who have worked hard to carve out a niche in a given market or activity, no matter how small, become established and are likely to stay in the informal sector, unless it is beyond doubt that they can benefit from working in wage employment, or from formalizing their businesses. This is seldom the case. Indeed, even if informal businesses were to become formal and pay taxes, most would still be too small to qualify for loans from commercial banks. Finally, people who try to re-enter the job market after years of informal work face stiff competition from younger, more qualified entrants.

Self-Employment and Poverty

By far the main reason self-employment is now in the limelight is that, in the absence of other sources of income or social safety nets for the poor and jobless, promoting self-employment is more cost-effective and equitable than conventional poverty-reduction strategies. In this context, it is interesting to note that, when asked what their main constraints are, the poor almost invariably say that they are the lack of money and the lack of access to credit. But lack of credit is but one of many constraints. The poor also lack endowment with land and productive assets, and have too few skills and too little education.

Microfinance programs that provide working capital for self-employment can alleviate some of these resource constraints, especially when financing is combined with basic training to teach business skills. This makes informal activities more productive, and improves the quality of life of microentrepreneurs and their families. The beneficial impact is greatest when women in poor households are taught basic business skills. When women are given a chance to earn money from viable activities, their families' health and nutrition improve. Illnesses become less frequent, and infant mortality, pregnancies, and birthing-related injuries decline when women have material incentives to space births. More generally, microfinance and self-employment can be used with great effectiveness to empower women and ethnic minorities, giving them greater control over their lives.

But, even though there are remarkable examples of upward social mobility among the clients of some of the institutions that are reviewed in this book, self-employment seldom breaks the vicious circle of poverty. When it does, the impact of self-employment seldom reaches beyond households or small rural communities. It cannot bring about economic change at the "macro" level, or eradicate large-scale poverty by laying the foundations for sustained economic growth and development. This is the case, even in countries where the majority of economically active people work in the informal economy. Although informal work is then the only way the majority can survive, most people remain at, or close to, the poverty level.

Activities in the middle tier of the informal sector have the greatest overall income effect. In microfinance programs that lend to the middle-tier poor, clients gradually manage to accumulate savings, and become a steady group of repeat borrowers with low arrears. Their businesses anchor families and communities, and ensure the financial stability and sustainability of the microfinance institutions that work with them. But even steady middle-tier businesses have limitations that constrain their growth and income potential; they engage in small-scale, low-productivity activities, and use out-of-date technology that cannot compete with manufactured goods. There are countless instances of craftsmen who are driven out of business, and lose their livelihood, when countries liberalize trade and begin importing goods from low-wage economies. When this happens, skilled artisans lose their livelihood and are forced to become petty traders, frequently relapsing into poverty.

The point is that self-employment is not a panacea. Poverty reduction on a large and lasting scale requires a multi-faceted approach for economic and social development. Self-employment and microfinance are necessary, but not sufficient components of that approach.

Notes

1. Hernando de Soto, *The Other Path: The Invisible Revolution in the Third World* (New York: Harper & Row, 1989), 152 and 166.
2. Hernando de Soto, 152 and 153.
3. Hernando de Soto, 167.
4. Hernando de Soto, 143 and 148.

3

Banking for the Unbankable

The previous two chapters discussed the roots of poverty, and the place of self-employment in the economies of developing countries. This chapter explains how, and from what sources, the poor and self-employed can obtain financial services that match their needs.

Microfinance covers a broad variety of institutional arrangements and approaches. They range from minuscule self-help groups with a handful of members, to huge organizations that have nationwide coverage and serve millions of clients. While all the large microfinance institutions promote self-employment as a means of reducing poverty, their approaches and target groups differ considerably. Poverty lending programs lend only to people whose income is *below* the level of absolute poverty. Most of their clients are women who have little or no work experience. In contrast, other microfinance institutions prefer to lend to the middle tier of the poor whose income is *above* the level of absolute poverty and who are already established as microentrepreneurs.

Differences in institutional arrangements and target groups are partly the result of social and economic factors. For instance, in villages in sub-Saharan Africa and South Asia, where the vast majority of people live in absolute poverty, rural microfinance programs are forced by circumstances to do poverty lending. Only institutions that work in towns and cities and in middle-income countries have more options in deciding which income group they will target.

As the country chapters in Parts II through IV will explain, population density and the state of infrastructure also have a determining influence on the size and outreach of microfinance programs, and on the cost of credit delivery. The largest microfinance programs, which serve millions of clients, are all in densely populated Asian countries that are predominantly agrarian. They work almost exclusively in rural areas. In highly urbanized Latin America, where poverty and informal activities are heavily concentrated in cities, microfinance is predominantly urban and the scale of the programs' activities is smaller than in Asia. Finally, in the sparsely populated Sahel and forested

39

areas of sub-Saharan Africa the terrain is difficult, and clients are hard to reach. African microfinance programs also face strong competition from informal credit arrangements in extended family groups. Working on a limited scale in difficult environments and with people who have virtually no savings, raises costs. In Africa the operating expenses of microfinance programs are much higher than in Asia or Latin America and depend on external funding and subsidies.

Banking on People

Regardless of the social, economic, and physical context, commercial banks are loath to lend to microentrepreneurs. They consider them unbankable because they have no credit history and own too few assets for loan collateral or other guarantees. Profit-driven banks have another reason for refusing to lend to the poor and microentrepreneurs: cost. The unit cost of credit delivery is high because it takes almost as much time to evaluate, approve, and process a loan of, say $300, as a loan of $30,000. Supervising and monitoring thousands of minuscule loans drives up costs even further.

In contrast, specialized financial institutions that make large numbers of small loans, sometimes in amounts as little as $20, manage to break even or even make profits. They can do so by being more flexible and adaptable than conventional banks; accepting alternatives to formal guarantees; and decentralizing and streamlining all decision making to bring down costs, and expedite credit approvals.

Most importantly, unlike commercial banks, where the poor feel ill at ease, microfinance programs *bank on people, not on money*. They establish relations of trust with their clients, and treat people with respect, even when they are illiterate, and only speak vernacular languages. This builds up people's confidence in their dealings with institutions that go out of their way to accommodate their needs and ease their apprehensions, and whose staff treat them as equals.

It is often argued that it is wrong to lend to microentrepreneurs, and to the poor in general, because the last thing a poor person needs is incurring debt. On the face of it, this makes sense. If a business is so small that it is unlikely ever to make enough money to repay a loan on time, if at all, encouraging to borrow is a fast lane to ruin. In fact, offering loans to people who are likely to be in default serves no purpose, since they would be worse off than without going into debt.

Refuting that argument is the collective experience of millions of women and men. They have shown that small loans for working capital or to buy equipment *can* have a significant economic payoff by raising their productivity and earning power. For the laundress who borrows dollars to buy a steam iron, the carpenter who can finally replace hand tools with an electric saw, the tortilla merchant who takes out a loan to buy a mechanical flour grinder, and the market vendor who has more goods on her stall, being able to produce or sell more goods means that they can earn more money and inch out of total poverty. For them, and millions of other microentrepreneurs, being able to borrow can be a way out of the vicious circle of impoverishment, moving onto a virtuous circle in which they begin accumulating some working capital, expand their income-generating activities, and achieve some upward social mobility, one step at a time. Their achievements rebut the "no debts" argument.

Character-based Lending

The financial innovation that made microenterprise financing on a large scale feasible is joint-liability lending to groups, in which people are responsible for each others' loan repayments. Barring few exceptions, group lending, where peer-group pressure creates moral collateral, is the norm in microfinance. But group lending is not risk free, and loan defaults can create contagion among borrowers; if people realize that others get away with not repaying their loans, there is a temptation to do the same, especially if defaulting is perceived as penalty free. Furthermore, groups create an endogenous risk of "free riding" by people who burden their co-guarantors.

One has to be realistic. The fact that most microentrepreneurs are denied loans by commercial banks does not mean that access to credit is a basic human right, or that poverty conveys entitlement to credit. Microfinance is not charity. It is a contract based on trust, in which a lender agrees to make a loan, and a borrower promises to repay the money with interest by a certain date. This means that lenders implicitly assume that their clients are willing and able to meet their obligations, while remaining alert to problems, such as the fact borrowers have few skills and no formal education. The bankers of the poor must always use caution and strict credit screening to eliminate potentially bad risks, regardless of people's needs. To make collective guarantees effective safeguards, they must make sure that co-guarantors trust each other. The "golden rule" of microfinance is that credit only makes sense if there is no doubt that borrowers will make good use of the funds, and that, after repaying the loans and interest, they will have enough money left to support themselves and their families, and begin accumulating personal savings.

Rigorous credit screening is also prudent business practice. It protects the integrity of the lending institutions, and safeguards the interests of their clients. If careless lending and massive defaults undermine an institution's financial viability and force its liquidation, existing clients are penalized by losing access to credit, and may even forfeit their savings. To limit that risk, and protect the institutions in which they are working, loan officers should approve loans only when it is beyond doubt that the people they are dealing with will use the funds productively. This means that they must visit clients before a loan is approved, and make a follow-up visit immediately after a loan is disbursed to make sure that the funds are being used as agreed. Loan officers must also maintain regular contacts with all their active clients, individually and in groups, to monitor their performance. Some microfinance institutions even offer interest-rate rebates as incentives for punctual loan repayments.

When prospective clients have no prior work experience or proven skills, which tends to be the case in poverty lending, offering borrowers basic training can improve credit quality. In such situations it is wise to begin with small loans that are increased in step with the clients' repayment capacity. If they do encounter payment problems with new clients whose small businesses fail, the safest course of action is to drop them after the first loan cycle.

Because lending is character-based and rests on peer-group pressure, some institutions do *morality checks* of prospective borrowers; they make sure that clients do not abuse their spouses, have no drinking or drug problems, and are not in arrears with other creditors. In some Muslim countries where polygamy is still practiced, the purpose of morality checks is sometimes to ascertain that men do not have more wives than they can support.

Of course, mistakes can and do happen, and the quality of credit screening varies. Some programs do not have enough experienced staff or adequate procedures to screen clients properly. Others, especially small donor-funded non-governmental organizations (NGOs), sometimes act nonchalantly. They use "cookie-cutter" credit checks and offer loans on a first-come, first-served basis. Lax credit screening then results in high delinquencies, which undermines the notion that self-employment and microfinance are viable alternatives to conventional poverty reduction. This is a disservice to all microentrepreneurs, and to those who are striving to improve their lives with small loans.

The Poor Can Be Creditworthy

The large number of well-managed microfinance programs has dispelled the notion that poverty and the ability to carry debt are inversely related. They have proven that even some of the poorest people can put credit to productive use, and earn enough money to raise their households' income *and* repay loans in regular installments—the largest poverty-lending programs have loan repayment rates that are as high as those of institutions that target middle- and upper-tier microentrepreneurs. In fact, expectations to the contrary notwithstanding, some of the smallest businesses are better credit risks than companies that have hundreds of thousands of dollars in turnover. It is not unusual for microfinance programs consistently to have repayment rates on the order of 98 percent, which is much higher than in most commercial banks. What is even more remarkable is that women are better payers than men. This means that poverty and gender cannot, and should not, be used as defining concepts to measure creditworthiness.

One should realize, however, that the poor are not better payers than the rich because they are better people, but because they have more reasons not to default. Foremost among them is access to credit. This is, in and of itself, one of the strongest incentives to remain punctual. If repaying a loan on time offers the assurance that credit will be available again, when it is needed, there is a degree of financial security. But the "carrot" of future loans must always be accompanied by the "stick" of zero tolerance of arrears. Only clients who are punctual payers should have repeat loans. Besides the assurance of continued access to credit, another good reason to repay a loan on time is peer-group pressure in group credit and the fear of scorn when letting one's co-borrowers down. This offsets the risk of free-riding.

Not surprisingly, default rates rise if credit is perceived as a gift, and defaulting carries no penalties. This happens when lenders are remiss in following up loan arrears, lend at heavily subsidized interest rates, or make it clear that there will be no repeat loans, regardless of repayment records. This explains why defaults are consistently higher in small programs that cannot assure continued access to credit, than in programs that already have large numbers of repeat borrowers.

The Vital Role of Savings

Savings provide a safety cushion for crises and contingencies, such as floods, illness, accidents, weddings, and funerals. To fulfill this role the funds must be readily available when needed. Only savings that are in a safe, accessible place give financial security. Beyond the financial security it conveys, saving is *always* better than accumulating debts, but very few people in the informal economy have enough cash to start a business without some form of credit. Those who can do so are probably not poor.

One of the biggest misconceptions is that the poor do not, and cannot save. Nothing is further from the truth. All but the poorest usually manage to accumulate *some* assets, but frequently do so in non-monetary forms which bypass the financial system. In pastoral nomadic tribes wealth and savings consist of camels, horses, goats, and cattle. In villages, people sometimes save to buy land. In Bangladesh I met several "landless" women who were using their savings to buy small plots of land, one bit at a time. But, because Islamic ownership and inheritance laws do not allow women to own land, they buy the land in their husbands' or sons' names. In cities, traders build up inventories, and artisans buy tools or materials. In many cases people simply hoard cash—literally under their mattresses—or pool their savings in voluntary associations outside the banking system. Others buy jewels with their savings, since this gives them access to pawn credit.

With the advent of microfinance, people who work in the informal sector had incentives to place their savings with the institutions that lend to them, rather than with commercial banks. But some of their money still ends up in the very banks that refuse to lend to them, and is used to make loans to big landowners and companies. This happens, for instance, in village banks, which are not licensed to hold funds and must place their clients' savings in a bank account.

Capturing savings is important for the institutions themselves. It leverages their lending potential, limits—or even eliminates—the need for external funds, and is a key to financial sustainability. Savings also makes it possible to perform local financial intermediation by using local savings to make loans in the same communities.

The microfinance institutions that have been most successful at attracting savings from people who have never had a bank account are the ones that work with the middle-tier poor. They establish trust by offering instruments, such as savings passbooks, that are safe, simple, and pay a fair interest rate. The most outstanding case is in Indonesia. Before the financial collapse of 1997–98, savers in Bank Rakyat's village banking units outnumbered borrowers by a ratio of 6:1, and the amount on deposit was three times that of the loans outstanding.

Poverty-lending programs, whose clients' savings are extremely limited, try to instill the habit of thrift through *forced savings*, obliging borrowers to set aside a fixed proportion of each loan in a special fund. The problem is that access to forced savings serve as cash collateral for loans. This curtails the access to those savings for contingencies, and, because interest is charged on the entire loan, setting aside forced savings raises the cost of borrowing.

Adapting Financial Services to the Needs of the Poor

Microfinance has a long tradition. The first recorded evidence of a financial institution that loaned exclusively to small farmers and the truly needy is in 1614, in Amsterdam, when the city's magistrates and regents founded the Bank van Lening (the Lending Bank). The city's leaders wanted to make sure that small farmers and the poor could get affordable loans, to keep them out of the clutches of pawnbrokers—even then pawnbrokers had a bad reputation. The bank's original building still stands on one of Amsterdam's stately canals. The bas-relief above the main entrance shows a woman receiving help, and the inscription above it admonishes the rich to go elsewhere if they need loans. This bank charged interest at 4 percent to small farmers, and the poor paid no interest at all.[1]

Four centuries after this worthy precursor of microfinance opened its doors, there are close to 7,000 active microfinance programs with more than thirteen million clients, and about $8 billion in loans outstanding. Even so, they still only reach a tiny proportion of the people who could use loans productively and there is an enormous unfilled need for credit in the informal sector.

Family and kin are still the first sources to which people turn when they need cash or working capital. The best examples of mutual support is in extended families and kinship groups in Africa, where it is almost a sacred duty for people with a steady income to help less fortunate relatives. The alternative to borrowing from kin is to seek credit from a variety of informal and formal financial intermediaries. These range from informal arrangements that only offer short-term credit in limited amounts, to large regulated financial intermediaries that have a broad geographical coverage, a full range of services, and a strong emphasis on mobilizing savings.

As was noted in the two preceding chapters, widespread poverty in South

Asia and growing unemployment in Latin American debtor countries were catalysts for the creation of specialized credit programs. The largest among them already have several million clients, offer a full range of financial services, and are financially self-sufficient. The availability of microfinance on a large scale is nevertheless a relatively new phenomenon. To overcome people's initial reticence towards this novelty, microfinance programs must establish their credibility in villages and poor communities. They sometimes have to work hard to gain the trust of people who are not accustomed to dealing with financial institutions, and may be reluctant to experiment with new ideas. But once the initial reluctance is overcome, it is possible to attract clients by word of mouth.

The Grameen Bank is one of the best examples of a grassroots approach to building trust and acceptance in tradition-bound rural communities. Before it opens a new branch office in a small village, an advance team goes there to meet the people and explain the bank's philosophy of group lending. The advance team also gains the confidence of villagers by living modestly like them, and buying and cooking their own food.

Informal Lenders

Informal credit is the norm in communities where there are no microfinance institutions. Informal credit shares all the attributes of the informal sector. It is unregulated, has low entry and exit costs, and is entirely voluntary. There are only verbal promises to lend and repay. Courts do not, and cannot, intervene in these informal arrangements.

Moneylenders

Moneylenders have an important place in village society and neighborhoods, where they are sometimes the sole purveyors of credit. Many of them perform local financial intermediation by collecting savings—they sometimes call it "renting money"—and lending the funds in the same community. They only "rent" money when there is sufficient demand for credit, and the rate they pay to savers always depends on what they can expect to earn on loans. Some moneylenders also hold people's money in safe keeping so that they can accumulate capital, and shelter their cash from the demands of friends and relatives in extended families. Most safe-keeping arrangements involve weekly deposits. In return for these services, a moneylender's fee is usually one week's deposit.

Moneylenders live locally and know their clients. Their *forte* is being able to offer credit when it is most needed. Although they charge high interest rates, and sometimes use strong-arm methods to recover their money—which often earns them a reputation of "loan sharks"—for people who have nowhere else to turn, the convenience of ready access to cash outweighs cost. That is the case for market vendors whose profit margins can be as high as

100 percent. For them it is preferable to pay a high interest rate than to forego a trading profit.

Moneylending is frequently combined with other activities. For example, a neighborhood shop that sells food on credit until the next payday does moneylending of sorts, and factors an interest rate into the price of its goods. One unexpected form of moneylending is in Bangladesh, where some Grameen members use their small loans to become village moneylenders—in these cases it is the men who do the actual lending with their wives' loans. When a moneylender is also a landlord—a frequent occurrence in villages, where peasant farmers rent small parcels of land—people can get so deeply into debt that they become virtually indentured to their creditors.

Pawnbrokers

Pawnbrokers are moneylenders who demand collateral in the form of gold jewelry or other valuables. In the poorest communities they also accept clothes and household goods as security—during the depression of the 1930s, families in coal-mining districts in northern England regularly pawned their "Sunday best" clothes until the next payday, reclaiming them at week's end.

As a rule, pawn loans are only for a fraction of the assessed value of the collateral, sometimes less than half of it. If a loan is not repaid on time, the collateral becomes the property of the pawnbroker, and is sold. A rare example of institutionalized pawn lending on a large scale is in Peru's Municipal Savings and Credit Banks. They have driven local moneylenders and pawnshops out of business by operating their own pawn windows. The municipal banks only accept gold jewelry as collateral. Unlike pawnbrokers, the banks roll over loans on a weekly basis, as long as there is enough collateral and interest is paid at the end of each week. They are also cheaper.

Rotating Savings and Credit Associations (ROSCAs)

These are voluntary self-help financial arrangements among people who form a group, and agree to make regular (usually weekly) deposits in equal amounts. There is direct intermediation between borrowers and savers: the communal savings pool is used as a rotating loan fund, from which each member can borrow in turn. After each member has had his or her turn, a ROSCA either breaks up, or begins a new cycle. In either case, members withdraw their accumulated savings at the end of each cycle. Belonging to a voluntary association encourages thrift and financial discipline, and is a convenient way to accumulate working capital.

The unusual feature of ROSCAs is that there is no interest on deposits *or* loans. All loans are short-term, usually for a month or less. Otherwise members would have to wait too long for their turns. In any event, patience has its rewards: accumulated contributions grow over time, and the later one borrows, the larger the loans.[2] To avoid favoritism, associations use different methods to allocate credit. The most common ones are to assign turns by drawing. Others allocate loans in alphabetical order, or on the basis of need. Some ROSCAs use bidding, in which people can pledge to make larger contributions, in return for being able to choose when to borrow.

There are no restrictions on the use of funds. It can be for consumption, to deal with emergencies, or for working capital in one's business. The fact that loans are rarely for more than one month makes them better suited for trade than for production. However, at the end of a full ROSCA cycle accumulated savings may be sufficient to start or expand a small business.

ROSCAs are run by their members, and are based on mutual trust. This explains why they are mostly formed by people who live in the same neighborhood or work the same place, or by groups of friends. Proximity and familiarity create loyalty and are strong motivations to make regular deposits and repay loans. Fraud and defaults are rare, and the collective responsibility and peergroup monitoring are precursors of group credit with collective guarantees. But belonging to an association is not a badge of honesty. There is always a risk that those who borrowed early in the cycle will defect, rather than continue making more weekly contributions from which they do not benefit.

There are numerous variations on the theme of ROSCAs, and they exist in most countries. There is a vast nomenclature of names and acronyms for ROSCAs. In Francophone Africa they are called *tontines*. Elsewhere they are *susu*, or *esusu*. In Japan, they are called *tanamoshi*, a term that has been adopted by Japanese communities in Peru. In the United States, in the early nineteenth century, people who had no access to housing finance organized savings clubs. The members of the clubs made monthly deposits that were large enough to make it possible for one member per month to purchase a house. Unlike in ROSCAs, in these housing-loan clubs patience did not pay off: the first served could buy a house immediately. Also unlike in today's ROSCAs, the funds did not revolve. The associations dissolved as soon as all members had bought a house. ROSCA-type savings clubs still exist in the United States, mostly among small traders and shopkeepers who belong to the same ethnic groups. Korean self-help groups are among the most active.

In some countries ROSCAs are managed by commercial banks. In Argentina many of the larger ROSCAs pay fees to banks which assume the credit risk on loans to members, and protect the members' collective savings. In Peru a small credit cooperative (Impulso) charges a management fee to safeguard to deposits of ROSCAs in ethnic Japanese communities, and in Senegal FONGS, a national federation of farmer cooperatives, coordinates the activities of village-based savings and loans clubs.

Semi-Formal Lenders

Semi-formal financial intermediaries occupy the middle ground between informal lenders and large microfinance programs. They have no banking licenses, are not subject to banking laws and prudential supervision, and are not held to specific capital requirements. Because they are not licensed they may only collect clients' or members' savings if they place the funds in custody with a commercial bank.

Intermediaries in this category enjoy some advantages. Since they need no permits or licenses they are fairly inexpensive to set up, and their small scale is well adapted to working in villages and neighborhoods. They can also operate out of modest premises and involve their member/clients in day-to-day management and decision making. Another advantage is that small semi-formal arrangements are easier to replicate than large programs. This explains why semi-formal financial intermediation is expanding faster than lending by large microfinance institutions.

The two most common types of semi-formal institutions are village banks and NGOs that manage credit programs on behalf of donors and foreign sponsors.

Village Banks: A Complex but Easily Replicated Formula

Like ROSCAs, village banks are local, self-selecting groups of twenty to fifty people, usually from the same community. Village banking began as an experiment in the Bolivian Andes in the late 1970s. The first ones were organized by rural community leaders, and loaned to groups of smallholders without collateral. From the outset they encouraged savings and peer-group solidarity among their members, most of whom were men. They were an instant success and flourished until the mid-1980s, when the country's entire financial system was virtually decimated by hyperinflation.[3]

The Bolivian experiment led to the establishment of the Washington, D.C.-based Foundation for International Community Assistance (FINCA). FINCA promotes credit for self-employment to families in severe poverty by providing start-up funding for village banks. It finances its international programs with grants and donations. In 1995, after ten years in operation, it had already helped launch close to 2,200 village banks, through fifteen programs in fourteen countries, in Africa, North, Central and South America—surprisingly, none are in Bolivia. In that year alone these banks had disbursed about $13 million in new loans. In 1997, FINCA had 70,000 members (12,000 more than in 1995), $7.7 million in loans outstanding, and $3.6 million in members' savings. Repayment rates consistently average 95 percent.[4]

FINCA's village banks are *for* women, and managed *by* women. Men are not excluded, but are not exactly welcome either. Contrary to what their name suggests, village banks do not operate exclusively in rural areas, and also work in peri-urban areas and small towns. In practice, village banking is "community" banking, rather than rural banking—in Latin America they are called *bancos comunales*.

The FINCA model is highly organized and standardized. Each bank must elect a president, a secretary, and a credit committee. The committee coordinates and oversees the members' collective loan guarantees, screens loan applications, approves all new loans, and handles bookkeeping and internal supervision. The banks normally meet once a week, on the day loan repayments are due. Members are expected to attend these meetings, at which new loans are disbursed and new proposals are discussed.

All loans are for sixteen weeks, repayable in weekly installments, and average $110 per member. Lending is at market interest rates. There are no subsidies or interest-free loans. Loans to new members are always small. Savings are both voluntary and forced—members must save one-fifth of the amount they borrow, as a partial guarantee of repayment. Each subsequent loan cannot exceed the amount of the previous one *plus* the amount saved in the previous round. That means that a loan of $100 plus $20 savings, can be followed by a loan of $120, of which $24 must be set aside in savings. The next loan can be for $144, and $28.80 will be saved, and so forth.[5] Leveraging forced savings is important as it helps build up members' working capital. Before joining a village bank, three out every four FINCA members had no savings. By 1996 they were saving up to $50 per loan cycle.

During the start-up phase, when the banks' internal savings are limited, loans are funded by FINCA and the members are collectively responsible for the repayment of the funds. This generates considerable peer pressure since only banks that repay FINCA in full, and have no delinquent loans, qualify for new funding. As internal savings grow over time, the external funding diminishes and gradually goes down to zero.

Each village bank must keep two separate accounts with a licensed financial institution. External sponsor funds are placed in an *external account* for which the members are collectively responsible. Savings and funds from the internal cash flow that have not been used for new loans are deposited in the members' *internal account*. The members can decide how to use the funds from the internal account, and have considerable latitude in borrowing from it.

Because it is so standardized, the FINCA model can be used in different social and cultural contexts and has already been replicated in Kyrgyzstan. FINCA has also spawned replications and adaptations by major northern NGOs, such as CARE and Catholic Relief Services (CRS). CARE is one of the largest NGOs in the world, with headquarters in Atlanta, Georgia. It was founded by the US government in 1945 to provide emergency food assistance in war-torn Europe. In 1996 it had village banks and microfinance programs in more than seventy-five countries, including Thailand, Peru, and Bosnia, that had more than 90,000 clients. For its part, CRS is active in Thailand, Latin America, and Africa. Unlike FINCA , CARE and CRS emphasize social intermediation, and combine credit with non-financial services, such as community development, and health, nutrition, and environmental programs. Their village banks also have more flexible rules than the original model. Instead of lending for sixteen weeks at a time, they offer maturities of up to six months for activities that need longer repayment cycles.

Even some FINCA affiliates have experimented with different loan maturities. For instance, in El Salvador the Centro de Apoyo a la Microempresa

(CAM) has a special weekly loan program for local market vendors, who must repay loans in daily installments. Each client receives a card that must be punched as evidence of daily repayments. Only women whose cards had been punched each day, qualify for new loans in the following week.

One problem is that village banks are inherently weak—though democratic, collective decision making undermines accountability, and record-keeping is often lax. One way of dealing with these problems is to place village banks under the umbrella of a second-tier organization, or *apex*, to which they delegate several functions. The apex then becomes the conduit for donor funds, which are passed on to member banks, and mediates all contacts between its village banks and the government and central bank. The apex also provides support for institution building through training and technical assistance, and is responsible for the internal auditing, bookkeeping, treasury management, and prudential oversight of affiliated banks. In smaller village banks it is not uncommon for the apex to be represented at weekly meetings. This can mitigate, but not eliminate, the risk of fraud. A case in point is CAM. In 1995, collusion between one of its employees and a staff member in a commercial bank allegedly resulted in the diversion of a large sum of money in phantom loans. After FINCA intervened all diverted funds were reimbursed to donors and depositors. (CAM is no longer affiliated with FINCA.)

Local Financial NGOs: Conduits for Donor Funds

Local NGOs use third-party funds to finance their activities. They are usually small, have no capital, and depend on donor funds, both for their lending and to cover their operating expenses. Most sponsors are northern NGOs, such as Freedom from Hunger and Save the Children. These donors, who are not financial intermediaries, support local credit and poverty-reduction programs with seed capital and technical assistance. USAID, the United Nations Development Program (UNDP), the European Union, and European aid agencies also support financial NGOs.

Despite their prestigious sponsors, many local NGOs have governance problems, even when donors set guidelines for lending and credit evaluation. The most common issues are poor credit screening, low repayment rates and loan recovery, as well as inadequate financial controls and loan-classification standards, and inefficient accounting and information systems. This plethora of problems has created unwillingness about the reliability and accountability of NGOs as intermediaries for microfinance programs. In reality, many NGOs are prudent and diligent financial intermediaries, and some have been so successful that they became stepping stones for specialized banks and finance companies. In Bolivia PRODEM, an NGO established by ACCION International, founded BancoSol, and in Kenya K-REP, the country's largest financial NGO, was re-incorporated as K-REP Bank.

A frequent criticism of NGOs is that many of them are advocacy groups that promote social programs, using loans to promote social objectives with scant attention to credit quality. On this point, one has to bear in mind that social intermediation offers valuable services in marginalized communities, and that giving basic training to unskilled, illiterate clients can be essential for the success of microfinance programs in the poorest countries and communities. In Bangladesh, BRAC is the epitome of successful blending of credit and social objectives. It makes participation in social programs a condition for access to credit and charges a nominal fee for those services.

Non-Bank Financial Intermediaries

This group includes credit unions, savings and loans cooperatives, and municipal savings banks. These are all formal intermediaries that can mobilize savings and deposits.

Credit Unions

Credit are non-bank financial intermediaries that are based on the principle of mutuality, which involves ownership by members: they lend exclusively to member-shareholders. Whereas joint-stock companies are run for the benefit of shareholders, mutualist organizations are run for the benefit of their members who are usually drawn from professional and affinity groups, such as teachers, farmers or civil servants. Mutuality has its roots in Roman law and has thrived in Europe in various forms since the eighteenth century. In Latin America credit unions were founded in the early 1900s by European immigrants. The mutualist movement gained new impetus in the 1950s, 60s, and 70s when new credit unions were founded by the Roman Catholic Church and the Peace Corps.[6]

There are rural and urban credit unions. In either case, to qualify for a loan, members must be active savers in good standing and loan amounts are always set multiples of prior savings—usually three to five times the amount on deposit. Because credit unions are extremely efficient in mobilizing savings and deposits they can rapidly achieve financial autonomy and be independent from external funding, especially when they have more depositors than borrowers.

Most countries have credit unions. The movement is strongest in former French colonies in West Africa and in Latin America. The World Council of Credit Unions (WOCCU) is an international coordinating body that sets uniform accounting and credit standards for affiliated unions. All credit unions offer loans to self-employed, non-salaried clients, but only West Africa's credit unions devote most of their lending to microenterprises. In Latin America they mostly draw their membership from the middle classes, and lend primarily for personal use and consumption, and to small—rather than "micro"—enterprises.

Despite their potential for financial self-sufficiency, credit unions—especially, but not only, in Latin America—have a patchy track record, both in terms of individual savings mobilization and lending. During the 1960s and 1970s the Inter-American Development Bank (IADB) and the United States Agency for International Development (USAID) used credit unions as conduits for subsidized loans for social welfare. With lending rates that were too low to cover operating expenses, these credit unions could not offer competitive interest rates on deposits, or attract new members. This undermined their financial sustainability, and created dependence on donor subsidies. In other cases, governments used credit unions for political patronage to favor influential groups, such as large landowners, which politicized their activities. Later, during the 1970s, credit unions fell in disfavor in Brazil and other Latin American countries, where military juntas and dictators viewed the cooperative movement with suspicion. Finally, in the 1980s, most of the remaining unions were decimated by hyperinflation. Now, with the return of macroeconomic stability, credit unions are slowly regaining favor in Latin America. They have 5.5 million members—in some countries 3 percent of the population belong to credit unions.[7]

The fact that credit unions only lend to their members is a source of weakness: it is a disincentive to compete with other institutions for market share or use financial innovation to attract new clients. More generally, the credit unions' democratic rule of *one-member one-vote* results in poor management and creates governance problems by involving member-shareholders who have no financial training in financial decisions. Collective decision making also undermines accountability and creates poor governance. A more serious flaw is that many unions have inadequate accounting and reporting standards. These problems are compounded by *regulatory risk*, namely the fact that credit unions are often operating without proper regulation or supervision.[8] This is partly attributable to the fact that, in many countries, banking supervisors lack the expertise and resources to enforce prudential rules, and prevent governance problems in credit unions.

Savings and Loans Cooperatives

These too are mutualist non-bank financial intermediaries that have many similarities with credit unions. They work exclusively for their members, and loans are always a function of prior savings. Their origin dates back to 1840, in Germany, when a Mr. Raiffeisen, the mayor of a large village, founded a cooperative that loaned only to farmers who were its sole owners and shareholders. This first cooperative—named after its founder, it was called Raiffeisen Kasse—was so successful that the Raiffeisen model was replicated all over Germany, as well as in France, Belgium, the Netherlands, Scandinavia, Switzerland, and Canada, and Japan, and became the origin of an international cooperative movement. Holland's RaboBank, France's Crédit Agricole, Germany's DG Bank, Canada's Caisse Desjardins, and Japan's Norinchukin Bank—all of which began as small rural credit cooperatives, based on the Raiffeisen model—have become major financial institutions in their own right.

RaboBank and Caisse Desjardins have also founded consulting businesses that offer technical assistance to new and existing credit cooperatives in developing countries, including in Vietnam, Eastern Europe, and the former Soviet republics.

To preserve the one-member one-vote rule, the members of cooperatives can own only one share each. Unlike credit unions, rural credit cooperatives usually have a national apex, to which banking supervisors delegate a great deal of supervisory responsibilities. With the technical support of Quebec's Caisse Desjardins and others, cooperatives have strengthened their financial and accounting procedures. This helps overcome the governance and accountability problems that plague so many credit unions, and explains why credit cooperatives are generally more efficient and better managed. Peru's Municipal Savings Banks, the country's the main purveyors of microfinance, differ from the cooperative model in that they are owned by municipal councils who are their sole shareholders.

The Top Tier of Microfinance

The top tier in microfinance consists of major financial institutions that operate on a nationwide scale, and usually fall within the purview of banking laws and prudential regulations. Most, but not all, use peer-group lending. Each one has achieved considerable outreach among rural and urban poor and/or microentrepreneurs. Four of the "superstars" are Asian, and work almost exclusively in rural areas. Though much smaller than the Asian programs, Bolivia's Banco Solidario is also in the top tier. Other organizations that belong in this group are two US-based NGOs that have large international microfinance programs—FINCA, the pioneer of village banking, and ACCION International.

The Grameen Bank

Grameen is the world's most famous microfinance institution, and its managing director, Muhammad Yunus, is the guru of microfinance. He is generally regarded as the inventor of group credit, which he calls *social collateral*. Over the years Grameen has grown into a financial colossus that works exclusively in rural areas in Bangladesh. It has 1,100 branches, works in more than 37,000 villages, and has well over two million members. Grameen exemplifies poverty lending: 94 percent of its members are illiterate, landless women, from the poorest rural areas of one of the poorest countries in the world.

Unlike most other microfinance programs, Grameen has a rigid matrix from which it never deviates. After experimenting with various group sizes Muhammad Yunus arrived at a standard model: all groups are single-gender, have five people each, and groups must be organized into centers of eight groups each.

The Bangladesh Rural Advancement Committee (BRAC)

This is the only major nationwide microfinance program that is an NGO. Outside Bangladesh it is less well known than Grameen. This is surprising, given that its work with poor rural women is, in many ways, even more progressive than Grameen's, and has a more profound social impact. Like Grameen, BRAC has a large national branch network of lending offices, works mostly with women, and uses social collateral. It also has a national network of community schools, and helps women defend their legal rights.

Bank Rakyat Indonesia (BRI)

BRI is one of Indonesia's premier state-owned commercial banks. Alongside conventional banking, it manages a nationwide network of *village unit desa* (unit banks) that work exclusively with rural and peri-urban microentrepreneurs. These village unit banks operate throughout the Indonesian archipelago. With more than two million active borrowers, and about twelve million savers, they have proven remarkably adept at tapping rural savings. BRI's loans to microentrepreneurs are fully collateralized, which is unusual in microfinance. The units do not specifically target the poor and draw many of their clients from the top tier of the informal sector.

Over the years BRI's microfinance activities have acquired a reputation for sound management. A conservative approach in lending and a strong emphasis on deposit mobilization made the unit banks so profitable that they were subsidizing BRI's loss-making retail commercial banking. Now, as a result of Indonesia's protracted financial crisis and the near collapse of the economy, rising loan defaults and a shrinking savings base may put BRI's achievements in microfinance in jeopardy.

The Bank for Agriculture and Agricultural Cooperatives (BAAC)

Thailand's BAAC, which is not reviewed in this book, is also a hybrid. It is, first of all, a conventional state-owned agricultural development bank whose primary mandate is to finance agriculture, regardless of the size of the borrowers. Its microfinance activities consist in lending to landless sharecroppers and subsistence farmers. An interesting feature is that, unlike other leaders in microfinance, BAAC uses interest-rate subsidies on loans that consolidate the debts of small farmers who are on the verge of losing their land to their creditors. It also helps smallholders with credit, technical advice on marketing, product storage, and quality grading. Like Grameen, this bank has broadened microfinance to include on-farm activities, and has shown once and for all that the distinction between on- and off-farm activities is arbitrary and misleading. It too has been severely affected by Asia's financial crisis.

Banco Solidario (BancoSol)

Bolivia's BancoSol became the private commercial bank that lends exclusively to (urban) microenterprises. It is a member of the ACCION network, and ACCION is one of its major shareholders. What makes this institution unique is that it began lending as an NGO (PRODEM). The bank was founded in 1992, when it acquired PRODEM's loan portfolio, staff, and premises through a share-for-loans swap, which made PRODEM one of the bank's main shareholders.

ACCION International

Boston-based ACCION is an NGO that supports microfinancing programs in developing countries. It works exclusively with urban microfinancing programs. ACCION was founded in 1962 to address urban poverty in Latin America and began its activities by supporting a community development effort in the shantytowns of Caracas. Through the sheer volume and diversity of its activities it outranks all microfinancing NGOs, and has built a network of lending affiliates that spans the entire Western hemisphere. It currently has twenty-four affiliates which disbursed more than $1.3 billion between 1992 and 1997 in loans to the affiliates' 275,000 members. Since the mid-1990s ACCION has also been working in marginal communities in the United States. From 1991 to 1996 its affiliates had made $1 billion. By the year 2005, the target year set by the Microfinance Summit of 1997, ACCION expects to have two million clients and a loan portfolio of $11 billion. As just mentioned, its largest and most successful affiliate is BancoSol.

Measuring the Effectiveness of Microfinance

Microfinance programs that assure continued access to credit for the self-employed, and offer a safe haven to their savings, can "anchor" villages and marginal urban communities. This makes it essential that they become sustainable in their own right. Nothing is more disruptive for marginal communities than agencies that offer cheap loans one day and are gone the next, when their pool of funds has been used up. The three most commonly used benchmarks to measure the effectiveness, socioeconomic impact, and lasting power of a micro-credit program are: financial sustainability, institutional viability, and outreach.

Financial Sustainability

This is defined as an institution's ability to stand on its own legs, without external financial support, and operate without grants or subsidies. Reaching this nirvana involves several stages: partial recovery of operating expenses, full cost recovery and financial break-even, and making a net operating profit. Only programs that have reached the third stage are self-sustaining. The keys to sustainability are: charging loan interest rates that are high enough to cover costs, applying realistic fees for training programs and technical support, enforcing strict discipline on loan repayments, and controlling expenses. Programs that deviate from these cardinal rules rarely achieve sustainability.

One question is whether interest rates should be higher for small loans to the poorest borrowers to cover the higher cost of processing and supervising these loans. The argument in favor of doing so is that the only other source of funds for the poorest are moneylenders who charge even higher rates. But equality of terms is fairer, and it is possible to cross-subsidize small loans with the comparatively lower costs and higher profit margins on larger loans. This is only feasible in programs that have a sizable proportion of clients with large loans.

One of the trickiest problems in microfinance is that of subsidies. There are two types of subsidies: interest-rate subsidies and operational subsidies. It is often argued that *interest-rate subsidies* are justified on economic and social grounds, such as for rural credit programs that work in extremely poor, isolated areas. This is true, but, as a rule, interest-rate subsidies should be avoided because they are often captured by the non-poor. When there *is* cause to use such subsidies, they must be transparent and funded by donors who target specific social objectives, and there should be rigorous targeting to limit "leakages." One should also bear in mind that interest-rate subsidies create two types of problems. The first, which plagued Latin America's credit unions during the 1970s, is that lending at below-market rates makes it impossible to offer competitive rates on savings accounts, and erodes financial sustainability. The second is that borrowers often treat subsidized loans as gifts, which creates high delinquencies—loan repayment rates are invariably better in programs that lend at market rates than in those that offer low-cost credit.

Operational subsidies cover operational expenses for microfinance institutions that cannot recover costs, are not financially sustainable, and depend on donor subsidies and funding. A key point is that microfinance programs should never charge above-market interest rates to pass on their own inefficiencies to clients. This means that all fees and costs involved in credit delivery must be explicit, and that borrowers must be told how much they are paying for their loans.

On the point of operating expenses some practitioners of microfinance recommend that staff salaries be kept as low as possible to compress costs. This amounts to being "penny wise, but pound foolish." Pay scales should always be commensurate with experience, bearing in mind that low-paid staff are more likely than well-paid ones to accept bribes and collude with dishonest clients to supplement their wages. Low salaries are also a sure way to recruit poorly qualified staff. Grameen, BRI, and BancoSol have shown that it is preferable to save costs and attain financial sustainability by streamlining loan procedures, improving staff productivity, and standardizing reporting procedures, than by skimping on salaries. They have also demonstrated that decentralizing loan approvals to local managers saves time, as well as costs.

To minimize arrears lenders must enforce strict repayment discipline. They can also offer incentives for punctual repayment—BRI's unit banks motivate clients by offering an interest-rate rebate for each six-month period during which they have no arrears. The alternative is to allocate extra funds for loan recovery and offer staff a premium for the recovery of delinquent loans, provided the savings from recovering delinquent loans exceed the cost of doing so. PRIDE in Guinea, which has zero tolerance for arrears—and spends a lot to enforce that rule—falls in this category.

While conventional definitions of sustainability focus on financial aspects only, the alternative is to look at finance, capacity building, and outreach, and also to define sustainability in microfinance more broadly as the ability to help reduce poverty by supporting self-employment with microfinance and non-financial services.

Institutional Viability

This measures the efficiency, integrity, and quality of an institution's management and staff. It depends, among other things, on the quality and transparency of internal procedures, accounting standards, and auditing systems, which serve to control costs and minimize the risk of fraud. The key to institutional viability is the quality and level of education of professional staff and managers. Good procedures and manuals achieve little if people don't know how to use them.

Grameen and BRI are two institutions that excel in the quality of the professional staff they recruit. Both only employ university graduates with honors degrees, and Grameen only recruits post-graduates for its professional staff. Both institutions also have in-house training institutes for capacity building through staff induction and follow-up training. BRI has four regional centers that have all the facilities of modern university campuses. New recruits must undergo residential instruction at those sites. Regular refresher courses are mandatory and people who are eligible for promotion must enroll in management training. There is a separate instruction center for senior managers in Jakarta.

Others who do not have sufficient resources to strengthen institutional capacity and sustainability through in-house training use external technical assistance from donors or other programs. For instance, Grameen Trust trains the key staff of Grameen "replicators" with courses on group-lending methodology. Some programs also rely on expatriate staff from donor agencies to fill key positions. Those programs can only achieve institutional viability if they hand over responsibilities to local management teams. One example of successful hand over is PRIDE.

Outreach

Outreach is a key criterion of operational effectiveness. It is defined as the number of clients and market coverage, as a percentage of the total potential client base. Of the nearly 7,000 microfinance programs that were active in

1996, fewer than 750 programs had more than one thousand clients, and even fewer were approaching institutional sustainability. All but a handful of programs reach more than 1 percent of the poor and low-income households and microenterprises in their respective catchment areas. In the poorest regions and communities outreach can only be increased by lowering loan sizes.

Only two microfinance programs, Grameen and BRI's operations on the island of Java, reach more than 25 percent of their potential clients. Even BancoSol, whose total lending volume is greater than that of all the traditional commercial banks in Bolivia, only covered about 10 percent of its potential clientele. As already mentioned, terrain and other geographic factors have a bearing on outreach and financial and institutional sustainability. While only a handful of African microfinance programs have significant outreach, Asia's superstars of microfinance serve millions of clients.

Poverty Lending Versus Microenterprise Development

There are two different schools of thought in microfinance. The first considers credit as a vehicle to engage people who are below the poverty line in productive activities, and sees self-employment is a means to raise income levels and reduce poverty. Poverty lending was pioneered by the Grameen Bank. Other poverty lenders are BRAC, Grameen replicators in Asia, Africa, and Latin America, village banks, NGOs, and charities. They usually lend in small amounts of $100 or less, and the majority of their clients are women.

At the opposite end of the spectrum one finds programs that work only with people who are already established in business, and have a proven track record. For them, credit is a means of helping microentrepreneurs develop their activities to the point of becoming eligible for credit from commercial banks. ACEP, a Senegalese credit union, and Peru's Municipal Savings and Credit Banks are examples of this approach. Indonesia's BRI shares some of their philosophy, selecting many of its clients from the top tier of the informal sector, and making individual, fully collateralized loans. Some microfinance programs, such as Peru's CREDINPET, go even further, and actually expect their clients to graduate into the formal sector to remain eligible for credit. Among bilateral donor agencies that have a major involvement in microfinance, only USAID combines the twin objectives of poverty reduction and microenterprise development, and divides its lending equally among them. To keep the two programs separate, the agency uses $300 as the upper boundary for poverty lending.

Blending Credit with Non-financial Services

There also are opposing views on the subject of blending credit with non-financial services: the minimalist approach, and what I call the maximalist approach.

Minimalism is financial purism. It draws a clear line between financial services—lending and savings mobilization—and non-financial services. The rationale is that non-financial intervention, such as client training, is input intensive and costly, and that it requires specialized expertise that most microfinance programs do not have. Minimalists seldom practice poverty lending, and usually shy away from it.

Maximalism considers that non-financial services are warranted, provided that they are offered on a selective basis, that non-financial components serve a clear function, and that they are adapted to clients' needs. In such cases all non-financial services should be remunerated at cost. Most, but not all, poverty lenders are maximalists.

Non-financial services fall into two main categories: training and social services. *Client training* is an integral part of programs that work in communities where most people are illiterate and lack even the most rudimentary business skills. It serves to improve client performance, ameliorate the quality of the loan portfolio, enhance financial sustainability, and minimize arrears. Basic training normally covers the rudiments of bookkeeping and of running a small informal business. In programs that lend to rural women, improving their communication skills and giving them the information they need to become more productive can substantially raise their income, and help them make good use of loans. In peer-group lending basic training familiarizes people with the responsibilities of belonging to a group and gives advice on group formation.

Some lenders go beyond basic training and offer advanced courses on business management, accounting, and marketing techniques to help their more skilled clients become self-sufficient microentrepreneurs. One example of advanced training for larger loans are the business workshops (Ateliers sur l'Esprit d'Entreprise) which PRIDE Guinea offers to its more educated and promising clients.

Social programs range from offering counseling and advice on breast feeding and basic nutrition, to child rearing and family planning in some cases. Many NGOs make participation in the non-financial part of microenterprise packages a pre-condition for access to credit, but rarely charge a fee. Freedom from Hunger is an interesting example of an international NGO that successfully blends credit with training and social programs. It works exclusively with poor rural women in the poorest countries in Latin America and Africa, including Burkina Faso and Bolivia, where it sponsors local credit unions and credit associations. The centerpiece of this NGO's credit activities is its Credit with Education Program, in which it turns the associations' weekly meetings into classrooms. It teaches women the rudiments of nutrition, sanitation, immunization, and family planning. Based on its experience and successes in developing countries, this NGO has launched a program of community health advisers in the United States Deep South.

Summary

At this point, it is already possible to draw a number of preliminary conclusions. They are all based on common sense.

- Credit is not a right, and lenders must carefully assess the creditworthiness of microentrepreneurs, taking into account their ability to make productive use of money. First-time borrowers should only be given small loans to test their ability to repay, and lending for investment should be for longer periods than lending for working capital.

- Credit screening is of the greatest importance to reduce the risk of default and ensure the sustainability of microfinance institutions.

- Women are generally better and more reliable borrowers, and more punctual payers, than men. Unlike men, women seldom squander money; when they are given the opportunity to become self-employed their first priority is to feed their families.

- Microfinance programs that work exclusively with women and discourage male participation risk alienating men, and widening the gender gap, unless they explain their goals. Aware of that problem, the Grameen Bank regularly holds meetings with its members' husbands and sons, to teach them to respect their wives and mothers, and accept them as equal partners in the household.

- Mobilizing savings should be an integral part of financial services for the poor. Even the poorest should be encouraged to save, and microfinance institutions should attach as much importance to savings mobilization as to lending.

- It is in the savers' interest that deposit takers be regulated and held to the same prudential standards and capital ratios as commercial banks. Unfortunately, in many developing countries bank superintendencies are weak and understaffed, and ill-acquainted with microfinance. The alternative is to delegate oversight to the depositors themselves. This is already being done in credit unions and cooperatives, where members are also shareholders, and in voluntary savings associations where there is peer-group monitoring of members.

- Loan interest rates should be commensurate with credit risk. They should also be sufficient to cover the cost of making small loans, and leave a profit margin.

Notes

1. Simon Schama, *The Embarrassment of Riches* (New York: Alfred A. Knopf, 1988), 338.
2. There also are non-rotating savings and credit pools. In those cases deposi-

tors receive and borrowers pay interest.
3. *Village Banking: The State of the Practice,* United Nations Development Fund for Women 1996, 5.
4. FINCA *Annual Reports for 1994 and 1995* and Fact Sheets.
5. *Village Banking,* 1996, p. 10.
6. Westley and Shaffer, *Credit Union Policies* (Washington, D.C.: Inter-American Development Bank, March 1998), 3.
7. Brian Branch and Christopher Baker, *Overcoming Governance Problems: What Does It Take?* (Washington, D.C.: Inter-American Development Bank, March 1998), 1.
8. Jeffrey Poyo, *A Conceptual Framework for the Regulation and Supervision of Credit Unions* (Washington, D.C.: Inter-American Development Bank, March 1998), 14.

Part II

The Asian Pioneers of Microfinance

With close to two-thirds of the earth's inhabitants, Asia is the most populated continent. Its economies cover the entire range of income and development levels, from wealthy (but now recession-plagued) Japan to impoverished Bangladesh. Asia also includes several newly industrialized countries—the East Asian "tiger economies." Until the fall of 1997, when the East Asian economic miracle began unraveling and the tigers' currencies, banking systems, and stock markets went into free fall, they were among the few developing countries that had adapted successfully to the global economy and were benefiting from it. For more than a decade these countries—Indonesia among them—had some of the highest, most sustained growth rates in the world, as well as moderate inflation and limited public external debt.

The prevailing wisdom was that their success was the result of sound macroeconomic policies, comparatively equal income distribution, high domestic savings, and substantial investment in education and social and physical infrastructure. The reality was quite different; the miracle was largely the product of mercantilist policies and of selective government interventions to "pick winners"—the opposite of free-market mechanisms. Moreover, as is discussed in greater detail in Chapter 5, the tiger economies' success was built on a shaky foundation of crony capitalism, clientelism, ingrained corruption, and lax banking practices in which banks based lending decisions on personal and political relationships, rather than on economic merit. Also, there were no miracles of high productivity. To make their exports competitive the tiger economies could tap huge reserves of docile, low-wage rural labor, and manipulate their exchange rates.

The East Asian "miracle" began to unravel in 1997, when financial turmoil spread across the region and left most economies in disarray. What is astonishing is the pace and depth of economic disintegration in countries which the World Bank had long touted as examples that other developing countries should follow. But the consequences of East Asia's financial collapse are still difficult to assess. On the one hand, the former tigers have begun restructuring their financial systems, and are gradually purging the worst aspects of crony capitalism. At the same time, the crisis has taken a heavy social toll, with a resurgence of poverty and unemployment, sporadic outbreaks of food shortages, bursts of hyperinflation, and a surge of informal activities. These have obliterated most of the achievements of the last decade and, judging by the reaction of the populace in Indonesia and Thailand, may trigger a backlash against globalization.

The two chapters that follow review microfinance in Bangladesh and Indonesia. In Bangladesh the majority of the people live in poverty. The wage economy is still relatively small and there are but few industries—mostly garment factories and jute mills. In agriculture, jute and rice are the main cash crops, produced mostly by smallholders. Informal activities dominate small-scale production, trade, and services in small towns and villages.

Indonesia is different. Despite a severe recession, it still has some vestiges of the social kaleidoscope of East Asia's economic boom, which created one of the largest proportional increases in the number of dollar billionaires, while 350 million people were still living on less than $1 a day.[1] Like other tiger countries, Indonesia had more than a decade of sustained growth, during which it built modern industries and saw the emergence of an affluent professional middle class with all the trappings of nouveau riche consumerism—expensive cars, designer clothes, and the ubiquitous cell phones. Yet, rural areas remained mostly poor and there were vast urban informal sectors, mostly in trade and services.

Another difference between these two predominantly Muslim countries is that in Bangladesh Islam is conservative and conformist, especially in the countryside, where religion affects all aspects of life. Indonesia is more secular, and Islam is more adapted to the demands of modern life.

Microfinance in South and East Asia

As in other parts of the world, Asian microfinance is a product of the socioeconomic and geographic environment. High population densities, a comparatively low level of urbanization, and a high concentration of rural poverty explain why Asian microfinance programs are larger and have far more clients than those on other continents. Asia's four largest microfinance programs institutions are mature institutions that have been in business for a decade or more, and are institutionally and financially sustainable. They work predominantly in rural areas. A large proportion of their borrowers are women, many of whom are repeat clients who have already completed several credit cycles.

Because these institutions already cover a sizable proportion of their potential outreach, they are expanding more slowly than their younger counterparts in Latin America and Africa.

South Asia, one of the poorest, most densely populated parts of the world, has a fertile environment for microfinance. With an average of $295, microenterprise loans in South Asia are even smaller than in the sub-Saharan region. Extreme poverty also limits people's ability to save, and most programs use forced savings and external funding to leverage their lending potential. On the other hand, high population densities and vast outreach reduce transaction costs, except in the smaller financial NGOs that work in marginal areas. At $40, their average loans are among the smallest in the universe of microfinance, and their operations are highly dependent on donor funds.[2]

In Bangladesh, the South Asian country where microfinance is most developed, the Grameen Bank and BRAC dominate the field. Both do poverty lending, working almost exclusively with the poorest. They are also striving to empower women by challenging the social and religious conservatism that keeps women in an inferior position. Grameen's and BRAC's credit programs, non-financial activities, and operating procedures have become models for microfinance worldwide.

Another leading South Asian microfinance institution is India's Self-employed Women's Association Cooperative Bank (SEWA Bank). It is an offshoot of SEWA, a trade union of self-employed women, which was the result of the amalgamation, in 1972, of three grassroots movements: labor, cooperatives, and women's groups. SEWA espouses Mahatma Gandhi's philosophy of nonviolence and truth to achieve social change and empower poor women. Like Grameen, SEWA Bank finances the income-generating activities of village women. Its loans can be for as little as $1.

South Asia also has the highest concentration of Grameen Replicators, mainly in Bangladesh, India, and the Philippines.

In *East Asia* average income is three times higher than in South Asia, and the average size of individual loans to microenterprises is 50 percent bigger. There the two dominant microfinance institutions are Indonesia's BRI and Thailand's BAAC. As mentioned in Chapter 3, in both institutions microfinance is an outgrowth of other activities, rather than the primary vocation. Thai microfinance is also remarkable for another reason. During the period of rapid industrial growth, informal credit began expanding faster than formal financial intermediation, when rice farmers in the Bangkok area sold their land to industrial developers, and began using their cash to make loans. With the growing number of farmers-turned-moneylenders, informal credit became highly structured and competitive. Under the pressure of competition traditional moneylenders also became more sophisticated, exchanging credit information about individual clients, and offering longer-term housing and investment loans to the best-rated clients.[3]

4

Challenging Social Norms to Empower the Landless Poor in Bangladesh

The area that is now Bangladesh was conquered in the early thirteenth century by Muslim invaders who converted most of the population to Islam. In the sixteenth century the country became part of the Mogul Empire. Thereafter, until the middle of the nineteenth century, it fell successively under the domination of Portuguese, Dutch, French, and British colonial trading companies. In 1859, the British Crown took over the administration of Bangladesh from the British East India Company, and made it part of the Raj. After the partition of British India in 1947, Bangladesh became part of Pakistan.

When it gained independence from Pakistan in 1971, Bangladesh was one of the world's poorest countries where most people suffered from chronic malnutrition. The toll of human misery reached unprecedented proportions shortly after independence, when millions of people who had fled to India during the 1950s and 60s to escape Pakistani oppression returned home. In 1974 the country had its worst famine, during which more than 1.5 million people died of hunger.

A Cruel Climate in a Poor, Overcrowded Country

Most of the land area consists of the alluvial lower Ganges plain. There are more than seven hundred rivers in five major river systems—including the Ganges and the Brahmaputra—which converge into the huge Ganges delta and drain in the Gulf of Bengal. Rivers and waterways are the country's principal natural resources, as well as the greatest threats to the land and its people. The rivers abound in fish, the main source of animal protein in the diet, and provide irrigation and nutrients for paddy farming. Riverboats and ferries are the only means of reaching many towns and villages.

During the monsoon seasons the normally placid rivers become raging torrents that wreak death and destruction. The devastation is made worse by deforestation in the Himalayan high plateau, which causes river silting and more floods downstream. In 1987 Bangladesh had its worst floods in decades. Thousands died, scores were injured, and tens of thousands became homeless. Roads, dikes, and bridges were swept away, and countless houses destroyed. The following year floods covered two-thirds of the country, and more than 2,000 people died.

Tropical cyclones are even deadlier. In April 1991, a cyclone claimed more than 140,000 lives and caused more than $250 million worth of damage to land, crops, and livestock. Five years later, in May 1996, storms and tornadoes ravaged central Bangladesh again. They blew away eighty villages, killed 440 people and left more than 30,000 people homeless and injured. In 1998 yet another cyclone left much of the country, including the capital, Dhaka, under water, destroying crops and countless houses, and making hundreds of thousands of people homeless.

Monsoons and cyclones make everyday life difficult, even in a land that is accustomed to hardship and natural disasters. Far from easy at the best of times, travel and communications become virtually impossible at the peak of the rainy seasons. Then, floods interrupt bus and riverboat traffic, and remote settlements in the Ganges delta can be cut off from the rest of the country for weeks on end. Flood waters also destroy many of the narrow paths along the dikes that separate paddies. The ones that remain become muddy quagmires where people slip and slide, and can only walk barefoot. In the coastal regions, where floods and cyclones are most intense, the frail reed and adobe huts which make up most rural housing seldom last more than one year. Having to rebuild dwellings year after year saps people's energy and drains their meager resources.

To reduce the toll of natural disasters there has been massive investment in flood-control programs, an early-warning system for cyclones, and cyclone-proof shelters. Some of the shelters have been built with funding from BRAC's Post-Cyclone Rehabilitation and Development Project, and the Grameen Bank is financing the construction of flood-resistant houses. These measures have reduced casualties in the most vulnerable areas.

Desperate Overcrowding Everywhere

Culturally and ethnically this is one of the world's most homogeneous nations. Ninety-eight percent of the people are Bengali, and 90 percent are Sunni Muslims. Bangla is the official language. Islam was declared the state religion by a constitutional amendment of 1988, in this, the world's third-largest Muslim country (after Indonesia and Pakistan). Surprisingly, there are few religious fundamentalists, and relations between Muslims and the small Hindu minority, though often fraught with tension, are generally peaceful.

Barely the size of Wisconsin, Bangladesh has a population of 130 million. There are close to nine hundred people for every square kilometer of land area—more than three times as many as in India, and about the same as in equally overcrowded Java. Since much of the land consists of paddies and rivers, the actual population density stretches the boundaries of the imagination. This and high population growth are among the factors that trap Bangladesh in a vicious circle of poverty, and are driving it towards a "frightening demographic situation."[4] Between 1976 and 1995 the population grew by close to 50 percent, the same rate as in India, but much more than in China, where the population increased by 23 percent over the same period.

Overcrowding is not just an abstract concept. It is a tangible reality that affects all aspects of life, every day, everywhere. From dawn to dusk, pedestrians, cattle, carts, cyclists, and bicycle rickshaws vie for space on the narrow dikes along the rivers and paddies, and the rudimentary rural infrastructure is overloaded and stretched to breaking point. Inter-city transport consists of ferries, shallow-bottom riverboats, and "express" buses. Always overloaded with bundles of freight and clusters of passengers on their roofs, the buses barrel down the congested two-lane paved highways. To avoid cattle and pedestrians drivers hug the middle of the road, and there are frequent lethal head-on collisions.

In small towns and villages daily life revolves around the bazaar and the mosque. The bazaars, always incredibly crowded, are the places where the buses stop, and where barbers, scribes, rickshaw drivers, tea-shops, craftsmen, and merchants ply their trades.

Bangladesh has so few tall trees that it imports hardwood utility poles from the United States, and dried cow dung supplements wood as a domestic fuel. The dung is mashed into foot-long "kebobs" on reed sticks, and dried in the sun. After dusk, when women begin preparing the evening meal, villages are covered in acrid smoke from hundreds of dung fires, making the air virtually unbreathable. At night the bazaars too are shrouded in smoky darkness, lit only by the kerosene lamps and small fires of market stalls and food stands.

The capital, Dhaka, has a modern government center, and the usual clusters of large private residences and luxury hotels in the embassy area. The rest of the city is hopelessly crammed, garbage strewn, ill-lit, and noisy. From dawn until well into the night the streets are clogged with rickshaws, smoke-belching three-wheel scooter taxis, and trucks and buses. There is no mass transit system and there are virtually no traffic lights or police. During rush hours most intersections become inextricable tangles of cars, buses, rickshaws, and bicycles that give gridlock a new meaning. Even there, wood and dried cow dung are the main domestic fuels. Air pollution from dung fires and vehicle emissions is often so bad that the smog obscures the midday sunlight. Electricity supply is erratic, with frequent power cuts and even more brownouts. Destitution is so overwhelming that entire city blocks are encampments of homeless people, many of whom are cripples who congregate near the mosques.

The availability of machine power and vehicles is so limited that most activities involve brute muscle power. Heavy freight, be it trees, huge loads of bamboo poles, or building materials, is hauled on wheelbarrows, buffalo carts, and flat-bed rickshaws, the poor man's substitutes for pickup trucks. What is remarkable, given the staggering poverty and rudimentary infrastructure, is that more than three-quarters of all Bangladeshis, even in the most remote villages, have safe drinking water from tubewells. That is one of the highest percentages for low-income countries, and almost four times as high as in Indonesia, where per capita income is four times higher.

Despite all these negatives, one's lasting impression of Bangladesh is the serenity and pastoral beauty of its landscape. Rice paddies form a delicate patchwork, crisscrossed by irrigation canals and rivers, where buffaloes wade, and shallow-bottom boats ply their trade. Paddy rice is grown year round, and the colors of paddies range from the tender green of new shoots to the lush shades of ochre of rice awaiting harvest.

An Economy Based on Agriculture and Cheap Textiles

Bangladesh is overwhelmingly agrarian. Its 86,000 villages are home to four out of every five people. Though this is by no means the world's poorest country—in Mozambique, the poorest of all, average annual income is only one quarter that of Bangladesh—more than a quarter of a century after independence the living conditions of most people are still piteous. In 1995 the standard of living was comparable to that in India thirty years earlier. At 66 US cents per day, the 1995 average income was only half that of Pakistan, and 70 percent that of India. Today well over half of all Bangladeshis live in absolute poverty, and only one in two men can read and write. Women's illiteracy is even higher (74 percent) and almost universal in villages. The poorest in the lowest decile (that is, the lowest 10 percent of the income scale) have to make do with less than 20 US cents per day. Even after adjusting for purchasing power parity, this is far too little to buy enough food to lead a moderately active life, and stay healthy, and close to half of all Bangladeshis make do with less than the minimum daily calorie intake.[5]

Like many other low-income countries, Bangladesh has a large external debt, more than half of which is owed to the World Bank and the Asian Development Bank. This debt almost quadrupled between 1980 and 1995. At $16.4 billion it was the equivalent of 56 percent of GNP, and three times the value of annual exports.[6] With one out of every five dollars earned on exports going to foreign creditors, debt service is a drain on the economy.

Agriculture accounts for one-third of national income, more than two-thirds of employment, and one-fifth of all exports. Most villagers are landless farmers. Those who are better off sometimes own water buffaloes, and hire out their labor to till their neighbors' paddies. The industrial sector is dominated by jute production and garment manufacturing. Jute is the country's "golden fiber" and its main cash crop. It is grown on the same land as paddy, and farmers rotate crops. Jute is even more labor-intensive than rice and absorbs much rural labor. Bangladesh produces three-quarters of the world's raw jute, and 50 percent of all jute products. It also produces and exports cotton, leather, shrimp, and fertilizers, as well as coal—there are large coal deposits in western provinces that remained untapped until the early 1990s— some steel, and small amounts of petroleum and natural gas. Exports of jute and sisal (woven jute matting), long the main sources of foreign exchange, slumped with the advent of synthetic fibers and have been supplanted by cotton garments, which now represent two-thirds of all exports.

Recent years have seen a burst of growth in the highly profitable garment industry. In 1995, it exported $1.5 billion worth of clothes to the United States, and was a major supplier of T-shirts in Europe. Altogether there are close to 1,200 garment factories in Bangladesh, many of which are owned by investors from South Korea and Taiwan. In Dhaka alone, they employ more than one million young women and girls. The textile export boom was temporarily imperiled in late 1995 and early 1996, when political and civil strife paralyzed the country for weeks on end.

Working conditions in the garment factories are harsh. The women are paid a pittance—$30 per month for six-day weeks. For a little more than $1 a day they work twelve-hour shifts, in dusty, noisy sweatshops. Although their wages are miserly by international standards, these jobs are much sought after because they pay quite a bit more than informal work. Until recently the garment factories employed children who worked as hard as adults, and were paid even less. Under intense pressure from North American and European human-rights groups, the Bangladesh Garment Manufacturers' and Exporters' Association was forced to cooperate with international agencies and revise its labor practices.

Sexual Apartheid and the Place of Women in Society

This is a conservative Muslim country, where life's rhythm from dawn to dusk is set by the muezzins' calls to prayer, and five-times-a-day prayers and trips to the local mosque. Religious conformism is most pronounced in villages, where women's lives are shaped by a patriarchal social system that compounds the impact of religion. From the day she is born, a girl is a second-class citizen. For the rest of her life she has minimal opportunities to acquire new ideas, skills, or contacts, or to work outside the home. This creates a *sexual apartheid* that stresses women's reproductive role, trivializes their work, and excludes them from the public domain. Women are conspicuous by their absence in markets, streets, and public places. Even women from better-off families who have servants rarely venture outside the house, and a woman alone is always treated with suspicion. If they do go out, women are rarely by themselves, and try to hide from public view—when they carry women passengers rickshaw drivers always pull down their hoods.

The influence of tradition and religion is so overwhelming that the household is a woman's basic consumption and production unit. Even in the poorest families that live in hardship, their role is to serve men, bear children, cook, and do household chores. In Dhaka a rickshaw driver told me that his wife stayed at home with the children, while admitting that life was hard and that on many a day he earned too little to buy food for his family. At mealtimes, women and girls always eat after men and boys. When there is not enough to eat for everybody, women are more likely than men to go without food. Since young girls eat last and receive only what is left, they are more likely than boys to suffer from malnutrition, and have lower survival rates in childhood.

Domestic violence, though strictly condemned by the Koran, is widespread, and desertion and divorce are constant threats, especially for women who only bear daughters. Although the legal system is based on Common Law, under Koranic Law a man can divorce or desert his wife without due cause or going to court. In fact, some men divorce one wife after another, until they find one who bears them a son.

The social exclusion of women has a downside for men. Whereas in other developing countries it is women and children who work as market vendors, and trudge along roads, to and from markets and villages, bearing jugs of water, bundles of wood, and loads of vegetables, in Bangladesh it is men who do all the walking, carrying, and shopping. Social conformism is so pervasive that in Hindu households women's status is the same as in Muslim families.

Three sets of cultural and religious norms underpin sexual apartheid. *Samaj* is Bengali for "society" or "community." In daily life it means, among other things, that all household belongings are controlled by the head of house-hold—the husband or eldest son. Only men can own or inherit land. Wives have little or no say, even on matters such as the education of their children. In the conjugal household, in her husband's family, a woman's position is de-fined by her husband's status—the eldest son's wife is senior to others, and the mother-in-law is senior to all her sons' wives.[7]

Purdah is Urdu for "curtain." Strictly speaking, it refers to women's face veils. Purdah was imported from India when Bangladesh, as East Bengal, was part of the Raj. It governs a woman's conduct towards her husband, and is the core of institutionalized gender discrimination. Purdah applies only to mar-ried women. Once married, a woman must veil her face, speak quietly and, above all, avoid all contact with men, other than with fathers, husbands, sons, or close relatives. Even in mosques women are confined to a separate, cur-tained-off area, out of men's sight.

Islam reinforces women's social, economic, and ideological handicaps. The *Sharia* (Koranic law) gives women no freedom to act independently, and they may not work outside the home. A husband is his wife's guardian and protector (for widows with grown sons, the eldest son is his mother's guard-ian). Even in divorces and domestic disputes that are settled by the courts, a woman must be represented by a male guardian, whereas men can represent themselves.

There is also a *material basis* for women's inferior position, namely the fact that, whereas boys stay with their parents and support them in old age, when a girl marries—usually at a very young age, and oftentimes to an older man—she becomes a member of her husband's family. This means that she will not support her parents in their old age. That, and the continuing practice of bridal dowry, places a heavy burden on families, especially if parents go deep into debt to marry off their daughters. Not surprisingly, the birth of a girl is often seen as a curse, and spending money on girls' education is considered a waste.[8] Though school enrollment of girls is rising, it is still far lower than for boys, and girls seldom go beyond the first grade. All too often, they stay at home, doing household chores, or working in the fields.

Jotsna's Story

Jotsna is a young Bangladeshi widow. She has two small children, a daughter of three and a nine-year-old son. Her story is typical of that of the women who are members of Grameen and BRAC. For the last ten years she has been living in the same tiny mud-brick house, in a small village in Mymensingh District in northern Bangladesh. It takes more than one hour to walk to Charnilaxmia, the nearest town. The village has no electricity, but there are latrines, and communal tubewells with safe drinking water.

Like all the people in her village, Jotsna is extremely poor. Hardship is an integral part of her life. She has only the barest essentials. Her house has an earthen floor that stands just above the average flood level. The roof leaks and is patched with banana-tree leaves. It has been like that for years but Jotsna has too little money to have it re-thatched. Inside there is a bamboo bedstead, a bed quilt, some clothes, and a few pots and cooking utensils. There are no windows and the door post is so low that it keeps sunlight out, and one must stoop to go inside.

Like her own mother, Jotsna married when she was barely a teenager. Her elder sister's husband, a rickshaw driver, arranged her marriage to one of his friends who was also a rickshaw driver. As tradition demands, after her marriage she was confined to the house, doing household chores and bearing children, and rarely ventured outside the village. The couple had to make do with the pittance her husband earned with his rickshaw. A few months after she became pregnant for the second time, Jotsna found out that her husband had another wife and family. Though polygamy was tolerated in the past, it is frowned upon nowadays, and Jotsna felt bitter and debased by his betrayal. To make matters worse still, her husband deserted her and the children. He went to live with his first wife, and was killed in a traffic accident a few weeks later.

Jotsna, who used to blame her husband for all her misfortunes while he was alive, was overcome with grief by his death. She felt no more anger, only sadness and despair. Penniless and already seven months pregnant, she turned to her neighbors for consolation and help. They comforted her as well as they could, and helped her by giving her food. After her daughter was born, the neighbors looked after her little boy for a few days, to let her recover.

Respite was short-lived. Still weak from a difficult pregnancy, Jotsna had to pull herself together to help her neighbors with the rice harvest. For her work she received a sack of broken rice and some vegetables, which was barely enough to feed herself and her children. After the harvest she was no longer needed and her neighbors could not afford to feed her any longer. With no other income, Jotsna began begging in the bazaar in the nearby town. She had reached rock-bottom.

Jotsna says that she will never forget the day when the manager of the newly opened Charnilaxmia branch of Grameen Bank came to her village to talk about credit programs for landless women. When they were told that Grameen would give small loans to groups of women who wished to start their own businesses, Jotsna and her neighbors could hardly believe it—even the local moneylender had refused to give her credit. Soon after Grameen's visit, Jotsna and four of her neighbors decided to form a group, and applied for a loan. After a week of induction training, her group was formally recognized by Grameen's area manager. A few days later Jotsna got her first loan of Tk.1,600 ($40).

In most situations this would be too little to provide working capital for any kind of business. Yet it changed Jotsna's life. She used the money to buy rice, oil, sugar, and a few cooking utensils, and began making rice cakes which she sells to women in her village and to market vendors. With what she earns by doing this, she has enough money to buy food for her two children and look after her aging father. After she received her second loan, Jotsna began making plans, dreaming of sending her children to school, and of living in a house with solid walls, a metal roof, and more space to sleep and make rice cakes.

Jotsna is a local celebrity. Because she has shown how, with a small loan, a poor, illiterate village woman can improve her life, Grameen decided to make a video about her.[9] Late one afternoon, in November 1995, after a full day's work, the manager of the Charnilaxmia branch, two of his colleagues, and I went to Jotsna's village to show the video. We piled into three bicycle rickshaws, laden with a TV set, a VCR, and a heavy-duty car battery. We arrived in the village at dusk. When we began unpacking our boxes dozens of giggling children were pushing and shoving around us. At first, they seemed even more intrigued by my presence than by what was about to happen. But, as soon as all the wiring and connections had been sorted out and the TV set flickered into action, children, young women, and mothers with babies sat in tight rows on the ground, their eyes glued to the set. Their husbands tried to look nonchalant, milling around in the back, smoking, but could not resist peering at the screen. Most villagers had never seen a TV show, let alone right there, in their very own village about one of their neighbors. This made it really special. A bit shy, and overcome by all the fuss, Jotsna sat at the back of the crowd. But what a smile when the audience hooted and clapped at the end of the video presentation!

What surprised me most was that this outing was nothing exceptional for the Grameen branch manager and his colleagues. It was part of their commitment to the bank's members, which is the quintessence of Grameen's work ethic and philosophy. Far from being dedication beyond the call of duty, going to a distant village after a full day's work, and walking back in total darkness, while carrying heavy boxes (because there are no bicycle rickshaws late at night) was all part of Grameen's commitment to reach out to poor women.

The Grameen Bank: Working to Empower the Landless

Grameen Bank means "village bank." It is one of the world's largest and best-known microfinance institutions. It targets landless women who are among the "poorest of the poor" and began life as an experimental project, in Chittagong, in 1976.

Its founder, Muhammad Yunus, likes to tell the story of how he came upon the idea of Grameen. It began in 1972, when he returned to Bangladesh shortly after Independence, after seven years in the United States. There he had completed his Ph.D. in economics at Vanderbilt University, in Tennessee, with a Fulbright fellowship. Back home, Yunus became the head of the Economics Department of the University of Chittagong and wanted to help rebuild his poverty-stricken country. There he was teaching elegant theories, at a time when people were dying of hunger during a calamitous famine. Yunus says that he soon became disenchanted with his profession, which had taught him nothing about how to eliminate hunger and poverty, and bore no relationship to the real world.

Right outside the campus, in the village of Jobra, he met a group of women who were trying to make a living, weaving mats and baskets which they sold in the local market. To buy straw, the women had borrowed from a money-lender. After repaying their loan, they had practically no money left. For all their hard work, they did not have enough money to buy food. Outraged, Yunus tried to convince the manager of the Janata bank on the university campus to give the women a loan. The manager turned him down, telling him that the women were not creditworthy and had no skills. Yunus decided to find out for himself. With $30 of his own money he made a loan to forty-two women. To his surprise, they repaid the money punctually.[10] An even greater surprise was that these minuscule loans had made a significant difference for the women.

Having made his point, Yunus went back to the local bank, only to get rebuffed again. Time and again he was told that lending to landless, illiterate women made no sense and that he would have to be their personal guarantor. After much time, and many more rejections, Yunus decided to launch the Grameen Project. He did this with the help of Krishi bank (the agricultural development bank) and the Janata bank, and support from the Bangladesh Central Bank.[11] The Grameen Project began lending in 1976 as the Experimental Grameen Branch, working out of a sub-office of a Krishi bank branch in Jobra. On its first day of business it loaned 52,000 takas ($1,500) to 24 villagers. By the end of the summer it had $15,000 in loans to four hundred villagers, one hundred of whom were women.[12] The project soon expanded to other districts. By the end of 1982, it had eighty-six village branches whose annual lending volume reached $5 million.

The experiment was so successful that the central bank passed the Grameen Bank Ordinance in September 1983. Shortly thereafter the Grameen Bank was incorporated as an independent bank, with its own capital and shareholders. The shareholding is mixed. At first, two-thirds of the bank's shares were held by the government, and the remainder by its borrowers. By 1995, the government's share was only 8 percent, and Grameen's members owned the remaining 92 percent.

Managing to Empower

Grameen's work embodies the crusading spirit and single-mindedness of its founder and managing director. Muhammad Yunus is more than a banker. He is a charismatic leader who is determined to change the world, and create an environment in which the poor can help themselves. To his credit, he is a tireless advocate of a world without hunger. Although or, perhaps, because he is a member of his country's establishment Yunus has never shied away from challenging social norms. Quite the contrary. What is refreshing is that Yunus still has all the verve of a young activist. At conferences, and in his numerous books and articles, he repeats tirelessly that poverty is a denial of human rights and that poverty was not created by the poor, both of which are true. He also likes to state that "credit is a basic human right," which it is not. But provocative hyperbole makes people think, which is the whole purpose of Yunus's discourses.

To break the vicious circle of poverty and empower impoverished landless women, Grameen creates an environment that gives them self-esteem and provides for productive activities. The bank is attentive to details, and never indulges in paternalism. It calls its borrowers members, *never* beneficiaries. Moreover, rather than doing things *for* people by offering them subsidized credit and an integrated package of poverty reduction, Grameen lets people decide for themselves whether to become members or not. It is up to them to act and change their lives.[13] To those who do, the bank offers small loans, so that they can develop independent activities and raise their social and economic status. This advocacy of individual self-help as a way out of poverty challenges the doctrine of conventional welfare programs, which do things for people and engender a passive attitude.

Grameen's greatest achievement is to have dared to challenge the religious establishment, and shown poor, uneducated women how to overcome sexual apartheid and patriarchy, and change their own and their daughters' lives by becoming economically active. This is no trivial matter for women who, for the first time in their lives, are "included," and encouraged to take initiatives. The women's independent activities raise their social and economic status in their households and communities, and challenge the authority of husbands, religious leaders, and village elders. For these reasons, Grameen has been branded as anti-Islam. Religious conservatives often spread wild rumors about the bank, and its staff and members occasionally face open hostility. In the early years, hostility sometimes escalated into violence, and several branch offices were set on fire. This no longer happens. But some husbands still beat their wives to keep them from joining Grameen, and the bank's more vocal opponents oftentimes try to prevent its workers from entering their villages. One of the reasons Grameen has been able (despite some opposition) to successfully challenge social and cultural norms, is that its actions do not threaten the economic interests of the country's large landowners and urban elite.

Better living standards in members' families are also changing the men's attitudes, and domestic violence is abating. But Grameen still has to go to great lengths to educate men who resent the fact that their wives or daughters have learned to fend for themselves. That is why zone managers organize regular workshops for husbands, to tell them that mutual respect is essential and that their wives are equal partners. They try to change men's attitudes towards their wives and women in general, by making them feel a part of Grameen's credit and empowerment work. The workshops also give men an opportunity to voice their concerns and ask questions. I attended such a workshop in Mymensingh, in northern Bangladesh. Not speaking Bangla, I could not understand what was being said but, judging by the demeanor and body language of the fifty men who were there, it was obvious that they were interested. They listened attentively, nodded repeatedly, and asked the zone and area managers many questions. That too is "managing to empower."

Turning Banking Principles Upside Down

Yunus rightly says that banks are symbols of terror, where illiterate people feel helpless and intimidated, and are at the mercy of others. To maximize outreach and gain the confidence of illiterate, landless villagers, Grameen has turned conventional banking wisdom on its head. Instead of telling people to come to the bank, managers and staff go to the villages. There, it is the members who control the situation, and they gain confidence. The only exception to this rule is that loan disbursements take place at Grameen's branch offices. Staff spend so much time in the field that Yunus calls them "barefoot bankers."

Whereas most microfinance programs only lend to people who are *above* a certain income threshold, Grameen does the opposite. To be eligible for loans, people's income must be *below* the absolute poverty level. Yunus often says that he prefers lending to women who have no prior experience of income-generating work, and that the less they know, the better. While some of Grameen's borrowers are not "the poorest of the poor," most of its clients are indeed extremely poor landless women. But the pressure on Grameen to demonstrate its viability is considerable, which can detract from the original focus on poverty.[14]

Lending with Social Collateral

Grameen's structure and administrative procedures are standardized, down to the smallest details. To become members, people must meet three basic criteria: they must live in rural areas, be landless (they may not own more than a half acre of land), and be organized in single-gender groups of five members. Preference goes to women—95 percent of Grameen members are women.

The groups are self-selecting and form "centers," each of which has a maximum of eight groups. Once a year each group must elect a new chief and secretary, and the members of a center elect a new center chief and deputy chief. The members of each group are jointly responsible for the repayment of each others' loans. In small villages, where there is little privacy among neighbors, collective responsibility functions primarily through peer pressure. If any member fails to repay her loan, the entire group is penalized by being denied credit as long as the arrears have not been cleared. This creates a moral obligation for members to remain punctual on their weekly loan repayments, and help each if they have problems in doing so. Peer groups are also effective deterrents against moral hazard: if a member shows bad faith, the other women can exert pressure on her, and collective responsibility becomes *social collateral*. As additional safeguards against loan defaults, each group's first loan is disbursed in stages. First, two members receive their loans. As soon as they have paid the first weekly installment the next two receive theirs. The last person to receive a loan is the center chief. If all members repay punctually, a group qualifies for a second loan cycle in which all loans are disbursed simultaneously.

Before a new group can qualify for loans, its members receive one week's induction training. The training workshops for new members are at the core of Grameen's social development and empowerment program.[15] They coach new members on Grameen's rules and regulations, explain what the "Sixteen Decisions" mean, and teach illiterate people how to sign their names. Each branch is responsible for organizing workshops in its district, and branch assistants are the instructors.

On the last day of basic training, the participants must pass a knowledge test. Each one must be able to recite the Sixteen Decisions and sign her name on the simple loan document. This is followed by a brief recognition ceremony. A new group can only be recognized by an area manager if each member passes the test, including signing her name. Signing one's name may not seem much, but is a symbolic act that gives a real sense of accomplishment to an illiterate person. It is quite moving to see an illiterate woman painstakingly write her name in full public view, surrounded by her neighbors. Attending a recognition ceremony and becoming members of Grameen are milestones in members' lives.

The Sixteen Decisions[16]

The Sixteen Decisions are Grameen's social-development constitution. They form the basis of center life and discipline. What is interesting is that, rather than being a corporate credo that is imposed from above, the Decisions were formulated by a group of women center chiefs at a national workshop, in 1984. The chiefs used their own experiences and aspirations in formulating the decisions:

1. We shall follow and advance the four principles of Grameen Bank— Discipline, Unity, Courage, and Hard Work—in all walks of our lives.

2. Prosperity we shall bring to our families.

3. We shall not live in dilapidated houses. We shall repair our houses and work towards constructing new houses at the earliest.

4. We shall grow vegetables all year round. We shall eat plenty of them and sell the surplus.

5. During the planting seasons we shall plant as many seedlings as possible.

6. We shall plan to keep our families small. We shall minimize our expenditures. We shall look after our health.

7. We shall educate our children and ensure that we can earn to pay for their education.

8. We shall always keep our children and their environment clean.

9. We shall build and use pit latrines.

10. We shall drink tubewell water. If this is not possible, we shall boil water and use alum.

11. We shall not take dowry at our sons' weddings, neither shall we give dowry at our daughters' weddings. We shall keep our center free from the curse of dowry. We shall not practice child marriage.

12. We shall not inflict any injustice on any one, nor shall we allow anyone else to do so.

13. We shall collectively undertake bigger investments for higher income.

14. We shall always be ready to help each other. If anyone is in difficulty, we shall help him or her.

15. If we come to know of any breach of discipline in any center, we

shall all go there and help restore discipline.

16.   We shall introduce physical exercises in all of our centers. We shall take part in all social activities collectively.

The Weekly Center Meeting: Discipline in Action

Each center has a center house, built by the members and their families. The houses are open, low-walled bamboo and reed structures that have pride of place in each village and also serve as the village meeting place. In the poorest villages that cannot afford to build a center house, the "center" meets in a clearance in the middle of the village.

Each center meets once a week, in the presence of the branch assistant responsible for that center. Meetings always take place on the same day of the week. Attendance is compulsory. During the meetings members squat on the floor in eight rows, one for each group of five. Each member has an assigned place: group chairwomen always sit to the left, facing the Grameen assistant; group secretaries sit next to them; the group whose chairwoman is also the center chief occupies the first row. Other members also have their assigned places, in each group row. Though this may seem excessively formal, it makes it easier to identify absentees. Even so, at the beginning of each meeting there is a roll call and the center chief must report who is absent, and for what reason.

Grameen expects strict discipline from its members. At the beginning of each center meeting, all present—the members, the Grameen officer, and visitors—stand at attention. The members greet Grameen staff and visitors with a military-style salute. Staff and visitors return the salute. As soon as the greeting ceremony is over, the women do calisthenics—stretching their arms, and repeatedly squatting and standing up—and recite Grameen's social credo: "Discipline, Unity, Courage and Hard Work." When addressing a Grameen staff, a member must stand up and salute. At the conclusion of a meeting, all present stand at attention, salute each other, and the women recite the Sixteen Decisions.

Branch staff are expected to be role models who set the tone at center meetings and in contacts with members. I attended several center meetings. On each occasion, the staff arrived on time, and were well groomed and courteous. They treated the women with respect, as equals, not as poor underlings, and made me feel part of the meetings by introducing me to the members, and telling me what was happening. At the weekly meetings, bank staff often act as counselors, giving advice on personal matters. At times, they help settle marital disputes and problems with landlords.

The weekly meetings are held in full view of the women's husbands and children, and of other women who are not yet Grameen members. The women are therefore encouraged to treat the weekly meetings as more than formalities, to repay loans and discuss new ones. They are social events that give them the opportunity to interact with each other, and with male bank workers and visitors. When addressing bank staff, members make eye contact and usually drop their face veils. On many occasions the women asked me direct questions—"Are you married?"; "Do you have children?"; "Why have you come here?"; "Do you grow rice?"; "Does Grameen work in your country?" When it was my turn to ask them questions, they replied without embarrassment and did not mind being photographed. Their behavior surprised me, because it was quite unlike the demureness one encounters outside the village centers, and a total departure from women's socially conditioned reserve in contacts with men.

Although such small details may seem unimportant, daring to challenge socially oppressive norms, and doing so without being self-conscious about it, is empowerment. By their actions and comportment at the meetings, the women set examples for other villagers, and Grameen uses the weekly meetings to disseminate its social philosophy. The almost military discipline with which the meetings are conducted always comes as a surprise to most people on their first visit to a center, and would be treated with derision in Africa or Latin America. But discipline makes sense in the social context of rural Bangladesh, where women have internalized the notion that they are worthless burdens. For them, saluting people, removing their face veils, making eye contact, doing simple exercises, and reciting the Sixteen Decisions helps build self-esteem and confidence. It also teaches women simple, yet effective, ways to improve the quality of life in poor rural communities, helps them change their habits, teaches them to eat more balanced diets and use basic standards of hygiene, and challenges patriarchal gender bias. By the same token, for women who have never acted independently, it is no small matter to be elected chief of a group or center, and to have public responsibilities. Even the act of electing someone conveys a sense of power, and instills democratic principles.

Circles Within Circles

Grameen's management structure can best be visualized as "circles within circles," where five-member groups make up the innermost circle. The next circle is comprised of the centers. Going on from there, increasingly wider circles are made up of Grameen's branch offices, area offices, zonal offices, and the all-embracing head office, with a staff of four hundred.

Staffing structures, seniority levels, promotions, pay scales, and workloads at each organizational level are standardized. Each of Grameen's twelve zonal offices supervises an average of ten area offices, each of which is responsible for about ten branch offices. Zonal offices have a staff of thirty-five, area offices a staff of six. Each branch office is responsible for a maximum of 2,400 members—that is, 480 groups in sixty centers—served by six branch assistants, each of whom is responsible for a maximum of ten centers, or four hundred members. Every working day, come rain or sunshine, branch assistants visit two of their ten centers. When member loads at a branch reach their maximum capacity, Grameen opens a new office, rather than increase the staffing and workload of an existing branch.

A typical branch has a manager, an assistant manager, six branch assistants, and a peon. Branch assistants are rotated every year to service a new set of ten centers. Men are almost always posted outside their home areas. This, and frequent rotations of managers at all levels, is designed to prevent the occurrence of favoritism or vested interests, and provides safeguards against fraud and collusion. Social conservatism nevertheless still prevents female staff from working away from their home areas. Moreover, while all the men have bicycles, the women on Grameen's staff must walk because saris make cycling impractical.

Because Grameen expects strict personal and group discipline from its members, it is equally demanding with its staff. It expects total dedication from managers and field staff at all levels. The bank's corporate culture also encourages all staff to be creative and to take initiatives and responsibilities in their work, and to be accountable to both their seniors and their subordinates. Contacts between staff and managers are always informal, and managers are told to treat junior staff and center members as equals, never as subordinates. Senior staff have an open-door policy, and staff and managers at all levels are encouraged to learn by listening. This encourages junior staff and managers to discuss problems openly. Dress is casual, which fosters an atmosphere in which junior staff and villagers feel at ease.

From the very outset, branch staff are fully immersed in village life. Before a new branch is opened, its future staff are sent to villages in the area to explain to people what they will do. They set an example by living as modestly as the villagers, building their own humble huts, and cooking their own food. Managers at all levels also make a point of remaining close to the bank's grassroots in villages. They regularly visit branch offices and attend center meetings. As far as I could tell, most of them do so with tact and courtesy, as observers, rather than as superiors of the local field staff.

While there inevitably is some hierarchy in a bank which has more than two million clients and 1,100 branch offices, senior managers have no perquisites of rank, such as fitted carpets, private dining rooms and bathrooms, and plush offices. The only exception is that zone managers have the use of a Toyota Landcruiser and a driver. This is necessary, because they cover large areas and remote villages, and sturdy cars and good drivers are indispensable on Bangladesh's dangerous roads. Area managers usually have motorcycles. But to avoid the appearance of favoritism, they lease them from Grameen. Salaries are good by local standards, but by no means exaggerated, and the bank's staff live modestly. As befits a bank whose clients are poor, Grameen's buildings, from its Dhaka headquarters to zonal and branch offices, are modest. Many of the branches are located in old buildings that have no running water or electricity, and the branch assistants' living quarters sometimes consist of bunk beds in the back of the office. Even the bank's headquarters in Dhaka are spartan, with furniture that is identical to that of branch offices—all the office furniture, even that in Yunus's office, is built in village workshops, to Grameen's specifications.

Accountability, Decentralization, and Staff Qualifications

To ensure maximum accountability, all decision making is participatory, fully public, and highly decentralized, and day-to-day management is based on delegation, transparency, and zonal autonomy.

Delegating basic decisions and tasks to the groups and centers is a basic tenet of Grameen's organization. Involving members in basic decision making and financial control is a key aspect of empowerment and social collateral. It also saves money by reducing transaction costs and overheads, and helps branch offices carry relatively large client loads. To make sure that delegation works in practice, group chiefs are responsible for the collection of the members' weekly loan installments, which they hand over to branch staff at the center meeting.

There is also full transparency of all decisions and actions involving the centers. Loan disbursements at branch offices are made in public, in full view of the branch staff and of each group's members and their husbands. This is a further safeguard against fraud and collusion. For its part, zonal autonomy gives zone managers full responsibility for setting the agendas and priorities for the areas and branches they control. At their annual conferences zone managers are also involved in setting the policy and program priorities for Grameen as a whole.

Grameen also puts great emphasis on staff and member training at all levels. It has demanding criteria for staff recruitment. All professional staff, including senior branch staff and branch managers, must have Master's degrees. Other branch staff must have completed secondary education.

Before taking up field assignments, new staff must undergo intensive training that emphasizes coping with real-life situations, and full immersion in the reality of rural poverty. After attending a two-day induction course at Grameen's Training Institute in Dhaka, all newly recruited professional staff are sent to a branch office for field training. Thereafter, they receive additional instruction in one of Grameen's three in-house training centers. Before they can be promoted to branch manager level and assigned to a posting, professional branch staff must complete a two-year preparation program, during which they undertake managerial assignments and internships in various branches and area offices.

Grameen also tutors its members, beginning with a week-long induction course for new groups, and continuous follow-up training at center meetings. There is also skills' training, and the bank organizes birth-attendant workshops, and mother and girl-child workshops to broaden women's awareness of their roles and improve their skills in managing their small businesses.

There also is an intensive in-house training program for women who are elected center chiefs. To that effect, each area office organizes annual, week-long workshops for the new center chiefs in its area. To impart a sense of responsibility and decision making, participants in these workshops are broken up into teams that partly set their own agendas. Members of each team must elect a new team leader for each day of the workshop.

Credit Delivery

During the long gestation period, before Grameen was formally established as a bank, Yunus tested different formulas and worked by trial and error to determine optimal loan sizes, the frequency of loan repayments, and the size of individual groups and centers. He also tried different loan types. Originally the bank only offered "general and collective" loans. They are for one year and must be repaid in equal weekly installments of 2 percent of the loan and interest due. On average, they account for 70 percent of all loans. These loans cannot exceed $250, the equivalent of the average annual per capita income, but many times that of a rural family's annual income. Only few members borrow that much. Most women borrow around $100, and loans are sometimes for as little as $40. Over the years Grameen has expanded its range of loan products, and adapted its lending to the members' changing needs.

General loans remain the entry point and still represent more than three-quarters of all lending. To qualify for any other type of loan, a member must either already hold, or have fully repaid, one or more general loans. Other short-term loans include:

- *Seasonal loans for agricultural inputs*. They cannot exceed $75, and must be repaid after the harvest. They have maturities of six to twelve months and may be repaid in a lump sum.

- *Family loans* for members who have completed four general loan cycles. Like general loans, they mature in one year and can be for up to $250, but are granted for family income-generating activities. What this means is that husbands are the main users. The rationale is that giving men access to credit and making them benefit from their wives' successful record as Grameen members in good standing strengthens women's position in the family.[17]

- *Tubewell loans* for the construction of shallow tubewells and *sanitation loans* to build latrines, which are for two years. All active borrowers are eligible. These loans are granted to individuals or to groups, as joint loans. Tubewell loans cannot exceed $250, sanitation loans $37.50.

By type of activity, general loans for cow fattening and raising milk cows are in the highest demand and usually account for around a quarter of all loans, and crop cultivation for a further 20 percent. The problem with financing the purchase of livestock is the risk of illness in frail animals which are raised by people with no experience in animal husbandry. Moreover, cow fattening takes a long time, consumes resources—animal fodder and loan repayments—and generates no income or profit until the animal is sold. This means that borrowers may face difficulties making their weekly loan repayments, especially if their cows die.

New loans are funded with the cash flow of repayments on existing loans. If a branch disburses more than it takes in on loan repayments on any given day, area and zone offices cover the shortfall at an internal transfer price of 12 percent, which leaves a net spread of 8 percent for the branch.

Grameen also provides *housing loans* to women who have completed two general-loan cycles without any arrears, and are able to take on more debt. These loans have ten-year maturities. They are offered only to individuals, not to groups, and can be for up to $625. These loans finance solid, cyclone-proof houses that are built to Grameen's specifications. They cover the cost of building supplies and materials, and the families must provide the labor. By May 1998, Grameen had financed close to 440,000 houses, and the families of one out of every five of its members were living in cyclone-proof houses.[18] Housing loans are collateralized: Grameen retains title to the house until the loan is fully repaid. Because Koranic law does not allow women to own property, husbands automatically acquire title when housing loans are repaid.

Mobilizing Members' Savings

Because Grameen's members are poor by definition, the bank uses forced savings, which serve as back-up loan guarantees:

- Members must make weekly contributions of one taka (3 US cents) to a Children's Welfare Fund, which finances education for members' children, at schools that are run by the members.

- There is a group tax of 5 percent of the amount of each loan. It is deposited into a Group Fund, which functions as a group's collective savings' pool. Each group manages its own fund. The women can borrow from it for special occasions, such as weddings, or to make loan repayments. In May 1998 cumulative savings in Group Funds were close to $180 million.[19]

- Groups must pay 25 percent of the interest due on any loan into an Emergency Fund, which is managed by the Dhaka head office. The money in this fund is an insurance against loan defaults due member's deaths or illness. Members cannot borrow from the Emergency Fund.

- Upon joining the bank, each member must purchase one share of the bank, with a value of $30. This is payable in installments. No member can own more than one share.

Grameen's Sustainability

In May 1998, Grameen had twelve zonal offices, 111 area offices, 1,112 branches, 65,960 centers in 38,551 villages, and more than 2.3 million members, 95 percent of whom were women.[20] This enormous outreach leaves no doubt about institutional sustainability. The bank has also achieved extremely fast growth. It passed the $1 billion mark in disbursements in March 1995. By June 1997, cumulative disbursements had already doubled to $2 billion, and were approaching $2.5 billion in May 1998. Annual loan disbursements now exceed $400 million.[21]

Fast growth and great outreach were achieved without losing the original grassroots focus. According to senior managers, at the time they become members, only very few people have incomes and assets that exceed the bank's income threshold for loan qualification: ownership of *less than* a half acre of land, and no prior experience of income-generating work. They also report that there are no documented cases of rich farmers qualifying for loans. On the other hand, many existing members do own more than a half acre of land. The fact that long-standing members who are no longer extremely poor stay in their groups and centers is normal and fully justified. Doing otherwise would mean expelling women who would still have no other place to obtain credit, and actually penalize good repayment records.

After more fifteen years of sustained growth, and with an increasing number of replicators around the world, Grameen is institutionally mature and sustainable. It has dedicated, well-trained field staff, who work with a sense of mission and commitment. The cadre of senior and middle mangers are seasoned professionals who "came up through the ranks." They have extensive field experience and remain dedicated to the bank's mission. Though internal procedures and reporting, accounting, and auditing systems are hampered by a lack of computerization, Grameen has developed reliable procedures and standardized forms and reports. Familiarization with these procedures is an integral part of staff training.

Financial sustainability is beyond doubt. All lending activities follow prudent banking principles. The bank controls costs and recovers all its operating expenses, has instilled strong loan-recovery discipline among its staff and members, and consistently high repayment rates make loan losses unlikely. At the village level, branch offices usually break even after five years.

However, even though reliance on subsidies is diminishing, Grameen is not yet financially self-sufficient. During 1993, 45 percent of all liabilities were represented by foreign loans—not grants—some of which have matured since then.[22] The only remaining grant was a mere $616,000 from the Ford Foundation. In terms of actual subsidy dependence, in 1994, subsidies represented about 4 percent of total assets, down from 23 percent in 1987.[23] The bank has also begun drawing funds from the local capital market. In 1995 it sold $163 million in medium-term notes with Bangladeshi commercial banks. Even though the notes were guaranteed by USAID, that issue was a big step towards financial independence.

Non-Banking Activities

Grameen has spawned several non-banking programs which are managed by non-profit group companies that are legally distinct from the bank.

Grameen Trust is the main non-banking affiliate. It is funded by foundations, and multilateral and bilateral agencies, including USAID, GTZ (the German overseas development agency),[24] and the World Bank. Its main functions consist in providing technical assistance, training programs, and seed capital for Grameen replicators. In 1998, there were already sixty-two replicators in Bangladesh and nineteen other countries in Asia, Africa, Europe, and the Americas.[25]

Grameen Trust also does research on poverty reduction, operates seven pilot health centers, develops software for the computerization of the bank's operations, and manages all in-house publications, including the Grameen Dialogue.

Social-conscience-driven companies are socially conscious non-profit ventures which are the outcome of a Studies, Innovation, Development and Experimentation Program (SIDE) which is implemented by the bank's research and development departments, with financing from donors.[26] SIDE has been experimenting with new ideas and technologies, and with new forms of individual and collective ownership. The socially conscious ventures include:

- Grameen Uddog has helped revive Bangladesh's tradition of weaving cotton fabric on hand-looms. With loans from Grameen, village women weave cloth, and make shirts and blouses, following a design by Bangladesh' best-known fashion designer. The bank markets the garments under the "Grameen Check" label. In 1997, it sold $20 million worth of Grameen Check in Europe.

- Grameen Fisheries Foundation has taken over several hundred money-losing fish ponds from the government. It operates a successful fish and shrimp farming business, staffed by members.

- The Grameen Agricultural Foundation does agricultural research on non-traditional crops and technologies.

- Grameen Leasing, which began in 1994, covers rickshaws, wheelbarrows, livestock, and power tillers. The annual rate is 20 percent, over a period of up to three years. Full payment conveys title to the lessee. Leases are only made to individuals.

Grameen's most ambitious business venture is Grameen Telecom. Its goal is to bring cellular telephone services to poor villages. The Norwegian telephone company Telenor, Marubeni of Japan, and a US telecommunications company have pooled together with Grameen to form Grameenphone. Launched in 1997, this company will sell cellular telephones to Grameen Telecom, which, in turn, will sell the telephones to center members. The goal is to create a rural communication network in Bangladesh, which currently has only two telephone lines per 1,000 people—compared with 602 in the United States. The target is to have 500,000 cellular phones in centers by the year 2003. The women who buy the phones will receive loans from Grameen. They will become local "phone ladies," who will make a living from providing telephone services in their villages, charging a small fee for each call.[27]

Cellular telephones would undoubtedly be useful in rural areas, where communication infrastructure is notoriously deficient. But this project still begs the question of how these battery-powered machines will be recharged in villages that have no electricity. The same goes for another tentative project, Grameen Cybernet. Even if this venture manages to acquire and distribute a large number of desktop and laptop computers, it is difficult to envision an Internet provider that will find users among center members in dirt-poor villages.

Finally, Yunus intends to launch Grameen Securities and Management to manage members' savings in their retirement. What this brings to mind is a futuristic view of village matrons who have individual retirement accounts, place orders to buy or sell securities through the phone ladies, and access their accounts online on their village computers.

Life in a Village Branch

In the Mymensingh District, in northern Bangladesh, on the border with India, I visited some of Grameen's oldest and newest branches. When I arrived in Dhaka in November 1995, there were violent strikes and political demonstrations. I was sent to the field immediately after receiving an introductory briefing at the head office, and began my stay in Mymensingh the next day. I spent my first week there in the area office, with the area manager, Shek Abusayeed, his wife, Nargis Sultana, and their two young children. Because there were no separate quarters for visitors my visit caused some commotion. Shortly after my arrival, a massive bedstead was ceremoniously wheeled in from a nearby branch office on two flat-bed rickshaws. With much banging and shouting, the bed was assembled in the manager's office, which became my living quarters. There I shared the space with two desks, several chairs and file cabinets, and the manager's motorcycle.

Because political unrest was almost as intense in Mymensingh as in Dhaka, the manager locked up the building at 7 P.M. for everyone's safety and protection, and I could not venture out alone after dusk. To make up for this, neighbors dropped by to talk, drink tea, and ask me questions about life in the United States and about my impressions of Bangladesh.

The family had a young live-in maid, the daughter of a member. Nargis Sultana and the maid spent much of the day preparing meals in a dark, smoke-filled, windowless kitchen. Squatting on the floor, they spent hours cutting up meat, chopping vegetables, and grounding spices for succulent curries. We ate curries three times a day—since there was meat or fish twice a day, I suspect that the family's diet was richer during my stay than on other occasions. To prepare these meals Nargis and her helper had only three cooking pots, a dozen plates, and a few spoons and knives. Cooking meant balancing the pots on a small clay stand, over a smoky wood fire. The same pots had to be used to fry vegetables and boil rice. The family's only sign of luxury were three armchairs, a coffee table and a black-and-white television set. For daily ablutions the family (and I) used a standpipe in the yard.

I accompanied Shek Abusayeed on his daily supervision visits to several branches in his district. On one such visit, we attended the last day of a week-long training workshop for center chiefs. It took place in a faraway rural branch, tucked away amidst paddies. The office was located in the middle of the village. It happened to be a market day, and the farmers had tied up their goats, cows, and water buffaloes to the gateposts of the office. What made the occasion remarkable is that, at lunchtime, Grameen's male staff served the women and ate after them, a complete reversal of the usual roles. The expression of delight and amazement on the women's faces is difficult to convey.

After Mymensingh, I went to a branch office in Charnilakmia. This office opened in August 1992. In November 1995 it already had more than 1,500 members, all of them women, and had disbursed well over $400,000 in loans. Arrears averaged 6 percent, which was above Grameen's total average.

At the branch office I spent time with the branch manager, Provash Das, and his family. Office accommodations in Charnilakmia are typical of the bank's more modern offices. It is a solid, brick and concrete, one-floor building. It is owned, and was built by, Grameen. There is running water and electricity. The office consists of a large L-shaped space, where each staff member has a desk. The manager has no private office. The furniture is identical to that in other branches. As in most new branches, the building has a small dormitory for visitors, and one for staff members who have transferred from other areas.

In the morning, when the staff visited their centers and the manager was either at center meetings, or in the zonal office, the office was deserted. Afternoons were quite different. Back from their center meetings, the staff had to count all the cash of loan repayments and complete paper work. Later in the day, different groups came to the office to receive their loan disbursements. Even though this branch has electricity, it has no computers or fax machine—these are available only in the head office and zone offices.

The manager and his wife are both Hindus. They and their newborn daughter were living in a two-room apartment behind the office. Before the evening meal Provash spent time playing with his daughter and changed her diapers, a thing which not many men would (or could) do in Bangladesh. After supper Provash, his wife, and two junior staff—both of them Muslims who had recently transferred to his branch office—spent the rest of the evening watching television. The young men also cuddled the baby. The atmosphere was extremely friendly and easygoing. Evening meals were simple but plentiful. Breakfast and lunch consisted of fruit—mostly bananas—and boiled rice.[28]

Meeting Grameen Members

Thanks to Grameen staff who kindly acted as my interpreters, I was able to talk at some length with several Grameen members. What follows are excerpts of these conversation.

Habina is a widow. She has three children, two daughters and one son. Though only fifteen years old, her son already works as a rickshaw driver. Habina has a general loan of $75, which she has used to buy plates and bowls that she sells to her neighbors. Her brother-in-law, who lives in nearby Mymensingh, bought the crockery for her. Her son went to fetch it with his rickshaw. After making weekly loan repayments of $1.90, paying her son's $2.50 weekly rental fee for the ricksha, and buying food, Habina can save about $5 per month. She is keeping her savings until she has enough money to lease a small plot of land, where she will grow vegetables.

Nurjahan is a third-time borrower. She has used her loan of $85 to buy two heifers for fattening. She also husks paddy. Her husband is a laborer in a jute mill. The family's weekly income is sufficient to cover the weekly loan repayment, household expenditures, and save about $8 per month. Nurjahan and her husband are using their savings to buy a half acre of land, one bit at a time. The land will be in her husband's name. As soon as he gets title to the land, Nurjahan will stop husking paddy, and grow vegetables on the land.

Najna is also a third-time borrower. With her loan of $120 she has bought two oxen with which her husband does contract ploughing. She manages to save about $3 per week, and in four years she and her husband had already accumulated $300 in savings from his ploughing and sharecropping of a potato field. They too are using the money to buy a small parcel of land to grow potatoes. This family's savings was considerable by local standards. But Grameen is loyal to long-standing clients and will not "graduate" them out of its program, even when they no longer qualify as poor or landless.

Hasina is a jeweler. She is married and has one son. As a second-time borrower she has a loan of $90, with which she has purchased old silver bangles from her neighbors. She uses the silver to make earrings. When we visited Hasina, her husband had locked the tool box while he went to the market. This suggested that the husband, not Hasina, was using the loan.

What is striking in the first three cases is the effect of Koranic law, which prevents women from owning or inheriting land. This is why as a widow, Habina could only lease a plot of land. In contrast, Nurjahan and Najna, both of whom had husbands, could use their savings to buy small parcels of land, albeit in their husbands' names.

Grameen's Achievements in Perspective

Because of the charisma of its founder and managing director, Grameen is often treated like an icon that should not be criticized. This has the paradoxical effect of making some observers overly judgmental and critical when they discuss Grameen. What follows may help put some of the criticism and praise of Grameen in perspective.

- *Grameen is breaking down gender bias and defying social taboos to empower women*: This is clearly beyond dispute. It can be seen in the women's demeanor at center meetings. The bank is also encouraging its members to stop the debasing practice of bridal dowry and to take control of their own fertility—birth rates are lower among members than non-members. There is also evidence that nutrition, health, and education levels are higher in households which belong to Grameen, than in those that do not.[29] Women nevertheless remain constrained in their economic activities. For example, if they use their loans to buy chickens or small livestock, their sons or husbands must go to the market to make the purchases. If women want to sell their products outside their villages, again husbands and sons do so on their behalf.

- *Empowerment is changing women's attitudes and social behavior*: It does. The habit of electing group and center chiefs and secretaries has made women aware of the importance of using their right to vote. As a result of this, women's participation in local and national elections is much higher in "Grameen" villages that in villages where it has no presence. In the last national election, in June 1996, women's votes tipped the balance in electing the Sheik Hasina—the daughter of Sheik Mujibur Raman, the independence leader—as Prime Minister.

- *Managers have internalized the culture of empowerment they promote*: From my own observations they have done so, to a point. In its offices the bank still adheres to traditional gender roles: in branch offices women serve the men; women only work in their home areas and walk to centers; fewer than 10 percent of the staff are women and only a few are managers. On the other hand, Grameen has gone out of its way to assign important roles to poor women who are its members. Eight of its thirteen directors are women who were elected by the centers. Better still, when Muhammad Yunus traveled to Brussels to accept a prize from King Baudouin, one of the bank's members accompanied him.

- *The bank lends without collateral*: It is true that Grameen demands no collateral as a pre-condition for lending, and that it uses peer pressure as its main form of security. However, equipment, livestock, and poultry remain the bank's de facto property until a loan has been repaid in full. The members' savings in emergency funds provide additional security and, for house-building loans, the bank retains title buildings until the loan are repaid in full.

- *Grameen has one of the highest loan repayment rates*: The bank's own data show that arrears are consistently below 2 percent of loans outstanding. But it must be noted that loans are not considered delinquent until arrears reach two years. Nevertheless, recovery rates exceed 97 percent one year after the loans are due, and close to 99 percent within two years.[30] Thus, loan recovery is more than satisfactory, by any standard. Moreover, Grameen does not reschedule loans, except when natural calamities such as cyclones and floods cause hardship to members. In such cases, the "repayment clock" is put on hold until the crisis is over.

- *The pressure to make loan repayments can be a source of financial stress and cause hardship*: Peer-group pressure and the bank's strict discipline have instilled a strong sense of financial responsibility in members. They always do their utmost to remain punctual, even when making weekly repayments is difficult. For instance, because of the generally poor genetic quality of Bangladeshi cattle, cows often die young. This causes financial stress for women who have debts, with no means of generating cash to repay their loans. In one of the centers I visited two of the women told me that their cows had died. To remain punctual on their loan repayments they were both working in a local cigarette factory, and were using most of their meager wages to remain up-to-date on their weekly repayments. Both said that the women in their groups had helped them. Over and beyond accidental financial hardship, lending for activities such as cow or goat fattening is a source of financial stress because these activities do not generate short-term income to pay the weekly loan installments

- *All loans achieve the goal of raising family income and living standards*: General and family loans, and housing finance usually achieve their goals—respectively generating income and providing hurricane-proof shelter. Grameen estimates that it takes ten to fifteen loan cycles for its members to graduate out of poverty. But there have inevitably been some failures, and not all lending is successful. The highest rate of failure has been in joint-venture loans, which were first introduced to finance the purchase of shallow tube wells. Because those wells are shared by several families, the loans were made to centers, a departure from group lending. The problem was that tubewells raised complicated questions about location and shared use. The loans were discontinued, and replaced with financing for deep tubewells, which also had some problems. Other joint-venture loans are for the purchase of paddy-husking machines, and for joint ventures by entire centers. They include leasing land, ponds, and fisheries, and purchasing power tillers and threshers.[31] On the whole, joint-venture loans have been among Grameen's most troublesome activities. There were misunderstandings among recipients, and cases of appropriation of the funds by individuals. Grameen has taken over the joint enterprises that became defunct and is phasing out these loans.

- *The income-generating activities the bank finances are low skill and of low productivity*: This is true, and is the case in virtually all microfinance programs. Informal activities which are financed by small loans rarely break out of low-skill, low-technology environments, and cannot achieve economies of scale. Moreover, in rural Bangladesh, tradition almost forces women to engage in activities that are extensions of home-based work, which limits productivity even further. Livestock fattening and fish farming, which account for over a third of loan usage, can be done in a village. The same is true of paddy husking, food processing, and trading, which account for the bulk of the rest. The problem is that these types of activities only provide marginal additional household income, because the women receive little training, and get no support form extension agents. Women's social isolation is also perpetuated because there is no tradition of cooperative work in non-traditional activities outside the homestead.

- *Manual accounting and complex procedures are inefficient*: Because many branch offices have no electricity, and none have computers or fax machines, all record keeping and bookkeeping is done by hand in ledgers, in which staff record loan repayments and disbursements, tally the various savings funds, and record the cash surplus, if any. Weekly and monthly summary reports in branches and areas are also done by hand, and involve a multiplicity of forms. These reports are consolidated by the zone offices on computers, and sent to Dhaka. Zone managers always have up-to-date weekly summaries of the financial position of branches and areas in their zone; senior managers in Dhaka always have up-to-date monthly accounts and financial statements.

- *Grameen has a high drop-out rate*: The drop-out rate was comparatively high in early years, and increased in relative terms from about 5 percent in 1985, to 15 percent in 1991.[32] With a total membership of around one million at that time, this represented an annual membership turnover of 150,000,000. Drop-out rates are higher in new branches than in mature ones and are higher among men than women (respectively 22 percent and 14 percent in 1991). Some of this is the result of women joining a center in another village, after they marry, which shows up as a drop-out in the center they leave. Drop-out rates have stabilized and become insignificant during the 1990s, but there have been slight variations in total membership. It declined by more than 5,000 during the first quarter of 1996 and by 7,000 between November 1995 and July 1996, respectively 0.24 percent and 0.34 percent of total membership.[33]

- *Though women are the borrowers, their husbands are often the ones who use the money*: According to the bank's staff, on average two-thirds of loans to women are used by them for their own activities.

The remainder is used by their husbands or elder sons, or for a family-run microenterprise with "family loans." This does not run counter to Yunus's philosophy, which is to empower women by giving them a greater say in their families *and* raise the families' incomes. When a household, rather than a woman alone, uses a loan, the very fact that the woman is the gateway to credit gives her greater say on how to use the money and increases her bargaining power in the family. The danger nevertheless exists that husbands "steal" their wives' loans. It happens, but only seldom. When it does, group members sometimes rally together to force the scoundrels to give the money back.

- *Loans are not always used for the stated purposes*: While the bank prides itself on driving moneylenders out of the villages, some of its own borrowers are perpetuating money-lending practices by using their loans to lend money to other women in their villages.

- *There is too little emphasis on mobilizing members' savings*: Savings potential is limited in poor families, many of which had only limited contacts with the cash economy before joining Grameen. Members already make forced savings in the Group Funds, and members are gradually accumulating voluntary group savings.

The Bangladesh Rural Advancement Committee

BRAC is an NGO which began operating in 1972 as a small committee to bring relief and rehabilitation to resettle people who had fled to Pakistan during Bangladesh's War of Independence, as well as others who returned home from India after Independence. Since then, BRAC has expanded its scope to include activities designed to promote rural development, alleviate poverty, and empower the poor in village communities. Except for visits to several BRAC village schools, I was unable to spend time with its other village projects. What follows is based on my notes on meetings with senior managers at BRAC's headquarters in Dhaka, and on the organization's 1994 annual report.

Credit Programs

Like Grameen, BRAC lends to landless women and focuses on poverty lending. The core of its credit programs is rural development, for which it establishes village organizations of the poor, offers credit, and encourages savings. Poor village women are the principal target group of BRAC's Rural Development Program, which makes small loans to women and organizes training programs. Eighty percent of village-organization members are women.

In 1986, this program was linked with the Rural Credit Program. By the end of 1994, there were active village organizations comprising 1.4 million households in more than 40 percent of all villages. Both programs are managed by area offices, each of which covers roughly about 130 village organizations has up to 7,000 members. All program organizers are field managers who mobilize rural men and women to form village organizations.

BRAC only finances rural projects that have an economic and social potential. There is no collateral. Loans are to individuals—unlike Grameen, it does not lend to groups—and range from as little as $12 to $175. Maturities range from one to three years, with a flat interest rate of 15 percent. Members of village organizations can combine different loans at any one time, for different purposes. In 1994, BRAC had about $54 million in loans outstanding. Loan recovery rates are only fractionally lower than at Grameen. Members' voluntary savings average 50 US cents per week. Members must also place 5 percent of each loan in a savings account. At the end of 1994, their total savings amounted to $16 million. In November 1995, BRAC was preparing to formalize its financial service activities and to create a bank.

Support for Village Schools

BRAC has two school programs. Non-formal primary education in villages was launched in 1984, with twenty-two experimental schools for children aged eight to ten. By 1994, there were close to 29,000 primary schools, with 800,000 children. The second school program offers basic education for older children, aged eleven to fourteen. In each three-year course, there is a student-staff ratio of 33:1, which compares favorably with public schools in the United States. The education programs help fight the anti-girl bias. Three-quarters of the students are girls, and practically all the teachers are women. BRAC sponsors scholarships of $1.50 per month to send promising students to formal secondary schools.

In each village I visited to attend Grameen center meetings, there was a BRAC school. The schools are simple one-room bamboo structures. There are no benches or chairs. During lessons, the children squat on straw mats on the earthen floor. They have no pencils or paper. Instead, they use chalk and slate boards, and keep their chalks in recycled aerosol canisters.

In 1994, BRAC opened an office in Nairobi, under the auspices of UNICEF, to advise African countries on non-formal rural education. At that time, it was also expanding its school programs in urban centers—Dhaka, Chittagong and two other major cities. For the teaching of English as a second language, it is also experimenting with interactive radio instruction.

BRAC's Other Programs

BRAC manages a nationwide rural health program of oral re-hydration therapy to combat the consequences of diarrhea, which is a major cause of infant mortality. By 1994 it had reached 13 million families. Its health programs also cover family planning, water and sanitation, health and nutrition, immunization, and preventive health care.

As part of its Rural Development Program, BRAC organizes income-generating programs, in cooperation with leading international NGOs and the government of Bangladesh. They include poultry raising, pisciculture, vegetable and maize cultivation, rural nurseries for reforestation, tubewell irrigation, and sericulture in village mulberry tree plantations. Each program is supported by intensive training. Management is participatory and decentralized, and program planning is "from the bottom up."

BRAC supports women's off-farm activities outside the traditional homestead, and finances women-owned village eateries and grocery stores. It also has a Human Rights and Legal Education Program which helps women defend themselves against illegal, unfair, and discriminatory practices. The aim is to empower the rural poor by raising their awareness about their basic rights, and by giving women information, without which they cannot defend their rights, or fight exploitation.[34] BRAC also funds experimental village carpentry workshops, and yarn and cloth dying. It markets its members' handicraft in its store ("Aarong") which has outlets in Dhaka, as well as in London and Vancouver.

Lessons from Bangladesh

Grameen is the best-known of all microfinance institutions. Numerous books have been written about it, and Yunus has received several prizes and awards. In fact, among the bank's staff there is also something of a Yunus personality cult. Visitors are often asked if he should receive a Nobel Prize—Peace? Economics?—or become President of the Republic. Each office has a large notice board with press cuttings from around the world about Yunus's latest speeches, travels, awards, and meetings with queens and first ladies.

This is not to belittle Yunus's achievements. He has accomplished more than anyone could hope for. Grameen is his creation and, during twenty years at the helm, he has made it a model of good governance and management. Yunus has also used the limelight with great effectiveness to draw the world's attention to the plight of the landless poor. Through his actions and relentless criticism of the failings of international development aid, he has also been instrumental in making the World Bank refocus its development strategy. Poverty reduction, which had almost vanished from the institution's agenda, is again its number one priority, at least officially. The World Bank's lending for microenterprise development, and its sponsorship of CGAP (see Chapter 11) and the Microfinance Summit, are the result of intensive lobbying by Muhammad Yunus. In other areas, the replication and adaptation of the Grameen model in other impoverished countries and communities is a great success. Last but not least, Yunus has given true meaning to empowerment by daring to challenge the religious conservatives, and teaching landless women how to help themselves.

One interesting aspect of Grameen is that the growth of its membership and outreach is characteristic of a mature institution. Total membership was already close to two million in August 1994, and its growth has slowed down considerably since then. One the other hand, disbursements and loans outstanding are growing fast, which suggest a rising income and debt-carrying capacity among the bank's members.

In comparison with publicity-conscious Grameen, BRAC is Bangladesh's Cinderella. It does not publish numerous pamphlets, nor does its managing director travel the world, or tell international agencies how to go about their business. Yet, over the years, BRAC has perhaps achieved even more than Grameen in terms of women's empowerment, and it covers almost as many villages as the latter. The fact that it does so more humbly is to its credit. By focusing on training, helping create village organizations, funding schools and health programs, and supplementing its fast-growing credit program with social intermediation, its activities have an extremely broad and profound social impact. Moreover, by showing women how to defend their rights head-on with legal actions, BRAC's Human Rights program challenges the religious establishment even more openly than Grameen's actions, and BRAC does as it preaches: almost one quarter of its staff are women—two-and-a-half times more than in Grameen—and many occupy managerial positions. This too is empowerment.

Through its other programs, BRAC is helping change the lives not only of individuals, but of entire impoverished communities. Most of all, its emphasis on schools will ensure that future generations of young women will grow up better able to defend themselves against prejudice.

One final observation is that, because Bangladesh is so overwhelmingly rural and agrarian, the urban poor have received too little attention. The time has come to introduce microfinance for income generation in Dhaka, Chittagong, and other cities. BRAC has already taken action to reduce urban illiteracy by establishing urban schools.

Postscript

Since the time of writing, the floods that wiped out crops and infrastructure across Bangladesh in 1998 have ruined more than half of Grameen's and BRAC's members. Their crops, houses, and livestock shattered by the floods, they are poorer than ever and cannot keep up their weekly loan repayments. This tragedy also shows that even the most "solid" microfinance institutions cannot take the future for granted; massive arrears are threatening the very existence of both institutions. Grameen has too few loan-loss reserves to forgive its members' debts, *and* give them desperately needed bridging loans. According to Muhammad Yunus, the bank will need $100 million to survive.[35] Similarly afflicted by client distress and loan arrears, BRAC's activities are also in jeopardy and it will need up to $50 million in external funding to continue lending.

Notes

1. Michael Walton, "The Maturation of the East Asian Miracle," *Finance and Development* (September 1997), 7
2. See *An Inventory of Microfinance Institutions in South Asia,* The World Bank, 5–7.

3. Dirk Steinwand, "Moneylending in Modern Times," in *Financial Landscapes Reconstructed*, edited by F.J.A. Bouman and O. Hospes, Westview Press, 1994.

4. *BRAC Annual Report 1994*, 27

5. Syed Ahmedduzzaman, *The Nation*, Bangkok, February 11, 1996.

6. UNCTAD, *The Least Developing Countries*, 1996, 31, and *WDR 97*, 246.

7. Rahnuma Shehabuddin, *Empowering Rural Women: The Impact of Grameen Bank in Bangladesh* (Dhaka: Grameen Bank, 1992), 52.

8. Muhammad Yunus, *Grameen Bank, Experiences and Reflections* (Dhaka: Grameen Bank, 1991), 15.

9. There are countless "Jotsnas" in Bangladesh. Their stories feature in *Jorimon and Others: Faces of Poverty*, published by the Grameen Bank.

10. There are many detailed accounts of Grameen's origin. One of them can be found in *The Grameen Reader*, Part Two, edited by David Gibbons (Dhaka: Grameen Bank).

11. Yunus, *Grameen Bank, Experiences and Reflections*, 22–24.

12. David Bornstein, *The Price of a Dream* (New York: Simon & Schuster, 1996), 51–52.

13. Susan Holcombe, *Managing to Empower* (London: Zed Books, 1995), 53.

14. Bornstein, *The Price of a Dream*, 191.

15. Andreas Fugelsang and Dale Chandler, *Participation as Process—Process as Growth* (Dhaka: Grameen Bank, 1993), 122.

16. Gibbons, *The Grameen Reader*, 150.

17. Fugelsang et al., *Participation as Process*, 109.

18. *Grameen Dialogue 35*, July 1998.

19. *Grameen Dialogue 35*.

20. *Grameen Dialogue 33*, January 1998.

21. *Grameen Dialogue 31*, July 1997, 1

22. Grameen Bank *1993 Annual Report*, including its audited financial statements.

23. S. Khandler, B. Kahlily and Z. Khan, *Grameen Bank, Performance and Sustainability*, The World Bank Discussion Paper 306, 1995.

24. GTZ stands for *Deutsche Gesellshaft fur Technische Zuzammenarbeit*.

25. *Grameen Dialogue 35*, 16.

26. Fugelsang et al., *Participation as Process*, 72–73.

27. *Grameen Dialogue 28* (October 1996), 13.

28. The point of this digression is to illustrate the spartan life style of Grameen's managers and their families.

29. Abu N. M. Wahid, ed., *The Grameen Bank, Poverty Relief in Bangladesh*, (Boulder: Westview Press, 1993), 59–63.

30. *The Grameen Bank, Poverty Relief in Bangladesh*, 57.

31. *The Grameen Reader*, 35–36.

32. *Grameen Dialogue 20*, July 1995.

33. *Grameen Dialogues 25, 27* and *28*.

34. BRAC *Annual Report 1994*, 16.

35. *The Financial Times*, October 1, 1998.

5

Bold Experiments with Unit Banking in Indonesia

With 13,677 islands Indonesia is the world's largest archipelago. It straddles the equator for more than 3,000 miles, from the northern tip of Sumatra to the border with Papua New Guinea in the southeast. The total land area is roughly three times that of Texas. It is divided into twenty-seven provinces and two special regions, Jakarta and Yogyakarta. Only about half of the islands are inhabited. Some are tiny uninhabitable atolls, while others, such as Sumatra, Java, Kalimantan (Borneo), Sulawesi, and Irian Jaya (the former West New Guinea), are larger than most European countries. The level of "civilization" varies greatly among the islands. Irian Jaya, for instance, is one of the most primitive regions in the world, where people have only recently abandoned the use of stone axes, and men's "clothing" consists solely of bizarre penis gourds.

For centuries this widely scattered archipelago was home to thousands of kingdoms and sultanates. Today, Indonesia's 200 million inhabitants make it the fourth most populous nation and the largest Muslim country. The principal ethnic groups are Javanese, Sundanese, Madurese, and Malays. Population densities vary enormously from island to island. The extreme is Java, where 110 million people are crammed together on 7 percent of the country's land area at a rate of more than 800 inhabitants per square kilometer. This is twice the population density of Japan and about the same as in Bangladesh. Taken by itself, Java would be the world's eleventh largest country. In contrast, Irian Jaya, which is three times as large as Java, has fewer than three million inhabitants.

Environmental protection is lax and deforestation and environmental damage are on a par with that in the Amazon forest. In 1997, uncontrolled forest fires in Sumatra and other islands destroyed vast swaths of pristine rain forest. That environmental disaster, which was caused by fires to clear forest land for profit—some of it by logging companies controlled by the Suharto family—was exacerbated by an El Niño draught. The fires burned for weeks, covering large parts of East Asia in a dense cloud of smoke that obscured the sun for weeks on end. In the smoke-filled areas children and elderly people suffered from respiratory diseases; economic activity slowed down; ships collided; an airplane crashed in the smog; and crops failed in Indonesia and neighboring countries.

Building a Nation

Molding this huge archipelago into a single nation was a lengthy process, which began in the eighteenth century, when all of today's Indonesia, except Portuguese East Timor, became the Dutch East Indies. At first, colonization was carried out by the Dutch East India Company, the Royal Charter Company that founded Holland's colonial empire in the East Indies and ruled its far-flung possessions from its headquarters in Batavia (now Jakarta). Early colonialism introduced coffee and other cash crops to Java, as part of its "cultivation system." That system worked in connivance with Javanese aristocrats to extract forced crop deliveries from small farmers. It also encouraged Chinese immigration to provide labor for Java's plantations. This set in motion a cycle of overpopulation, monoculture, and poverty the effects of which are still felt in parts of the country. Towards the end of the eighteenth century, mismanagement and a decline in trade forced the East India Company into bankruptcy, and the Dutch Crown took over colonial rule.

The Indonesian nation state which took shape under Dutch colonial rule is largely a product of the pan-Asian, anti-Western ideology propagated by the Japanese troops that occupied Indonesia during the second world war. Like the pan-Germanic ideology of German invaders, which aroused Flemish nationalism in Belgium during the two world wars, the Japanese awakened Indonesian nationalism. The colony declared independence from Holland on August 17, 1945, two days after Japan's surrender. The Dutch tried to hold on to power, but were defeated in 1949 after a bitter war of independence.

Sukarno, the leader of the nationalist movement under Japanese occupation, became Indonesia's first president. His twenty-year rule was plagued by attempted military coups, economic mismanagement (more about this later), and mass discontent at the country's extreme poverty. Famines regularly ravaged Java and the other islands, and several thousand died of hunger during the 1950s. Returning from a state visit to Indonesia in 1953, then Vice President Nixon said that "In no other country we visited was the conspicuous luxury of the ruler in such striking contrast to the poverty and misery of his people. Jakarta was a collection of sweltering huts and hovels. An open sewer ran through the heart of the city."[1] Under Sukarno, living conditions were actually worse than under colonial rule, and the country remained politically fragmented.

Most of the president's support had come from the Indonesian Communist Party (PKI). Sukarno gradually lost PKI and popular support in the mid-1960s, and was stripped of most of his executive powers after a bloody coup by left-wing army officers in 1965—the "year of living dangerously." He was ousted the following year by a young right-wing colonel by the name of Suharto, who quashed the rebellion with US support. Even before assuming power Suharto began exterminating PKI members and sympathizers. Several hundred thousand people (some estimates say two million), including many ethnic Chinese, were massacred in 1965–66. Co-opted as President in 1966, Suharto began forging Indonesia's diverse cultures and ethnic groups into a single nation. He did this by imposing a standardized national school curriculum and making Batan Indonesian, a modified form of Malay originally spoken only in Jakarta, the official national language.

Even so, linguistic unity remains a distant goal in this country, where some 700 native languages and dialects are still spoken. Religion is the strongest bond among the people of this scattered nation, 87 percent of whom are Muslims, and Bali is the only island where Muslims are a minority. Indonesia's secular Islam is better adapted to the modern world than that of most other Muslim countries. Women take an active part in work and social activities and can mix openly with men, and *purdah* is rarely practiced. But in small towns and villages many women, and even schoolgirls, wear head scarves (*chadors*) and long dresses.

Controversial Transmigration

Transmigration, which already began under Sukarno in the 1950s, is one of the government's most controversial social integration programs. Its ostensible purpose was to alleviate rural poverty and ease overcrowding in Java, Bali, and Lombok, by moving their "excess" populations to distant Kalimantan, Sulawesi, and Irian Jaya. By 1995, more than 2.5 million people had been resettled, but the population grows so fast in Java and Bali that transmigration did little to improve living conditions. At the same time, transmigration was deeply resented in the outer islands, where this thinly veiled way to "javanize" them had a damaging social and environmental impact. In Irian Jaya it disrupted the hunting-and-gathering life style of tribal communities, but did not create new institutions to alleviate social tensions.

Transmigration also caused serious environmental damage in areas where settlers cleared swamps and rainforests, to make space for houses and fields. Some of the worst deforestation was the work of resettled subsistence farmers from Java. They were accustomed to rice farming on volcanic soils and did not know how to adapt to a different environment. Their slash-and-burn methods destroyed fragile tropical forest soils, in areas where soil composition and water supply were not suited for rice cultivation.[2] The isolation and lack of proper infrastructure in many areas of settlement also meant that farmers had no access to markets to sell their produce.

Transmigration also included the involuntary relocation of thousands of landless farmers and laborers, and of slum dwellers from Jakarta and other big cities. Those people, who had no education or skills, and could not fend for themselves in an alien rural environment, became burdens for the areas of settlement. Altogether the program was a failure, and many settlers live below the poverty level and are destitute.[3]

Early Growth Based on Oil

Until the late 1960s Indonesia was one of the poorest countries. During the first decade after independence it had to make crippling debt repayments to Holland and most large businesses were still under Dutch control. Thereafter, Sukarno's "Guided Democracy," from 1959 to 1965, was a total failure. The government squandered foreign loans on prestige projects and armaments, and expropriated British- and Dutch-owned companies in a vain attempt to regain popular support. Desperate to salvage his government, Sukarno launched a campaign of self reliance in 1965, withdrawing the country from the World Bank and IMF.[4] This too ended in failure because, by then, Sukarno had already lost executive power. The legacy of his hapless economic management was a per capita GDP of $50, one of the lowest in the world, and only half that of Bangladesh in the same year. In 1970, two out of every three Indonesians were still living in absolute poverty.

After seizing power, Suharto reversed his predecessor's policies. Indonesia rejoined the multilateral institutions, and was among the first to adopt an IMF stabilization plan.[5] Suharto's government also introduced an ambitious development strategy, implemented in a succession of five-year plans. To that end, it passed legislation protecting foreign investors against nationalization, awarded logging concessions to Japanese and American companies, and boosted exports of tropical timber. The government took advantage of its vast oil reserves to raise oil exports and generate cash for investment in large industrial projects and modern technology.

During the 1970s, when oil prices were high and rising, oil revenues represented more than two-thirds of the annual budgets. They were used to finance social and physical infrastructure, and fund a wide array of subsidized credit lines. There were special credit lines for paddy farmers to boost production and achieve rice self-sufficiency, and credit lines for small businesses. Other credit facilities, which were combined with trade protection, financed investment in new industries, such as steel, plastics, and petrochemicals. Until the early 1980s, directed subsidized credit made up close to half of all bank lending.[6]

Oil revenues were also invested in "human capital." To encourage school enrollment the government eliminated fees for primary schools, built more and better schools in villages, and promoted the education of girls. This made Indonesia one of a handful of developing countries where the gender gap in education and school attendance is insignificant. Enrollment in primary schools is universal, and adult illiteracy is among the lowest in the developing world.

The strategy of supporting the economy with directed subsidized credit was feasible as long as oil prices remained high, and oil revenues filled the state's coffers. To its credit, when oil prices began falling in 1983, the government changed tack rapidly. It could do so because, having borrowed relatively little from foreign banks, Indonesia had no debt crisis. The change of course was supported by a World Bank structural-adjustment loan which stipulated, among other things, that the financial sector should be reformed, interest-rate subsidies phased out, and trade liberalized. As part of the same program public spending on industrial projects was replaced with a mix of privatizations, market incentives, and mercantilist policies.

The strategy paid off. The reforms gradually weaned the economy from over-dependency on oil, and, at a time Latin America was mired in its lost decade, Indonesia's growth and the pace of industrialization accelerated during the 1980s. GDP growth averaged 6.1 percent during the second half of the eighties, and climbed to 7.6 percent after 1990. By the mid-1990s Indonesia was heralded as a success story. With a 1995 per capita income of close to $1,000 this formerly poor nation had become a lower middle-income country, putting it in the exclusive group of Asia's newly industrialized "miracle economies." [7] It had a stable currency, the rupiah, annual inflation that remained consistently below 10 percent, and high domestic savings and investment that fueled capital accumulation and industrialization. In 1995, industry already represented 42 percent of GDP, compared with only 17 percent for agriculture. Even so, agriculture, fisheries, and forestry still account for about half of total employment. Agro-industrial export crops include coffee, fruits, and tropical beverages. The increasingly diversified industrial base produced textiles, plywood, cement, fertilizers, and locally assembled electronics.

Strong growth and political stability under Suharto's rule became magnets for foreign investment in new industrial ventures, and large inflows of speculative money in the Jakarta bourse and in real estate drove up the price of financial assets and property. The most conspicuous yardstick of economic success was the modernization of Jakarta. This sprawling metropolis of more than fifteen million people, long notorious for its appalling poverty and ramshackle infrastructure, had re-invented itself. The glamour zone of the new downtown formed a "golden triangle" with a state-of-the-art financial and business center, luxury hotels, and air-conditioned shopping malls that rivaled those of Bangkok and Singapore. At the height of the boom Jakarta had one of the world's highest per capita ownership of Mercedes Benz motor cars, and a runaway construction boom that was largely financed by Japanese banks. In the golden triangle gleaming new steel-and-glass buildings stood side-by-side with partly finished office towers, amidst a forest of cranes. Work-in-progress on new expressways and a rapid transit system added to the confusion by creating terminal rush-hour gridlock.

Financial Collapse and Economic Implosion in 1997

Indonesia's astonishing economic success and political stability deceived foreign investors and the multilateral development agencies for years. What was overlooked—or conveniently ignored—was that political "stability" came at the price of harsh repression of political and ethnic dissidents, by an autocratic regime that brooked no dissent. Moreover, Indonesia's economy combined the remnants of a nationalist command economy with the worst excesses of crony capitalism, amidst corruption and nepotism on an unparalleled scale. No major project or investment could go ahead without the President's approval, or without giving big cuts to his sons and daughters, and political protégés. Suharto's six children and closest cronies also skimmed off billions of dollars in rigged bids for concessions and privatizations. They owned or controlled several industrial conglomerates and banks, as well as toll roads, the clove monopoly, the plywood cartel, and timber concessions.[8] Suharto's eldest daughter, who controlled all the major toll roads, was nicknamed "tutut" for the honking of cars approaching the toll booths. Before Suharto's downfall in May 1998, the combined net worth of his family was estimated at $16 billion.[9]

The economy was also undermined by the fact that, instead of continuing to fund rural infrastructure and education, the government was pouring vast amounts of state resources into uneconomical prestige projects, such as a domestic aircraft industry, to assert Indonesian technological prowess. It also spent hundreds of millions of dollars to bail out the clove monopoly, controlled by one of the President's sons, and gave $1 billion in subsidies to the "national" car industry in which Suharto's youngest son had a major stake.[10]

This corrupt system remained unchallenged for years, and managed to survive and prosper for years because the fear of repression and growing urban affluence had created an apolitical urban middle class. Ignoring or overlooking tell-tale signs of trouble—the lack of democracy, widespread human-rights violations by the armed forces, rampant corruption, and crony capitalism that was undermining the banking system—the World Bank stated in 1995 that Indonesia had become another East Asian dynamo, and praised its growth as the product of traditional outward-oriented policies and an abandonment of selective industrial policies.[11]

Cronyism and lax banking practices could be ignored as long as the economy continued to grow, the rupiah remained stable, and the banks could keep on rolling over the mounting number of weak, technically non-performing loans. Thus, the international community continued to brush off concerns. In its 1997 Annual Report, released at its annual meeting in Hong Kong, in September 1997, the World Bank expressed confidence in the region's stability, despite serious signs of weakness in the banking systems. The report stated that: "Although there are some concerns about the fragility of the region's banking systems, the risks of loss of confidence in banking systems would be easy to overstate, since most East Asian countries have a more robust external and fiscal position than countries that have faced banking crises elsewhere. The prospects for continued high growth in coming years remain sound, provided countries undertake the necessary important reforms."[12]

So much for the World Bank's insight. The Asian miracle began to crumble one month later, in October 1997, when the Thai banking system collapsed under the weight of bad loans, dragging down Indonesia, Korea, and Malaysia in its wake. Thailand's banking and financial crisis rapidly engulfed the entire region, and foreign investors began withdrawing their funds en masse. By late October 1997 the weakness of the Jakarta and Bangkok stock exchanges had spilled over to Hong Kong and Seoul. The ensuing region-wide stock-market meltdown had ripple effects that made share prices tumble in Hong Kong, Europe, and New York. Like Mexico in 1994, Asia's crisis showed that being in the global economy can bring more perils than rewards, and that chaos can set in when countries rely on short-term speculative funds, which foreign investors can withdraw almost instantly when they lose confidence.

To put Indonesia's problems in perspective, the economic collapse and loss of value of the rupiah were so severe that, by early 1998, the dollar GDP had lost close to 80 percent of its value, down from an original $228 billion in 1997, to a revised $50 billion.[13] On a per capita basis this put the country at about the same level as Haiti, Mali, and Bangladesh, in the lower tier of low-income countries. More than two decades of economic growth were wiped out in a matter of months.

As can be seen from the sequence of events that followed the region-wide stock-market crash of October 1997, the worst-case scenario materialized despite massive, but largely futile foreign intervention to avert an implosion of Indonesia's economy.

- In November 1997, the IMF stepped in with a bailout of $23 billion to ward off economic collapse and restore investor confidence. To that end, it imposed the habitual package of austerity measures, including abolishing subsidies on staples, such as cooking oil and rice, to reduce budget deficits. Singapore and Japan, the World Bank, and the US Treasury topped up the bailout to $43 billion.[14]

- In the weeks that followed, the government was forced to close sixteen insolvent banks, and consolidated the state-owned commercial banks into three big institutions, one of which was BRI.[15]

- The IMF's intervention did not manage to stabilize the situation or restore investor confidence. By late November the rupiah had lost almost 32 percent of its value, and the stock market continued to fall.

- Over the New Year the crisis deepened even further, amid mounting fears of political instability and well-founded doubts about the government's commitment to implement the necessary reforms.

- Anti-Chinese riots and looting of food stores spread across provincial towns in early January, causing vast destruction, hundreds of casualties, and increasing food shortages.

- Meanwhile, the rupiah continued to loose ground against the dollar—by late January 1998 it had lost more than 80 percent of its pre-crisis value—-and the Jakarta stock market was still in free fall. The precipitous drop of the rupiah virtually bankrupted companies that had piled up large amounts of dollar debts, and they stopped making repayments on a total of $65 billion in overseas loans.[16]

- In an attempt to restore stability, and ensure compliance with the terms of the IMF bailout, the United States, Japan, and the IMF sent several high-profile missions to Jakarta, in January, February, and March 1998. The managing director of the IMF met with Suharto in January to negotiate new terms for the bailout. He also wrested several concessions from Suharto, forcing him to break up the cartels and monopolies in which his children and friends have substantial interests. The IMF also forced the government to scrap projects it considers unjustified, the national car and passenger-plane projects among them.

- These various missions still failed to ensure even a semblance of commitment to reform from Suharto, and the economic situation continued to deteriorate. In early February 1998, the economy was grinding to a halt. Work had stopped at building sites and road infrastructure projects all over the country.

- By then, even the IMF's economists could no longer make reliable forecasts. Estimates of the number of people who would be jobless after scores of offices and factories would not reopen at the end of Ramadan already ranged as high as nine million.

- There was also a deepening policy stalemate that gradually turned into a tug of war between the IMF and Suharto. The IMF threatened to suspend the bailout, while an undaunted Suharto snubbed the IMF with a stern third-worldist attitude.[17] He refused to implement some reforms and reversed earlier ones, trying to gain time and preserve a hint of legitimacy in the run-up to the March presidential elections.

- After more than thirty years in power Suharto was co-opted to a seventh term in office on March 12, 1998. This was to be his shortest term. Less than three months later his power base crumbled in the face of massive demonstrations by students who had occupied the grounds of the national parliament. After the army had killed several students, mass revolt exploded, and Suharto stepped down, handing over power to his Vice President, R.J. Habibie, on May 21, 1998.

- Since May 1998, the new president has pushed through some democratic reforms, and purged the army of officers guilty of human-rights abuses. He also obtained a major concession from the IMF: in a sixth and final round of negotiations of the bail-out package, the IMF relented and no longer made the elimination of food subsidies a condition for its support.

- Yet, from April to June 1998, the economy shrank by an unprecedented 16.5 percent, a deeper contraction than any other country during the last fifty years, and government estimates were that 80 million people—40 percent of the total population—were living in poverty.[18] This was a four-fold increase over the level of poverty before the outbreak of the crisis.

- The impact of job losses has been heightened by the catastrophic devaluation of the rupiah, which fed an inflationary spiral. In August 1998, official estimates already put inflation at more than 70 percent, even though the central bank had taken protective action to quash inflation by raising interest rates.[19] Its intervention actually deepened the recession since higher interest rates forced cash-strapped companies into bankruptcy, causing yet more unemployment.

- In September 1998, Indonesia's economy was still on a downward slide, with no end in sight. Out-of-control inflation, food shortages, and mounting protests were threatening reforms, and putting Habibie's tenure in doubt.[20] The country's deepening crisis was also affecting the economic outlook as far away as Brazil and the United States, causing fears of a global recession.

Poverty and Informality in a Divided Society

Until 1997, Indonesia could pride itself on being one of the few developing countries where the percentage of the population living below the poverty line and the number of absolutely poor had declined, especially in rural areas.[21] The introduction of pest-resistant rice seeds raised paddy yields and improved nutrition, and massive investment in rural infrastructure and primary education also played a part in lowering rural poverty. The newly found prosperity was most evident in big cities, where the booming economy had created a young, nouveau riche urban middle class. There was also a super-rich minority of ethnic Chinese—they make up less than 5 percent of the population, but control much of industry and commerce—and the President's kin and friends.

Indonesia's growing urban prosperity and economic ascendancy long obscured the fact that, even before its economy collapsed, this was still essentially a poor country with deep pockets of rural and urban poverty, virtually untouched by years of growth. Even at its peak, in 1994 and 1995, the economy could not absorb the more than two million people who join the labor force each year, and 15 percent of the population were living in absolute poverty. After more than a decade of strong growth, in 1995, average *daily* income was still less than three dollars, and Indonesia's GDP was about equal to the combined revenues of two US corporations—Wal Mart and Exxon.[22]

Poverty is deeply ingrained in cities. A few miles away from the modern downtown, much of Jakarta is still a tangle of crowded slums and squatter settlements, where ramshackle dwellings are crammed along fetid, refuse-strewn streams, and amidst pools of filth and mountains of garbage. Living conditions there are almost as bad as what Richard Nixon described in 1953. People have no basic services or infrastructure, and no safe drinking water or sewers. There is also extensive poverty in the more remote islands, particularly in the areas of transmigration resettlement. But even the comparatively prosperous economic heartland—Java, Sumatra, and Bali—still has large pockets of poverty.

The unprecedented economic collapse of 1997 and 1998 was much more severe than what Latin America experienced during the lost decade, and is undermining the country's social fiber. It has exacerbated poverty and hardship across the entire country to an unprecedented degree. Inflation was also fueled by the fact that unscrupulous merchants had been selling existing stocks of goods, which had been imported before the devaluation, at post-devaluation prices. This triggered the food riots and looting, and violence against ethnic Chinese. In Jakarta hundreds died when rioters set fire to shopping malls. Trapped inside, looters were burned alive.

The economic heartland in Java suffered proportionally more. In Jakarta entire city blocks were destroyed. There, and in other cities, idle factories, empty office buildings, and the rusting shells of partly completed building sites and abandoned public works became testimonies to the reckless, unsustainable expansion of the past. Hundreds of thousands of seasonal workers, including many from Bangladesh and Pakistan, lost their jobs in the building industry.

In early 1998, at the height of the crisis, the situation was so confused that there was no clear trend of how people were reacting to mounting unemployment and hardship. With nowhere to turn, foreign migrant workers were trying to avoid returning home. Among Indonesians, jobless workers were flocking to Jakarta in large numbers from other cities, in the hope of finding work. Others returned to their native villages, fleeing urban joblessness and hardship.[23] Their return in large numbers caused extreme stress in villages, straining the limited infrastructure, and burdening relatives whom they had supported for years with remittances.[24] The lack of money, despair, and forced idleness also provoked rising crime and domestic violence in normally tranquil villages.[25]

A further complication is that it will be impossible in the short run to offset some of the job losses by expanding exports. The companies that were still in business could not afford to make new investments, let alone import spare parts from abroad, to maintain or expand production. Thus, spiraling unemployment and rising poverty may be likely to continue.

A Flight to Informality and Microfinance

Most newly jobless—especially those who returned to their native villages—will somehow have to try joining the more than twenty million people who were already living in poverty and working in the informal sector before the crisis broke out. But, with as many as 60 million *more* people living in poverty, without jobs, it is difficult even to begin imagining how they will fare. For most new entrants in the informal sector the transition from wage work to self-employment in an alien environment will be difficult, if not traumatic.

Even before 1998 the number of microenterprises already represented one third of all businesses, mostly in trade and services. In provincial towns "public" transport consists mainly of bicycle rickshaws. In Jakarta there are tens of thousands of smoke-belching three-wheeled scooter taxis, and "motorcycle taxis" are a convenient, if somewhat dangerous, form of fast transit. There are also countless sidewalk food stalls and eateries (*warungs*) all over Jakarta, even in the modern downtown. During the building boom many *warungs* did good trade, catering for construction workers at the city's ever growing number of building sites.

Outside Jakarta, in tourist centers on Java and Bali, the informal sector was fertile ground for "guides," and for peddlers who plied their trade close to tourist sites and on beaches, selling trinkets and souvenirs. There is—or, at least, was—also a flourishing informal handicraft industry with a myriad of small workshops, where men make wood carvings, and women weave cloth in traditional patterns on hand looms, and make tie-dye saris and artificial flowers. In more remote areas, away from tourist sites, informal work falls into the more conventional pattern of farm labor, sharecropping, off-farm activities such as food processing, market vending, and small mechanical and repair workshops.

One possibility, of which there are few precedents elsewhere, is that Indonesia's economic downturn will be so prolonged that the informal sector will reach total saturation from new entrants, at a time there is a drop in the demand for the goods and services of informal businesses. This was already happening in 1997 in Jakarta, where the collapse of the real estate market and idle building sites had taken away most of the customers of fast-food stands. Also, people who no longer have jobs may prefer to walk, rather than spending money on pedicabs and motorcycle cabs, and a drop in tourism at a time of political and social unrest will inevitably cause less work and income for workers in the handicraft industry.

When they need financing for working capital or investment, Indonesian microentrepreneurs usually have access to a wide variety of sources of credit. Altogether, there are more than fifty active microcredit programs in Indonesia. Unlike in other countries, they include several banks. The reason for this is that the banking law obliges all commercial banks to set aside one-fifth of their lending for small businesses (meaning maximum loans of $100,000). Although few banks make loans of less than $50,000 and mostly avoid lending to small farmers and informal businesses, some of the smaller regional banks do support small businesses.

As already mentioned, BRI, one of the country's largest state-owned banks, has made small-scale lending in rural and peri-urban areas one of its leading activities and principal source of earnings. Another unique trait of Indonesian microfinance is that the informal sector has traditionally been a major source of household savings—at BRI rural savings on deposit in the village banking units have long been the bank's largest source of savings deposits, much of which was used by BRI's commercial-bank branches in corporate loans that had a much higher default rate than rural microfinance.

This pre-crisis situation will inevitably change, and the supply of credit to all sectors of the economy has already severely diminished after scores of insolvent banks were forced to close down. Even BRI has not been immune to delinquencies and solvency problems in its commercial-banking activities. Unchecked, those problems could threaten its village units. The remainder of this chapter is dedicated to reviewing the evolution and activities of BRI and of other micro-financing programs that try to emulate its activities. It also attempts to evaluate the fallout of the crisis of 1998 on BRI.

Bank Rakyat: The People's Bank

Rakyat means "people." In the universe of microfinance this is the only state-owned *commercial* bank that lends to microentrepreneurs, and its microfinance program is one the largest. Established in 1895, BRI is one of Indonesia's oldest banks. It was nationalized in the early 1950s, becoming the country's fourth-largest state-owned bank. In January 1998, at the height of the financial crisis, the government liquidated sixteen insolvent banks, and restructured and consolidated the state banking sector into three banks, one of them being BRI. Before this consolidation took place, BRI had more employees (43,000) than any other bank, and was the only one with a nationwide branch network serving all the inhabited islands, and remote rural communities.

What makes BRI unique is that it combines conventional retail branch banking, corporate finance, and international banking, with microfinance. The latter has grown into one of its core businesses—four out of every ten of its employees work in microfinance—as well as its main source of profits and deposits.

From Directed Credit to Microcredit: BRI's Metamorphosis

After BRI was nationalized, its banking activities were deeply influenced by the government's decision to use oil revenues to boost economic growth with directed subsidized credit. During the 1970s the bank became a conduit for subsidized farm loans, and it opened a nationwide network of village banks that operated alongside its urban commercial branch offices.

BRI's first government-funded farm-credit program was BIMAS, an agricultural diversification program with a subsidized credit component. Working through the village banks—the *unit desa*—this program offered loans in cash and kind, at subsidized interest rates, to rice farmers. Low-cost credit for in-tensive paddy farming was designed to increase crop yields, achieve self-sufficiency, and phase out imports of rice. BIMAS was a success. It brought the Green Revolution to Indonesia. Long a major importer of rice, the coun-try became a net exporter in the early 1980s. But success was temporary. Paddy production could not keep up with population growth, and in the mid-1990s Indonesia began importing rice again. Moreover, as tends to be the case with subsidized agricultural credit programs all over the world, BIMAS was a financial disaster. It suffered from bad loan repayments and was discontinued in 1985.

Alongside BIMAS, BRI also managed two other subsidized special credit programs—*kredit midi* for medium-sized businesses, and *kredit mini* for small enterprises. The three programs were funded in their entirety out of oil rev-enues that were channeled to BRI through Bank Indonesia, the central bank. The central bank assumed the credit risk on the loans and used BRI's unit branches as passive credit windows.

After 1983, when falling oil revenues forced the government to refocus its economic policies and phase out most subsidized credit, central-bank funding was cut. BRI was faced with a dilemma. It could close down its more than 3,000 village banks, which could not survive without government support. But this would have caused huge losses and made several thousand employees redundant, which was socially and financially unacceptable. The alternative was to salvage the village units by commercializing their activities. BRI opted for the latter. Drawing on its experience with *kredit mini* and *midi*, it turned the unit banks into self-sustaining operations, adapting their financial services to the needs of rural and peri-urban small businesses and microentrepreneurs.

The change of course was greatly facilitated by the technical help of a team of financial experts from the Harvard Institute for International Devel-opment (HIID) who had been assisting the central bank on banking reform, as part of the country's first World Bank structural-adjustment program. As it happened, phasing out subsidized directed credit and commercializing BRI's unit branches were among the conditions of the World Bank's loan. To ensure a quick and seamless transition from subsidized credit to lending-for-profit, BRI's management worked with the HIID team to make the necessary man-agement and organizational changes. These included:

- eliminating subsidies, and setting lending rates at a level that covered all operating costs plus a profit margin
- giving the same importance to savings mobilization as to lending, and introducing new savings products
- standardizing and simplifying loan documents and credit-approval procedures
- upgrading administration and accounting with standardized daily fi-nancial reporting by the village units, and computerizing local

accounting (by mid-1996, all units had computerized bookkeeping)

- tightening internal supervision and auditing, and focusing on problem-solving, rather than a compliance and enforcement

- relocating the units from the former BIMAS paddy-growing areas to local business centers and areas of proven business potential, and making them more client-oriented

- introducing a profit-sharing system for staff, and incentives for timely repayments by borrowers

Kredit Unum Pedesaan: Modular Management with an Emphasis on Training

The rural credit program of the reincarnated unit banks became known as Kredit Unum Pedesaan or KUPEDES (meaning "general rural credit"). It was launched in 1984, with the support of the central bank, which allocated the remaining funds from *kredit mini* and *midi* as a long-term loan to BRI to set up KUPEDES.[26] There was also financial support from the World Bank.

KUPEDES is delivered through a nationwide network of 3,500 village unit banks, most of which are carry-overs from BIMAS days. There also are 420 village service posts, and 350 mobile units. In 1995 they had a total staff of more than 17,000. The units are also clearinghouses for little rural credit cooperatives and village banks that are not part of BRI's network. Like Grameen, BRI has perfected its management structure. The keys of the success of KUPEDES are its simplicity (it is the village units' only loan product), modular management, ample delegation of authority to local units, and emphasis on training.

- Each village unit has a minimum of four staff, and a maximum of eleven. The minimum staff consists of a unit manager, a credit officer (*kreditman*), a bookkeeper (*deskman*) and a teller. If business volume requires expanding staff beyond eleven, a new unit is established in the same area. A *kreditman* can handle up to four hundred active clients, each of whom must be visited and supervised at least twice a year. Village service posts have a skeleton staff of two, a bookkeeper, and a teller, who report to the nearest unit.

- Unit managers can approve loans up to $2,000 and are responsible for their unit's performance. Credit officers process loan requests, are the primary point of contact with clients, do promotional work, and are responsible for the collection of payment arrears.

- Each unit reports to a Unit Business Manager (UBM) in one of the bank's 326 retail branch offices. Each UBM is responsible for four units, spending an average of four days a week on supervision and one day a week marketing and promoting loan products in his or her area. UBMs report to the *unit desa* officer in their branch. These are senior staff who must approve loans that exceed a unit manager's authority and are responsible for business development.[27]

• To ensure efficiency and quality in credit delivery, and facilitate career development, BRI has continuous staff training with regular refresher courses and management training. There are five regional staff-training centers, and one central training facility in Jakarta for senior staff. All training courses are residential. The instructors are all former *unit desa* managers. Each training center is a modern integrated campus, with a resident faculty, several class rooms and dormitories, canteens, sports facilities, and a residential enclave for faculty members and visitors. Staff induction courses last one month; career development courses range from five to seven weeks, depending on seniority. In addition, all staff must have a one-week refresher course every eighteen months.

Lending Terms

KUPEDES is the units' only loan product. All loans are to individuals—there is no group lending. Conditions are flexible, with maturities and loan sizes that are adapted to borrowers' needs and repayment capability. By the end of 1995, cumulative loan disbursements surpassed $7 billion, in 16.5 million loans, and annual loan disbursements had reached $1.3 billion to about 2.3 million clients, or about the same as Grameen's total membership in early 1998. From 1990 to 1997, the number of borrowers more than doubled, and the amount loaned more than trebled.

Unlike the Grameen Bank, which targets poor landless women, and Bolivia's Bancosol, which lends exclusively to urban microentrepreneurs, BRI's units do not target specific clients, sectors, or products. They finance working capital and investment for on- and off-farm activities, trade, and services, and non-farm workshops in peri-urban areas. (About 20 percent of the units are located in small towns and lend to urban clients.)

The units only lend to creditworthy customers. What this means is that, to qualify for a loan, new clients must already be established in business and offer two guarantees, respectively a life insurance policy that covers the principal and interest outstanding of the loan, and enforceable collateral. The life insurance premiums are factored into the lending rate. Collateral is in the form of assignment of title to the borrower's property or equipment, such as a motorcycle or machine. No loan can exceed two-thirds of the value of the collateral. This collateral requirement makes BRI unique among microfinance institutions, none of which demand collateral for their basic loans. The units also offer personal loans to salaried employees and the military. All personal loans are guaranteed by assignment of payroll deductions.

Working-capital loans can be for up to two years, investment loans for up to three years. Surprisingly, given BRI's policy of continual staff training, KUPEDES is a strictly minimalist program: the units offer no training or technical support whatsoever to their clients. Much of the lending goes to small entrepreneurs whose income puts them above the poverty level. In 1995 only 25 percent of the units' borrowers were women. By type of activity, about half of lending was for services and small shops. Agricultural loans represented 20 percent of the total. Most working-capital loans were for house construction and repairs.

In pre-devaluation US dollars, in 1996 loans ranged from as little as $100 to $11,000. Two-thirds of all loans were for less than $600, and only 3 percent of loans exceeded $2,000. All loans are at a flat, monthly interest rate, calculated on the original loan amount, not on balances outstanding. In 1996 the monthly rates ranged from 2 percent per month (or an effective rate of more than 42 percent per annum) for small loans, to 1.6 percent per month for larger amounts. Loan repayments are in monthly fixed installments, regardless of amount and maturity.

There are no other costs or fees. The monthly rate also includes a late-payment penalty of 0.5 percent which is reimbursed every six months to clients who have no arrears during the previous half year, and reduces the cost of small loans to 32 percent. That rate is sufficient to cover the units' operating costs, overheads, loan losses, and a profit margin.

A Blend of Large and Small Clients

My study tour of *unit desa* in August 1996 was arranged by BRI's International Visitor Program (see below). By coincidence, like in Bangladesh in November 1995, I arrived in Jakarta at a time of political unrest, during which several buildings were set on fire, and several people were killed in violent demonstrations—harbingers of 1998. My briefing on my first day at BRI's headquarters was cut short, when a bomb scare forced people to evacuate the building and, as in Dhaka the year before, I was immediately ushered off to the field. There I was accompanied by a representative of the visitor program and by staff of regional offices.

We went to western Sumatra and central Java, where we visited several BRI retail branches, and about a dozen *unit desa*. The managers of each unit took us to visit their clients. What struck me most during these field trips was the stark contrast between the modest premises of the village units and the twin steel-and-glass skyscrapers of BRI's Jakarta head office. (Some regional offices also have striking architecture that makes a statement about BRI's prestige.) Like Grameen, BRI clearly understands that, when dealing with small farmers and microentrepreneurs, keeping a low profile has its advantages. It creates an atmosphere in which clients feel at ease, and makes contacts between clients and the bank's staff more easygoing. Nonetheless, the *unit desa* are more formal than Grameen. Most unit managers and staff usually wear ties, and the women have smart pink uniforms. Office technology is also more advanced than in Bangladesh. All the units have electricity, telephones, faxes, and computers.

My hosts also took me to dozens of clients whose businesses were more reminiscent of some of the microenterprises I had seen in Guinea, Bolivia, and Peru. This shows that, at least some of the time, the *unit desa* work with clients whose income is at or below the poverty level. Most of these smaller businesses belonged to craftsmen. We also visited several small stores. What follows is a sample of these visits.

• *Retreading old tires.* Near Padang, Sumatra, a small workshop makes retreads from old truck tires. Even though Indonesia is a major producer of rubber, new tires are very expensive. Retreads, which are much cheaper, are in great demand despite the risk that the inner canvass and steel structures of the tires are weakened by age—many road accidents are the result of blowouts of retreads. This particular workshop is at the back room of a small house.

Making retreads is hard work. First, what is left of the previous tread must be scraped off with sharp files. Then a thick layer of new rubber is glued on the old tire carcass. This done, the new tread is heat-sealed and molded onto the tire under great pressure, at high temperatures, in what looks—and hisses—like a gigantic waffle iron.

The men who were doing this back-breaking work told me that they could make eight "new" tires a day by working a twelve-hour shift. They sell their retread tires to garages and trucking companies. It is good business because the demand for good retreads is virtually limitless. The men had been BRI clients for over three years and had a loan of $650, which was guaranteed by assigning title to the "waffle iron."

• *Making pulpits for mosques.* One mile up the road from the retread workshop is the workplace of a master woodcarver. He and three apprentices have specialized in carving verses of the Koran in elaborate calligraphy on curved teak panels. Their only tools are sharp chisels and hammers. Once finished, the panels are dove-tailed into a seamless assembly to make an elegant pulpit. The carver, a gentle hunchback who spoke fluent English—a rarity in Indonesia—said that his work was in great demand and that he had three more pulpits on order, which would keep him business for at least two more years. He had learned his trade from his father, and hoped that his three young apprentices would carry on the tradition. The master carver had been a BRI client since 1990, and had a working-capital loan of $1,700, guaranteed with a mortgage on his workshop.

• *Stuffing* kapok *into mattresses.* In another neighborhood in Padang we visited a microenterprise that makes inexpensive *kapok* mattresses and pillows. (*Kapok* is white vegetal fiber—it is made from bleached tree bark—that closely resembles cotton.) Squatting on a concrete floor under a porch, young women spend their working days sifting through huge mounds of *kapok*, fluffing the fiber, and stuffing pillows and cotton mattresses by hand. They usually work in a thick cloud of kapok dust, but have no masks. The owner had a loan of $400. He imports the fiber from Java, and sells his products in the local market.

• *Using water buffaloes to make bricks.* Of the hundreds of microenterprises I saw while doing research for this book, one of the most memorable experiences was my visit to a small brick factory near Bukkittingi, in West Sumatra. Artisan brick factories and kilns are customary landmarks all over the third world, especially in the clay-rich alluvial plains of South and East Asia. This one is in the hills, tucked away behind rice paddies. It is a small family-run business, where people and beasts work harder than anyone could imagine. The "staff" consists of eight water buffaloes, two men, and one woman. They all work equally hard, except that the buffaloes work in shifts of two, and have four times as much rest as the three people.

Making clay bricks is messy, back-breaking work. Day after day, a team of one man and two buffaloes spends long hours mixing clay in a huge, deep pit, thirty by thirty feet, under a thatched roof. The roof keeps rainwater out of the pit, but makes heat in the pit suffocating. The clay is mixed with a wooden plow which the buffaloes drag. Slipping and sliding, knee-deep in the clay, the man must coax and hit the exhausted beasts to make them go around the pit. When I was there, the animals came close to sinking into the gooey mass and dragging the man down with them.

The man's wife, an emaciated woman, works by the side of the pit. Scooping big dollops of clay from the edge of the pit, she molds bricks, using two short planks and pat-a-cake movements. She stacks the new wet bricks four-high, on boards on a wheel barrow. As soon as she has made three dozen bricks, she wheels the heavily laden barrow uphill over a narrow gangplank, into an open-sided shed. There she unloads the wheelbarrow, and stacks the bricks in tight rows so that they can dry before they are fire-baked. Hers is Herculean work, almost like building a pyramid single-handed, *and* making the bricks for it. (Back in Washington, I weighed bricks on my bathroom scales. Two standard dry red bricks weigh about eleven pounds. This means that three dozen *wet bricks*—the woman's average load per barrow-full—weigh well over two hundred pounds. To this, one must add the weight of the barrow, and pushing that heavy load uphill dozens of times a day.) The woman who was doing all this work was still young and had a baby. Yet, she was toothless, haggard, and prematurely gray. If nothing else she bore witness to the fact that working conditions in the informal sector can be harsh.

On a normal day, the owner of the factory takes turns with his workman at mixing the clay, firing the kilns, and feeding the buffaloes. His wife looks after the woman's baby and prepares meals for the crew. This business was a long-standing BRI client, with a working-capital loan of about $700, guaranteed by a mortgage on the factory's land.

• *Making scales in Yogyakarta.* The ancient city of Yogyakarta in central Java is the most active center of traditional Javanese arts, as well as Indonesia's second most important tourist center, after Bali. The city has countless monuments, and several museums, universities and academies. Borobudur, one of East Asia's largest and most splendid Buddhist monuments, is only a few miles from the city center.

Not far from these monuments is a small smithy. It too is a relic from another age. Working in sweltering heat and semi-darkness under a thick bamboo thatch, four blacksmiths forge iron rods into sturdy scales for local market vendors. Any day of the week the smithy is a scene from Dante's *Inferno*. The eldest man stokes two furnaces with huge leather bellows. Stacked with iron rods, the furnaces spew sparks into the blackened thatch. Working in stifling heat and humidity, in front of the furnaces, impervious to the risk of fire, the other three blacksmiths rhythmically pound the white-hot iron rods into shape with huge sledgehammers, never missing a turn, or pausing for breath.

The blacksmith's house, barely a shack, has no electricity, running water, or lavatory. It is always filled with acrid smoke and soot from the furnace. There are no modern comforts, not even a proper bed for the blacksmith, his young wife, and their newborn baby. The smithy has been operating since 1994. The owner said that, by working thirteen hours a day, six days a week, he and his crew could make about eighty scales a month. He had a $900 loan from BRI. Fortunately there is good demand for his scales, which he sells for about $15 to market vendors in Yogyakarta. This leaves him a gross profit margin of 30 percent, or about $360 a month, after buying the rods, coke, and the cast-iron casings and tin pans for the scales. Out of this he pays his workers and makes monthly loan repayments of $55. He was working hard to save enough money to build a new roof over his smithy and buy a bed and a transistor radio.

The Top Tier of BRI's Clients

The clients we visited ranged from typical microenterprises to fairly large businesses with several employees. These visits and conversations with unit managers confirmed that much of the units' lending is for businesses in the upper tier of "small." While this improves recovery rates, reduces overhead costs, and raises profit margins—processing large loans is less costly than small ones—it does little to reduce poverty. Four of the businesses I visited were in this category:

- One was a furniture factory in Yogyakarta, which I already described in Chapter 2. It has a staff of thirty in three workshops, and uses two small trucks to ferry materials and furniture between the three sites. The owner supervises her workers and keeps the accounts.

- The second was a silk weaver, also in Yogyakarta, who produces richly embroidered ceremonial wedding gowns and dresses. The weaver's exclusive, hand-woven designs are in great demand for weddings and special occasions, and cost several hundred dollars. Most gowns are shipped to wealthy clients in Jakarta, Singapore, and Kuala Lumpur. These two businesses had been BRI clients for several years and had loans of approximately $5,000.

- The third "large" business was a state-of-the-art fish farm, on a lake in the highlands of western Sumatra. The fish are bred in large tanks that are partially immersed in the lake. The farm breeds five different fish species in ten different tanks. Hatchlings are kept in separate tanks. The farm's three workers clean the tanks, feed the fish, and monitor the growth of the hatchlings. The grown fish are sold in local markets and supply the owner's modern lake-shore restaurant. This client had a loan of 20 million rupiahs—about $8,300 at that time— which put him in the upper range of KUPEDES. Surprisingly, this business, which clearly did not "need" BRI, was a client of a small, recently opened unit. It also had a much bigger loan from a commercial bank.

- In central Java we visited a producer of nut chips—a blend between walnuts and potato chips—who employs sixty young girls, fifty of whom work on contract at home. Theirs is tiring, monotonous work. Working in teams of three, they must par-boil dozens of pounds of nuts in a huge cauldron, then smash the nuts, one at a time with a flat stone. Working ten hours a day, each team could produce about one hundred kilograms (220 pounds) of chips. For this they earn the equivalent of $5 a day, *per team*. The production process struck me as somewhat unhygienic. All the work was done on a dusty floor, where the workers were squatting in the dust, amidst mounds of nuts and stacks of chips. The owner of this business had been a BRI client for several years, and had a loan of about $5,000.

Tapping Rural Savings

One of BRI's greatest successes is that its unit banks have been able to tap Indonesia's huge pool of rural savings. They do so by offering safe savings products, at attractive interest rates. At the end of 1995, the *unit desa* had $2.6 billion in fifteen million savings accounts. Individual savings accounts outnumbered loan accounts by a ratio of more than 6:1, and the amount of deposits was three times that of KUPEDES loans outstanding. Total deposits more than tripled between 1990 and 1995, and the number of accounts doubled during the same period. While the majority of savings accounts belong to KUPEDES clients, farmer cooperatives, banks, schools, municipalities, and some larger businesses also deposit their funds at the unit banks. One of the reasons BRI is so successful in capturing local savings is that, in most small villages, its unit banks are the *only* bank. This gives them a virtual monopoly. BRI's units offer two basic savings products:

- SIMPEDES—it means "general rural savings"—was introduced in 1984, at the same time as KUPEDES. In 1995, it accounted for roughly two-thirds of the units' total savings mobilization. At that time there were close to nine million SIMPEDES accounts, with average balances of $185. BRI is also making a conscious effort to broaden the base of its rural depositors by including larger businesses and government agencies. Depositors can make unlimited withdrawals without penalty. These deposits have slightly lower interest rates than for urban deposit accounts.

- SIMASKOT, the other type of savings account, was introduced in 1989 to attract deposits from the clients of urban unit banks and BRI branch offices. Although the clients of rural units can open such accounts, few do so, even though interest rates are higher than on SIMPEDES. The rather unusual explanation for this is that urban customers are more discerning than rural ones and expect higher yields. At the end of 1995, SIMASKOT represented less than 14 percent of all savings deposits.

BRI and the village units also offer time deposits in the form of certificates of deposit, with varying maturities and rates of interest. Time deposits represent 10 percent of all deposits. Like all banks in Indonesia, BRI must also accept deposits from participants in the national savings program which targets small deposits, including deposits from children and students. It represents about one-third of BRI's total deposit base, but is little favored by rural clients. Finally, there are a small number of Giro deposits, which emulate the Dutch model of post-office savings deposits.

One of BRI's innovations, which partly explains why it attracts more savings than any other bank in the country, is that branch offices and unit banks combine deposit interest rates on both types of savings accounts with regular lotteries for their account holders. All clients who have a minimum balance of $4 in their account are automatically included in lotteries. These are held every six months at BRI's commercial branch offices.

The value of the prizes at lotteries is a function of the importance of the units or branch offices that organize them. In BRI's Bukkittingi branch, in West Sumatra, the first prize for the August 1996 lottery was a Toyota minivan. By contrast, in Padang, where the unit's presence is less important, the first prizes were more modest motorcycles. As for the smaller units, the main prizes are mopeds and TV sets. The lottery drawings at major branches are always festive occasions that generate much free publicity. The prizes are exhibited for several days on a stand, behind a podium. On the day of the drawing the local police chief, military officers, and other dignitaries are guests of honor. Before the drawings there are speeches, music, and popular signing. All prize winners are cheered by the crowd.

At the end of 1995, the units' total deposits were almost three times as large as their loans outstanding. Some units commonly have ten times as many depositors as borrowers, and virtually all units have surplus funds. Those funds are transferred to the BRI branch office in each unit's district. Branch offices can either use the funds for their own lending, allocate them to another unit or branch office, or transfer the excess funds to regional offices, for use in the national network. Interestingly, despite its huge surplus of rural savings, BRI is not self-sufficient and is still dependent on external funding sources. These include $700 million in bilateral and multilateral credit, including a $102 million loan from the World Bank. Bank Indonesia also chips in, with a credit line of 3,000 billion rupiahs ($1.3 billion).

The transfer of excess funds is a major source of earnings for unit banks, given that the internal transfer price which is paid on surplus funds is much higher than the units' average cost of funds.

Evaluating the Unit Desa

BRI's *unit desa* network can boast major achievements that yield several lessons for other microfinance institutions:

- Until the crisis of 1997–98, this was one of the few self-sustaining microfinance programs. By the end of 1995, 96 percent of the units were making profits, and contributed more than 40 percent of BRI's total revenue.

- Rural lending no longer depends on external subsidies. The units charge interest rates that are sufficient to cover all operating costs, interest expenses, and a profit margin: the system of village banking as a whole is fully self-sufficient, which is exceptional in the universe of microfinance.

- Loan arrears are comparatively low and compare favorably with those of other microcredit programs. They averaged 3.5 percent in 1995, down from more than 9 percent in 1992. This compared with 13 percent arrears among BRI's non-KUPEDES clients. BRI's policy on arrears and on the recovery of delinquencies is strict.

- Rural outreach and coverage are enormous. There are BRI units, village posts or mobile units in all inhabited parts of the Indonesian archipelago. By 1992, the village units had made loans to 5 percent of all Indonesia's households, and were accepting deposits from one in every six households.[28]

Socioeconomic Impact

The bank's internal research shows that small enterprises with KUPEDES loans tend to grow faster than the economy as a whole, both in terms of business output, and enterprise income; household income of borrowers can double during a three-year credit cycle. The units' loans also promote job creation: BRI claims that small businesses that borrow from the units are able to increase their staffing by two-thirds of pre-enrollment levels. Some of the larger clients own businesses that have made the transition from micro to small.

Internal research also shows that the units' lending reduces poverty and that, after an average participation of three years, over two-thirds of formerly poor households usually graduate out of poverty.[29] Against this one must weigh the fact that the *unit desa*'s average loans are in amounts that are equal to 80 percent of per capita income (which is more than in virtually all other microcredit programs) and that fewer than 25 percent of their clients are women. Moreover, BRI states that the percentage of poor people among its borrowers is equal to the *national average* of poor, whereas most other large microfinance programs have a higher percentage of poor than the national average. In other words, in reality, the units do not aim to reduce poverty (although this may have to change, now that some 40 percent of the population are living below the poverty level). The World Bank's comment to the effect that KUPEDES shows that "It is possible to create a microlending program that serves the poor and is profitable and self-sustaining"[30] is, therefore, incorrect.

The socioeconomic impact of, and the jobs created by, KUPEDES are constrained by the fact that, unlike other microfinance institutions, BRI does not accept non-conventional guarantees. Instead, its units demand formal collateral, only lend up to two-thirds of the value of the collateral, and only lend to businesses that already exist. This policy is prudent and protects the quality of the loan portfolio, but it also makes it difficult to help launch new microenterprises, or develop the full potential of existing clients.

I found a clear example of this while visiting clients in Padang, one of whom was a talented, university-trained graphic artist. His workshop occupied the bedroom and main room of a small, ramshackle house, where the graphic artist, his wife, and two teenagers were designing and printing intricate silk screens, for posters, advertising material, and business cards for local companies—including for BRI's Padang office. Cans of solvent, ink, printing materials, trays of paint, and prints were stacked higgledy-piggledy in and on every available space and surface. The bed served as printing table, brushes were washed in the kitchen sink. In 1996, this small business, which had been operating since 1992, had just obtained a loan of $200. What astounded me was that this client's request for a slightly larger loan, which he could have used to expand his business and make working conditions somewhat more salubrious, was turned down because the loan collateral—title to a motorcycle he used to make deliveries to clients—could not justify a larger loan. In that and other cases BRI's lending practices severely curtail the bank's socioeconomic impact.

A second, oft-voiced criticism of the units' focus on savings mobilization is that they pull resources from rural areas to fund BRI's own loans to commerce and larger businesses in Jakarta and other cities. BRI is conscious of this fact, but argues that the units' surplus savings actually stay in the rural economy, where households and household enterprises generally are net savers, and slightly larger enterprises are net borrowers. What this implies is that, in BRI's mind rural savings *belong* in rural areas and it helps keep them there. Even if that were true, the argument misses the point altogether. What BRI *should say* instead is that its savings programs are offering a valuable long-overdue service to rural households that have no other access to savings facilities, and that it re-deploys surplus savings profitably.

Taking a broader view, BRI has followed the examples of Grameen and BancoSol, and is using its unit banking system to extend its international influence by training the staff of other microfinance programs. It does this through its International Visitor Program, which has been providing technical support to new programs and potential replicators since 1991. The program is operating as a special department at the head office in Jakarta, with funding from USAID. It hosts delegations from microfinance programs from around the world, which (used to) send people to Indonesia to learn from BRI's experience. Until the intense political turmoil and unrest of 1997 and 1998, BRI received about as many foreign visitors as Grameen. Like Grameen's international training program, BRI offers modular packages that range from one-day briefings to elaborate multi-week field trips and training programs. In the years since 1991 the Program has hosted delegations form Asia, Africa, Latin America, Europe, former Soviet Republics and the US. Judging by my own two-week visit to BRI, it is an example of efficiency and thoroughness, combined with exceptional hospitality.

BRI After the Financial Collapse of 1998

It is impossible to make a clear assessment of how BRI has been affected by the events of early 1998. At this point, in the late summer of 1998, one can only form some hypotheses about the effects of the credit crunch. A number of things could happen.

- Rising unemployment and the unprecedented flight to informality will increase the demand for microfinance, notwithstanding a diminishing supply of credit.

- At the same time, rising poverty, inflation, and generally lower earnings across the board are eroding the savings capacity of workers in the informal economy and of rural households. This will dry up the supply of loanable funds for BRI's village units and other microfinance programs.

- Given the severity of Indonesia's crisis, the informal sector will most likely see a sharp drop in the demand for its goods and services. This will cause rising loan defaults among the clients of BRI and other microfinance institutions. In the first stage, this will affect the weaker institutions, and cause solvency problems. But even BRI will be affected to a certain point.

- Small rural producers also will experience payment difficulties due to crop failures caused by the drought and forest fires of 1997. This too will increase arrears, and potentially reduce the demand for new credit.

- The quality of BRI's loan portfolio is also likely to be adversely affected by the effects of the devaluation of the rupiah and ensuing inflation on its clients' creditworthiness.

- On the other hand, subsistence farmers and small rural producers, some of whom are BRI clients, are less likely to be harmed by the crisis, and the consequences of inflation and the recession will take a longer time to unfold among in villages. One of the reasons for this is that farmers are food producers, not buyers, which shelters them from price hikes. They may even benefit from inflation by charging higher prices for the goods they sell in local markets.

- Turning to the liability side of BRI's balance sheet, the sharp depreciation of the rupiah, inflation, and lower incomes and savings will most likely increase the demand for cash, cause large withdrawals from savings accounts, and diminish the inflow of new savings. The partial dollarization of Indonesia's high- inflation economy will also dry up the supply of rupiah savings, which may cause liquidity problems for BRI.

- On the other hand, BRI has a reputation of quality, and could benefit from a "flight to quality" by clients of other banks who withdraw their funds from other institutions, placing place their savings in the newly restructured state-owned banks.

- Finally, as regards the intrinsic strength of BRI itself, structural weaknesses and solvency problems will only become apparent after a detailed evaluation of the quality of its non-unit commercial loan portfolio, and of how losses in its other banking activities could impinge on the units' ability to continue making rural credit. There already are indications that BRI has suffered major losses on delinquent commercial loans. But one element is clearly in BRI's favor. Unlike all the other commercial banks, it has minimal foreign-exchange exposure, so that the devaluation of the rupiah does not, in itself, constitute a threat to the bank.

Learning from BRI: The Village Credit Banks

The village credit banks—Badan Kredit Desa (BKD)—are scaled-down *unit desa*. There are 3,800 such village credit banks, all owned and operated by villages in remote rural areas in four provinces on Java. BRI's *unit desa* and branch offices are the clearing houses for the village banks in their districts.[31]

BKD was established in 1898, at about the same time as BRI. Its village banks are structured as cooperatives whose borrowers must also be shareholders and depositors. All the banks are small. The village banks, which are managed by the village elders, are open only one day a week, the day the weekly loan installments are due. The weekly meetings are normally held in the house of the village chief who is also normally the head of the credit committee. BKD's clients are much poorer and older than those of BRI's village units. Many are illiterate.

Lending is only for villagers. Most loans are for small-scale trading, and range in amounts from as little as $11 to a maximum of $450. All loans are repayable in weekly installments. Loan maturities range from one to nine months. There is a flat interest rate of 6 percent *per month*, which translates into more than 90 percent on an annual basis. To this one must add the compulsory savings of 10 percent of the loan amount. This explains why there are practically no loans at the upper end of its lending range. Borrowers who qualify for the upper range of loans can usually "graduate" to become BRI clients. Not surprisingly, the high cost of borrowing from BKD creates significant arrears which sometimes reach 20 percent of all loans.

In 1995, BKD had 1.6 million loans outstanding, for an amount of $113 million. All loans must be approved by the village chief. Clients must be of good character, have trading skills, and be able to use and repay a loan. Each BKD keeps a member register, listing the maximum amount any member can borrow.

The village banks also accept voluntary savings from their clients. Clients' voluntary and forced savings are deposited with the nearest BRI branch. The deposits are remunerated at the SIMPEDES interest rate, from which the banks deduct a service fee of 2 percent. BKD savers are automatically enrolled in BRI's lotteries for savers.

This is truly a shoestring operation. The "office" of one of the village banks I visited near Yogyakarta is a bamboo-covered porch, which it shares with the village kindergarten. Roosters were roaming between the tables, and the children in the kindergarten were peering through cracks in the bamboo screen to look at us. One of the village elders was the bank's treasurer. During our meeting he was accepting loan repayments from several, equally old and toothless men and women, sorting ruffled bank notes into neat little stacks.

At another village bank nearby, the postman and local police officer were members of the credit committee. They were assisted by a BRI *kreditman* who was the bank's de facto administrator-cum-supervisor. In fact, with its small scale of operations, minimal capital and lack of its own management, BKD owes its survival to the institutional support it receives from BRI and to the government's decision to keep it going.[32]

Yet, for all its limitations, and notwithstanding its near-usurious lending rate, this network of small village cooperatives plays a useful role in Java's rural economy. It provides access to credit to the most unbankable people, is an alternative to even more usurious moneylenders, and stimulates a modicum of commercial activity in marginal rural areas. It especially helps village women; two-thirds of clients are women, and, because there are no formal guarantees or collateral, BKD works with Java's poorest rural people.

Lessons from Indonesia

BRI's *unit desa* program contains a number of important lessons for other microcredit programs.

- Savings mobilization is the key for the sustainability of the units' lending. Their experience and track record show that rural savings can grow if small savers have access to safe, transparent and adequately remunerated savings instruments.

- Because rural savings have traditionally exceeded the units' lending volume, the units derive a large part of their profits from the internal transfer of excess liquidity to BRI's commercial-bank branches.

- Standardized management structures and procedures contribute to corporate governance and simple, well-focused credit programs and decentralized decision making work best for large networks of small banks. The *unit desa* largely owe their success to the fact that they offer only one loan product that can be tailored to clients' needs. Strong management and simple, modular structures are as important as regular supervision in ensuring good portfolio performance and low arrears.

- Incentive programs and staff training motivate good performance and staff loyalty—turnover among unit staff is minimal, and well below that of BRI's non-unit staff.

- When starting a new program, it is simpler to work with existing institutions. Moving from the defunct BIMAS rice-credit scheme to a new system of small loans on commercial terms would have been impossible if BRI had been forced to liquidate its existing network of rural offices and begun anew from scratch.

- Even a well-managed self-sustaining credit program with a good track record can be threatened by extreme economic instability and inflation.

- Looking beyond BRI, the collapse of Indonesia's economy in 1997–98 shows that there are limits to nepotism, corruption, and economic mismanagement. The irony is that this country, which managed to avoid excessive foreign borrowings in the 1970s, and remained unscathed during the debt crisis of the 1980s, repeated the mistakes of Latin America, amassing close to $140 billion in foreign public and private debt—but it did so twenty years later.[33]

- Public discontent has raised political awareness and unleashed grassroots protest against corruption in this normally politically apathetic country. Like Ferdinand Marcos in the Philippines, Suharto, one of the world's longest-reigning despots, was forced out of office by massive student demonstrations.

- The IMF also shares much of the blame for the collapse of Indonesia's economy, and for the potential contagion of East Asia's financial crisis into a possible global recession. Indeed, the IMF mishandled Indonesia's (and Thailand's) banking crisis by meting out the same remedies it had given Latin America fifteen years earlier. But, whereas deflation restored stability—albeit at enormous social cost—in Latin America in the 1980s, and dealt with fiscal crises, trade deficits, and rampant inflation, in Asia the IMF's intervention backfired, by imposing austerity on economies that were *already* in recession. This had a cumulative effect, accentuating the banks' solvency problems and job losses in industry.

- In early 1998, mass protests against food shortages and rising unemployment reached a crescendo, and the populace vented its ire on the World Bank's president. In February 1998 James Wolfensohn drew harsh criticism from community leaders during a visit to Jakarta. His critics chastised the World Bank for lending billions of dollars to the government, while turning a blind eye to corruption and the lack of political freedom. At the meeting, Wolfensohn had to admit that "We didn't get everything right in the past."[34]

Notes

1. *Lonely Planet, Indonesia* (Lonely Planet Publications, 1995), 31
2. Catherine Caufield, *Masters of Illusion* (New York: Henry Holt and Company), 1997, 119
3. *Indonesia, Strategy for a Sustained Reduction in Poverty* (Washington, D.C.: The World Bank, 1990), 74.
4. Cheryl Prayer, *The Debt Trap* (New York: Monthly Review Press, 1974), 71.
5. Prayer, *The Debt Trap,* 80.
6. Donald P. Hannah, *Indonesian Experience with Financial Sector Reform* (Washington, D.C.: The World Bank, 1994), 2 and 5.
7. Asia's tiger economies are (were) Korea, Malaysia, Hong Kong, Indonesia, Singapore, and Taiwan.
8. The clove monopoly owes its importance to the fact that Indonesian cigarettes (*kreteks*) are a blend of tobacco and clover.
9. George Aditjondiro, "Suharto and Sons," *The Washington Post,* January 25, 1998.
10. Aditjondiro, "Suharto and Sons."
11. Danny Leipziger and Vinod Thomas, *The Lessons from East Asia: An Overview of Country Experience* (Washington, D.C.: The World Bank, 1995), 12.
12. *World Bank Annual Report 1997,* 48.
13. Peter Montagnon, *Financial Times,* January 23, 1998
14. Geoff Spencer, *The New York Times,* November 2, 1997.
15. Spencer, *The New York Times.*
16. David E. Sanger and Seth Mydans, "Sudden Weakness Aside," *The New York Times,* January 18, 1998.
17. Peter Montagnon and Sander Thoenes, "Indonesia's Simmering Crisis," *Financial Times,* March 11, 1998.

18. Paul Blustein, Business Section, *The Washington Post,* July 11, 1998.
19. Sander Thoenes, "Indonesia in Big Interest Rate Increase," *Financial Times,* March 24, 1998, and Cindy Shriner, *The Washington Post,* September 10, 1998.
20. Cindy Shriner, "Economic Crisis Clouds Indonesia's reforms," *The Washington Post,* September 10, 1998.
21. *Indonesia, Strategy for a Sustained Reduction in Poverty* (Washington, D.C.: The World Bank, 1990), 1.
22. David E. Sanger, "The World Looks at Bali," *The New York Times,* January 18, 1998.
23. Keith Richburg, "Economic Crisis Spurs Unemployment," *The Washington Post,* March 6, 1998.
24. Paul Blustein, "Dreams Tumble with the Rupiah," *The Washington Post,* January 23, 1998.
25. Keith Richburg, "For Migrant Workers, Path from Boom to Bust Leads Home," *The Washington Post,* September 8, 1998.
26. Jacob Yaron, *Successful Rural Financial Institutions* (Washington, D.C.: The World Bank, 1992), 97.
27. Each UDO is responsible for nine to seventeen Units. If a Branch has fewer than nine Units, the UBM also performs the UDO function. If a branch has eighteen units, which is exceptional, there are two UDOs.
28. *OED Précis 104,* The World Bank.
29. *BRI Village Units,* promotional brochure of BRI's IVP program, 14.
30. *OED Précis 104.*
31. Bank Kredit Kecamatan (BKK) is another system of small village banks that bears many similarities with BKD. It too is located in central Java, and works exclusively in poor villages. Unlike the other programs that are reviewed in this chapter, it does not have a permanent staff. Instead, mobile units visit units once a week for loan collections and disbursements (see Jacob Yaron, *Successful Rural Financial Institutions* 92–93).
32. BRI supplements BKD's lack of capital with a long-term line of credit.
33. Sander Thoenes, "Indonesian Solution Prompts Doubts," *Financial Times,* February 12, 1998.
34. Keith B. Richburg, "The World Bank Under Fire," *The Washington Post,* February 5, 1998.

Part III

Informality and Microfinance in Latin America

When the debt crisis erupted in 1982, eleven of the seventeen most highly indebted countries were in Latin America. Their aggregate public external debt represented three-quarters of the debt of all the problem debtors and they had borrowed more heavily from commercial banks than the other debtor countries. In Argentina, Brazil, Chile, Mexico, Uruguay, and Venezuela commercial loans represented 75 percent or more of the external public debt. As was to be expected, the fallout of the crisis was much more severe than in other parts of the world, and the 1980s became Latin America's lost decade.

Of the three chapters that follow, Chapter 6 sketches the socioeconomic environment in Latin America in the early 1980s, and examines the after-effects of the debt crisis from the perspective of the region as a whole. It also gives an overview of microfinance in Latin America. Chapter 7 explains how Bolivia, the region's poorest and most isolated country, fared during the debt crisis. It goes on to review the activities of BancoSol and explains how new laws are creating opportunities to broaden the field of microfinance. Chapter 8 reviews the aftermath of 1982 in Peru. This country lagged behind Bolivia in undertaking stabilization and adjustment. In 1996 it had a brief spell of record-breaking growth. The chapter goes on to review recent developments in microfinance in Peru, including government initiatives in support of poverty lending and self-help groups. While Bolivia and Peru have relatively small economies, when compared with Latin America's giants—Argentina, Brazil, and Mexico—in both countries microfinance is more highly developed there than elsewhere in Latin America, and banking regulatory agencies are applying prudential supervision to microfinance.

6

Coping with the Lost Decade

Latin America stretches from thirty-two degrees north, at Tijuana in Mexico, to fifty-six degrees south, at Cape Horn in Chile. South America, which encompasses most of Latin America, is roughly twice as large as Australia. Brazil, its largest country, is bigger than Australia and has almost nine times as many inhabitants. Latin America is also the most urbanized part of the world. Close to two-thirds of its people live in cities. In the most extreme case, Argentina, almost 90 percent of the population is urban.

This region of great contrasts is geographically and ecologically one of the most diverse parts of the world. The Andean cordillera is the longest mountain range, and has the highest peaks outside the Himalayas. It follows the Pacific coast over a distance of 4,500 miles, from Panama to Cape Horn. The Amazon rain forest, which covers about half of Brazil's land area, and major parts of Bolivia, Colombia, Peru and Venezuela, is the largest remaining—but rapidly shrinking—tropical rain forest and ecosystem. With a course of 3,900 miles the Amazon is the second longest river after the Nile. Together with 11,000 tributaries, it has more than 20,000 miles of mostly navigable waterways. It is, by far, the largest watershed and the largest source of fresh water in the world. The biggest pristine wetland, the Pantanal, straddles central and western Brazil, and the northeastern part of Paraguay.

Latin America's ecosystems are also among the most-severely affected by the warming of surface waters in the Pacific—the phenomenon that is known as El Niño. In December 1997, after more than four months without rain, the water level had dropped by more than nine feet in parts of the Amazon basin and, in March 1998, forest fires raged out of control in the state of Rondonia, in northern Brazil. At the same time, torrential rains caused floods that ravaged the normally arid coastal plain in Peru, devastated crops in southern Brazil, and caused deadly landslides in the Andes, while abnormally warm ocean currents along Peru's coast decimated what remained of anchovy fisheries.

A Common Legacy in a Fragmented Region

Centuries of colonialism have created a veneer of continental homogeneity. All but Brazil, and three small countries to its north, were colonized by Spain, and Spanish is their national language. Several countries even revere the same "national" hero, Simon Bolivar, the Venezuelan general who routed the Spanish occupiers in the nineteenth century. Beneath this veneer there is immense social, ethnic, and cultural diversity, and social and political tensions are rife throughout the region.

Unlike many Asian countries most of which are culturally and ethnically homogeneous, in Latin America there is an ethnic division between the descendants of pre-Columbian Indians and people of European origin—the progeny of colonial invaders and more recent settlers. In Mexico, Central America, Ecuador, Peru, and Bolivia, Indians and *mestizos* (people of mixed European and American Indian ancestry) vastly outnumber the Caucasians. Chile, Paraguay, and Uruguay also have large Indian communities. Brazil has sizable Afro-American and Amerindian minorities and the largest concentration of ethnic Japanese outside Japan. Only Argentina is relatively homogenous. Except for a few Indian settlements on the border with Bolivia, Argentines are predominantly of Spanish, Italian, and German stock. Many Germans arrived after World War II when President Peron offered safe haven to Nazi war criminals. People of European descent dominate society everywhere, even in countries such as Bolivia, where they are a small minority. Without exceptions, class divisions reflect the ethnic divide and poverty is always most pronounced among indigenous "minorities." Indigenous cultures are rarely part of the mainstream, and in only a few countries are indigenous regional languages recognized as official languages.

Per capita incomes vary greatly across the region—in 1995 they ranged from $380 in Nicaragua, to $8,030 in Argentina—and income distribution is more skewed than in other parts of the world. In the most extreme case, Brazil, the top 10 percent of the population earns more than half the national income and seventy-three times more than those in the lowest decile. Given the high level of urbanization poverty is heavily concentrated in urban slums and shantytowns. Santiago's *poblaciones*, Mexico City's "misery belt," Rio's *favellas,* and Lima's *pueblos jovenes* (young communities) are home to tens of millions of people, many of whom live in abject poverty.

While the high level of urbanization makes rural poverty less dense than in other parts of the world, social conditions in the countryside are worse than in urban areas, especially in the Andean highlands and in Brazil's desolate northeast, where poverty is at a par with the worst of sub-Saharan Africa. Throughout Latin America the growing concentration of land ownership is matched by increasing landlessness—close to three-quarters of Latin America's rural population consists of landless peasant farmers, farm workers and sharecroppers.[1] Land tenure and access to land are burning issues that polarize rural communities. In the Andean highlands subsistence farmers live on marginal land and in Central America, land redistribution mandated by various peace accords is boycotted by landowners, and implementation is slow and patchy. In the northeast of Brazil disputes over land rights often become pitched battles between landless farmers and large landowners, and the conflict in Chiapas, in southern Mexico, is largely about land tenure in Indian communities.

Relations between countries are often tense, and border disputes occasionally escalate into armed conflicts. In 1969 a border dispute between El Salvador and Honduras became the infamous "football war." It was provoked by a contested goal during a qualifying soccer game for the 1970 World Cup. In 1995 an acrimonious quarrel between the presidents of Peru and Ecuador grew into an all-out armed conflict that flared up again briefly in July 1998.

Political, Criminal, and Domestic Violence

Latin America has a long, sad history of dictatorships, civil wars, and political violence. During the 1970s, tens of thousands of people "disappeared" or were summarily executed in Argentina and Chile, both ruled by brutal military dictators, and civil wars that lasted until the mid-1990s have left deep scars in El Salvador, Guatemala, and Nicaragua. The brutality of dictators and the military was matched by that of guerrilla movements, such as Uruguay's *Tupamaros,* Peru's Shining Path and *Túpac Amaru,* and Colombia's People's Revolutionary Army.

The political situation improved in the early 1990s. Dictators began giving way to democratically elected governments and peace was brokered in Central America, putting an end to conflicts that had disrupted economic activities, destroyed the infrastructure, and dislocated society. Guerrilla activity has also abated. But violence is so deeply ingrained that it is difficult to eradicate it. In post-conflict Central America the restoration of peace was followed by a surge in violent crime by demobilized soldiers and former freedom fighters. There, and in Brazil, Colombia, and parts of Mexico, delinquency and crime are fueled by extreme poverty and hopelessness. Armed robberies, murders, and kidnappings have reached critical levels, sometimes to the point of being threats to growth and investment. In Colombia and Mexico random assassinations and wars between rival drug cartels add to the tension.

Violence is not confined to the public domain. Depending on the country where they live, anywhere from 25 percent to more than 50 percent of Latin American women are victims of domestic violence. Moreover, women doing unpaid work in family businesses—that is, women working in their husbands' microenterprises—are more frequent victims of domestic violence than women who have jobs outside the family unit.[2] Domestic violence oppresses women, destroys their self-esteem, and diminishes their contributions to the economy and society. It also traumatizes their children.

The Lost Decade

The 1980s were one of the darkest and most turbulent periods in Latin America's history. Income and output fell for the first time since the end of World War II, and poverty climbed sharply.[3] As explained in Chapter 1, the roots of the lost decade lie in the massive foreign loans which the countries in the region had accumulated during the 1970s, and Mexico was the first country to crumble under the weight of its external debt.

By August 1982, when the Minister of Finance suspended all debt service to commercial creditors, Mexico owed the banks more than $58 billion, eighteen times more than in 1972.[4] In declaring a debt moratorium Mexico had acted out of necessity. Its debt-servicing capacity had already become stressed in 1981, and by 1982, the economy was in a dismal state when the price of oil—its main source of foreign earnings—was plunging. This, and sharply higher interest rates made it impossible to continue servicing an external debt that amounted to 31 percent of national income and was absorbing one-third of export earnings.[5] When President López Portillo left office at the end of 1982, after years of sustained growth national income was already declining, annual inflation was in triple digits, the value of the peso was plummeting, and capital flight had become a stampede.

In declaring a debt moratorium, the Finance Minister had acted on the assumption that, because the country owed the banks so much money, they would be conciliatory. As we know, the very opposite happened and the banks stopped lending, even to countries that were still able to service their debts. This bandwagon effect made solvency problems a self-fulfilling prophecy for all highly-indebted countries. By 1984 Argentina, Bolivia, Brazil, Chile, Colombia, Costa Rica, Ecuador, Peru, Uruguay, and Venezuela had all become problem debtors.[6]

Stabilization and Adjustment After 1982

The modalities and details of structural adjustment need not be repeated here (see Chapter 1). However, the severity of Latin America's debt problems, and the fact that the social consequences of adjustment were so profound, warrant another look at some aspects of the lost decade.

By 1982, when the debt crisis broke out, Latin America's problem-debtors-to-be all had large fiscal and current-account deficits and rising inflation. After Mexico's debt moratorium of August 1982, the IMF and United States hastily assembled the first multinational bailout and, following Mexico's lead, the region's ten other highly indebted countries gradually began undertaking macroeconomic stabilization and adjustment programs, and negotiated debt reschedulings with their commercial creditors to stretch out repayments.

The pace of adjustment and the political commitment to implement the necessary reforms differed among these countries. The process was most rapid in Chile under Pinochet's dictatorship, and reform also proceeded quickly in Mexico. On the other hand, after failing to agree with the IMF on the terms of its intervention, Argentina and Brazil attempted to deal with their economic problems with *heterodox* measures—that is, measures that differ from the "orthodoxy" of the free-market policies of IMF stabilization and World Bank structural adjustment. Reform and adjustment also lagged in Peru, where it only began in 1990.

Argentina's Austral plan of June 1985, and Brazil's Cruzado plan of the same year cast some light on how countries fared when they chose another path, and resorted to heterodox measures to deal with inflation and fiscal crises.

To curb inflation Argentina used a combination of wage, price, and exchange-rate freezes, introduced a new currency (the Austral), and the government promised not to print more money to finance budget deficits. The initial result was promising: the plan brought inflation down from an annual rate of close to 2,000 percent to about 2 percent per month. But respite was short-lived. In 1987, inflation was back with a vengeance, soaring to around 200 percent per year. But the plan had shown that it was possible to bring hyperinflation down—albeit briefly—to double digits without causing a major decline in economic activity, a rise in unemployment, or a reduction in the purchasing power of wages.[7]

For its part, Brazil's Cruzado plan aimed for zero inflation by abolishing the wage and price indexation that had fueled inflation. Like Argentina, it used price and wage freezes, and a new currency (the cruzado). But the central bank also decreed that all financial contracts be rewritten to take account of *future* inflation.[8] This rekindled the inflationary expectations that the plan had tried to quash. The expectations fed back into the economy and the program failed. By 1986 real wages were increasing and eroding corporate profit margins. There were shortages, black markets mushroomed, and there was generalized instability.[9] However, the balance of payments continued to deteriorate, and, like in Argentina, the gains were temporary.

The Social Debt of Adjustment

The multilateral agencies rushed to restore stability in debtor countries as fast as possible, but paid too little attention to the social consequences of their actions. Their reasoning was that rapid intervention would be politically acceptable, provided that no more pain was administered after the first, undeniably unpleasant, crunch.[10] In Mexico the crunch made national income fall by 4.7 percent *in real terms* in 1983,[11] real wages declined by almost 40 percent between 1981 and 1986, and job losses in the public and private sectors made unemployment rise by more than 60 percent.[12]

In 1988, when the social cost of adjustment was already evident, the *World Development Report* nevertheless stated that "lower incomes were necessary to compress demand and improve the external balance."[13] This is indeed what happened: in Latin America as a whole imports fell by one-third between 1980 and 1984.[14] The turnaround in foreign trade was especially dramatic in the two largest debtors, Brazil and Mexico. In barely two years, from 1981 to 1983, Brazil turned a $1 billion trade deficit into a $13 billion surplus, and Mexico moved from a $4.7 billion deficit to a surplus of $13 billion.[15] Sharply lower imports and the allocation of resources to debt service took their toll on investment. In Mexico gross fixed investment fell by 25.3 percent 1983,[16] and in Bolivia and Peru investment dropped by an average of respectively 17 and 12 percent *per year* between 1982 and 1988.[17]

Finally, cuts in public expenditure and the elimination of social programs made poverty rise everywhere. In 1983 the Mexican government cut the federal fiscal budget by half, official unemployment rose to around 15 percent, and 40 percent of the workforce was under-employed. There were comparable budget cuts in other countries. The social impact was such that, by 1985, 30 percent more Latin Americans were living in absolute poverty than in 1980, and between 1980 and 1990 the number of people living in poverty almost doubled, to 140 million, of whom 35 million were living in extreme poverty.[18] In the aftermath of the debt crisis, basic health and welfare indicators worsened throughout Latin America, making it one of the only parts of the world where maternal mortality during childbirth actually rose during the 1980s.[19] With fewer funds for public education the quality of education also deteriorated. This, in turn, worsened income prospects for those who had little or no education, and perpetuated the region's disparities in the distribution of income and wealth. Even the World Bank had to admit that "this decline (in income) placed a heavy burden on the poorest members of society, at a time when social spending was already being cut sharply."[20]

One aspect of stabilization and debt reschedulings about which very little was said at that time, is that some of the proceeds of structural-adjustment loans were actually round-tripping—the debtor countries were using some of the loans to clear up a part of their debt and interest arrears to the commercial banks. The result: by capitalizing unpaid arrears and borrowing large amounts from the World Bank and IMF, the external public debt outstanding of Latin America's largest debtors almost doubled in five years, from $125.5 billion in 1981 to $236.3 billion in 1986.[21]

Latin America in the 1990s

The severity of the recession of the 1980s makes it worthwhile to look at how the situation evolved during the 1990s, when the debt crisis was all but over. By the middle of the 1980s Argentina and Brazil had abandoned their attempts at heterodoxy. They had rejoined the orthodox fold, in the vanguard of financial liberalization, and had begun dismantling the corporate state in which various interest groups had been competing to extract rents from the state.[22] This altered the balance of power between the state and the private sector in both countries, and paved the way for large-scale privatizations. Both countries also introduced new currencies—the Argentine peso and the Brazilian real—whose value is tied to the US dollar. Argentina went on step further. It was among the first countries to introduce a currency board to stabilize its currency, and it adopted a constitutional amendment to maintain a fixed parity between the peso and the US dollar. In fact, the peso gained against the dollar and became overvalued, which hurt exports and employment. But pegging the exchange rates achieved dramatic reductions in inflation—in Brazil's case from more than 4,000 percent in 1994 to about 10 percent three years later.

Growth was also restored in most former problem debtors, sometimes with spectacular results. In 1994–95 Peru enjoyed a brief spurt of growth that even surpassed East Asia; since the beginning of the 1990s Chile's consistently high rates of investment and fast growth put it on a par with East Asia's tiger economies; and in Brazil, notwithstanding enormous income inequality and appalling rural and urban poverty that affects millions, price stability and an expanding employment base triggered a consumer boom in 1996–97. Last but not least, by the early 1990s investor confidence had been restored and private capital began flowing to the region in ever growing amounts, both as portfolio investment and in the form of foreign direct investment.

But progress has been uneven and inequitable: Latin America shares sub-Saharan Africa's unfortunate distinction of being one of only two parts of the world where poverty *increased* between 1987 and 1993.[23] Not only was there no trickle down during growth, but the gap between rich and poor, which had always been greater in Latin America than in anywhere else, became a chasm. The social debt of adjustment is still there, and is still awaiting *its* bailout. At a meeting in Barcelona, in March 1997, the Inter-American Development Bank reported that income disparities had not improved in the region and that unemployment had climbed to its highest levels since 1985.[24]

The widening income gap is causing an increasing polarization between a small minority of immensely wealthy people and an impoverished majority. Even in Chile, where the legacy of the free-market revolution of Pinochet's fifteen-year dictatorship are a dynamic modern economy, a buoyant stock market, and a modern financial system, inequality is brutal. In 1994 the lowest decile had a mere 1.4 percent of national income. In contrast, with 46 percent of total income, the highest decile was earning thirty-three times more than people at the bottom of the scale. While Chile's income inequality is not as extreme as Brazil's, with a ratio of 6:1 between the highest and lowest income deciles, income distribution in the United States is benign by comparison.

Repeating the Mistakes of the 1970s: Mexico's Peso Crisis of 1994

The underlying trend of greater economic stability in the region was interrupted by bursts of instability. The first episode, which began with Mexico's financial crisis and the ensuing recession of 1995, erased much of the progress of the previous years. What happened in 1994 is that, as in the 1970s, Mexico was once again relying heavily on external savings, this time in the form of massive foreign investment in short-term Mexican treasury bills. Moreover, rather that going into productive investment and social programs, those funds helped finance an import-led boom. What was different in 1994, and made problems more complicated than in 1982, was that, while commercial banks could not withdraw or cancel loans after Mexico's debt moratorium of 1982, private finance was more mobile. When foreign investors lost confidence in 1994, they sold large holdings of treasury bills and pulled out their funds. This made the linkages between shifts in capital and domestic interest rates and exchange rates more difficult to manage. To stem the outflow of funds, Mexico raised interest rates to over 100 percent, but the peso still lost value.

A meltdown of the capital market was avoided, thanks to rapid intervention by the IMF and the United States, which arranged a $40 billion bailout, with the support of the Bank for International Settlements.[25] This, the country's second bailout in just over a decade, stabilized the peso and brought Mexico back from the abyss. But the events of 1982 were repeated in more than one way. As in 1982, there was a band-wagon effect—the "tequila effect"—that spread contagion to other Latin American capital markets, which were also affected by large outflows of speculative foreign capital. Argentina suffered the most: unemployment jumped to 18 percent, in 1995; GDP fell by 4.5 percent; and there were massive withdrawals from the banking system.[26] But the scale of the contagion was limited compared to what *would have* happened to the rest of Latin America if Mexico had had no international rescue package.

In other words, much like the stabilization programs and structural adjustment loans of the 1980s, and the IMF's bailout of Thailand and Indonesia in 1997, the 1995 bailout of Mexico served primarily to reassure and protect investors. Once again, a collapse of the financial system was averted, and, even though foreign investors were bruised, they were not crippled. On the other hand, as had already been the case during the "lost decade," the cost of dealing with the peso crisis was socialized: in 1995 Mexico suffered its most severe recession in sixty years. By March 1995, 800,000 people had lost their jobs when companies and factories closed their doors, and a further 10 percent of the working population were working less than fifteen hours per week and became self-employed. The crisis was so severe that output declined by more than 9 percent during the first quarter of 1995.

This affected the entire population. Among the urban middle class who had benefited from the large inflows of foreign funds, and whose standard of life had improved since 1990, there were scores of instant "new poor" who could no longer afford mortgages, car loans, and credit-card debts when market interest rates on their debts rose to more than 100 percent. Many lost their cars, stereo systems, and home appliances to "repo men," and mortgage lenders began foreclosing on the houses and apartments of people who could not keep up with monthly payments.

In fact, the effects of the 1994–95 peso crisis lingered much longer than expected. By June 1998, the cost of dealing with the commercial banks' $65 billion in unrecoverable loans—a measure equivalent to the retirement savings of all Mexicans during the next twenty-five years—had become "a political time bomb on a short fuse."[27] In an unexpected rebuff to President Zedillo, Congress rejected his proposal to "subsume" the bank's bad debts under the national public debt.

The Fallout from Asia's Financial Crisis

The tequila effect had barely subsided when the aftershocks of East Asia's financial crisis threatened Latin America in the fall of 1997 and early 1998. This time Brazil, Latin America's largest economy, suffered the most. In November 1997 the central bank had to double short-term interest rates to more than 60 percent per year, to protect the real. This could not prevent a downward slide of the currency, which lost 15 percent of its value by the end of the year. The higher interest rates also brought parts of the economy to a halt. Ford, Volkswagen, and other car manufacturers stopped their assembly lines and closed their factories to avoid building up unsold—and unsellable—inventories. Investment plans were also put on hold. The decline continued in early 1998, with a steep rise in unemployment in January 1998, which cut across all sectors, from manufacturing to commerce and construction.[28] It is still too early to assess the consequences of East Asia's unfolding financial crisis for Latin America (and other parts of the world), except that higher interest rates and unemployment will cause an upsurge of poverty. Ominously, by the end of August 1998 Brazil's economy was showing signs of extreme weakness, raising the specter of a global recession.

Microfinance and Informality in Latin America

Latin America has always had sizable informal economies, and several specialized credit programs for small farmers and businesses pre-date the rise of informality of the 1980s. The region's high and increasing level of urbanization has shaped its informal sector, as well as the financial institutions that are working with it.

The predecessors of today's microfinance institutions were credit unions, rural savings and loans associations, farmer credit cooperatives, and agricultural development. Although these institutions had promising starts in the 1960s and could have prospered, over the years their viability and sustainability were undermined by government intervention and the politicization of lending. Instead of working with the marginal segments of society for which they were designed, credit unions, savings banks, and other community-based institutions were used by governments as vehicles for subsidized lending to large farmers, and to curry favor with landowners.

Later on, in the late 1970s and during the 1980s, high inflation virtually brought financial intermediation to a halt, and wiped out scores of these institutions. The book value of loans that pre-dated inflation was often eroded to the point of becoming meaningless, and it made no sense to attract deposits at the absurdly high interest rates of the 1980s. In Peru, which had the largest credit-union system in Latin America, the system came close to collapsing during successive waves of hyperinflation, and only a few of the original unions survived inflation of 7,000 percent in 1990.

Latin American microfinance underwent major changes during the 1980s, in response to the growing credit needs of the fast-growing urban informal sector. In most debtor countries rising unemployment and a shrinking employment base meant that self-employment had become the sole source of earnings for those who had lost their jobs. In Bolivia and Peru the informal sector rapidly became the dominant form of economic activity and the largest source of employment. By the end of the 1980s, two thirds of Bolivia's economically active urban population and 90 percent of its rural population were working in the informal economy. In Peru the share of wages in GDP fell from 51 percent in 1985 to 42 percent in 1990, and there was a steep rise in poverty and informal activities during the same period.

As in other parts of the world, there was feminization of poverty. This left its mark on microfinance through innovative grassroots approaches, such as

The Informal Economy and Evangelism

There is an interesting, but probably coincidental, link between the rise of informality and self-employment and the spread of evangelism among people in marginal communities throughout Latin America.

In the fifteenth century the Spanish Conquistadors brought Roman Catholicism to the Americas and it remained the unchallenged dominant faith for centuries. This situation is changing. From Central America to the Southern Cone, increasing numbers of people are deserting the Roman Catholic Church for evangelical faiths. Interestingly, those who espouse the new faiths are mostly poor and work in the informal economy. One possible reason for this is that, because the Roman Catholic Church has traditionally sided with the elites and defended the status quo, it is—rightly—perceived as the faith of the oppressors.

A more probable cause for the mass appeal of evangelism among the poor in Latin America lies at the heart of the Roman Catholic Church itself. The institutional Roman Catholic Church is largely hierarchical and undemocratic, and always involves intermediation by a priest, who accepts confessions and administers the sacrament. It is a religion of repentance and supplication. In contrast, evangelical preachers, most of whom are poor like their followers, preach a more individual interpretation of faith that embodies the concept of self-help, which is bound to appeal more to those who are already helping themselves.

Lima's Mothers' Clubs and communal kitchens. There, women's community work created original and effective coping mechanisms, and set up rotating credit funds for the club's members. At the same time, accelerating rural migration by rural dwellers who were desperate to escape poverty, landlessness, and violence resulted in the proletarianization of the formerly rural labor force.[29]

Government-funded Microfinance

In a number of Latin American countries, where formal microfinance is relatively undeveloped, governments use a mixture of budgetary resources and donor funds to finance microenterprise development. In Chile, the Ministry of Agriculture uses a blend of its own funds and multilateral financing to finance rural microenterprises, mostly managed by women. Projects that are funded in this manner include greenhouses for the cultivation of tomatoes and flowers in the country's chilly south, as well as llama and *vicuña* breeding in the Andean highlands. All loans are at market rates. The Ministry supplements external financing with additional resources for agricultural extension services and gender-focus groups. There is no fee for these services.

In Mexico, the government's Solidarity Program (Solidaridad) uses resources from the federal budget to finance a nationwide program of community-based projects (rural electrification, small-scale irrigation, rural road rehabilitation) and rural microenterprises. In some of the poorest states, including Chiapas, Oaxaca and Guerrero, Solidarity projects are co-financed by the World Bank. In Nicaragua, the Ministry of Agriculture funds rural microenterprises, using a blend of its own funds and financing form the World Bank.

The Leaders in Latin American Microfinance

Microcredit began expanding again as soon as lower inflation made financial intermediation possible. The first large-scale credit programs in the region were launched by North American financial NGOs, two of which stand out as leaders in their field.

As discussed in Chapter 3, one of them is FINCA, which provides seed capital to village banks in many parts of Latin America. In 1995 it had more than thirty-six active village bank programs—seven in Central and South American countries. It also has affiliates in the Dominican Republic and Haiti.

The second is ACCION International, which supports urban microfinance programs in fourteen countries in Latin America. Together these programs have about 65,000 clients, whose loans average less than $100. ACCION's best-known affiliate is Bolivia's Banco Solidario, South America's premier microfinance institution. ACCION has also helped launch ADEMI, a microfinance program in the Dominican Republic. In 1997 it was operating nationwide and had more than $35 million in 15,000 individual loans to local microentrepreneurs. But not all ACCION ventures are resounding successes: in 1995 its affiliate in Colombia, Finansol, which had 40,000 clients, experienced a severe financial crisis and deterioration of its portfolio. It was restructured with the help of ACCION.

The early successes of FINCA and ACCION have also led to a revival of credit unions and cooperatives in Latin America. For instance, acting with the support of the World bank, in El Salvador the government has depoliticized the national system of credit cooperatives, and placed it under a recapitalized apex, FEDECREDITO. By 1994 there were already over 1,500 second-generation credit unions in Latin America, with close to 2.5 million members. They had about $1 billion in loans outstanding, and close to $850 million in savings deposits.

The financing needs of Latin America's informal sectors have also attracted the attention of multilateral and bilateral lenders. The Inter-American Development Bank (IADB) has a continent-wide "2001 Microcredit Initiative," and Germany's overseas development agency, GTZ, is active in Peru and Bolivia, offering technical support to Peru's Municipal Savings Banks and Bolivia's most recent microfinance institutions, the Caja Los Andes. Major northern NGOs, such as CARE, CRS, and Women's World Banking are also involved in Latin American microlending.

Latin American microfinance is extremely dynamic and continues to evolve, as NGOs take advantage of new laws and regulations and become regulated financial intermediaries. In Bolivia, PRODEM may seek follow the example of Los Andes, and also become a non-bank financial intermediary, and, in December 1997, ADEMI received clearance from the Dominican Monetary Authority to become a bank, as Banco de Desarrollo ADEMI S.A. (BancoADEMI). The new bank will take over its predecessor's client portfolio and offer a full range of loan and savings services to microenterprises.

Notes

1. Michael Redclift, "Land, Hunger and Power: The Agrarian Crisis in Latin America," in *The Crisis of Development of Latin America* (The Hague: Center for Latin American Research and Documentation, 1991), 24.
2. "Domestic Violence," an *IDB Special Report*, Inter-American Development Bank, 1997, 1.
3. Pablo González Casanova. "The Crisis in Latin America as a Global Phenomenon," in *The Crisis of Development of Latin America* (The Hague: Center for Latin American Research and Documentation, 1991), 2.
4. By 1982 the private external debt of Mexican companies had reached $26 billion. *WDR 1982*, 249 and Leopoldo Solís and Ernesto Zedillo, "The Foreign Debt of Mexico," in *International Debt and the Developing Countries* (Washington, D.C.: The World Bank, 1985), 261.
5. *WDR 1982*, 249.
6. *World Debt Tables 1988–89*, Box 1, xviii.
7. Rudiger Dornbusch and Juan Carlos de Pablo, "Debt and Macroeconomic Instability in Argentina," in *Developing Country Debt*, National Bureau of Economic Research (NBER) Conference Report, edited by Jeffrey Sachs, 1987,

16 and 17.

8. Eliana Cardozo and Albert Fishlow, *The Macroeconomics of the Brazilian External Debt*, NBER, 1987, 78.
9. Cardozo and Fishlow, 80.
10. Harold Lever and Christopher Hume, *Debt and Danger: The World Financial Crisis* (London: Pelican Books, 1985), 69.
11. Leopoldo Solís and Ernesto Zedillo, "The Foreign Debt of Mexico," in *International Debt and the Developing Countries* (Washington, D.C.: The World Bank, 1985), 278.
12. Susan George, *A Fate Worse than Debt* (New York: Grove Press, 1988), 121.
13. *WDR 88*, 65.
14. E. V. K. FitzGerald, "Latin America in the World Economy," in *The Crisis of Development in Latin America*, 9.
15. Angus Maddison, *Two Crises: Latin America and Asia, 1929–38 and 1973–83* (Paris: OECD), 78.
16. Solís and Zedillo, "The Foreign Debt of Mexico."
17. *World Debt Tables 1987–88*, xviii.
18. *World Debt Tables 1987–88*, xiii and Juan Luis Londoño and Miguel Székely, *Distributional Surprises after a Decade of Reforms: Latin America in the 1990s* (Washington, D.C.: Inter-American Development Bank, March 11, 1997), 6. Mimeo.
19. *Where Women Stand*, Global Fact Sheet of the International Center for Research on Women.
20. *WDR 88*, 65.
21. *WDR 1983*, 178–179, *WDR 1988*, 252–253.
22. For more details see Shahid Javed Burki and Sebastian Edwards, *Dismantling the Populist State: The Unfinished Revolution in Latin America and the Caribbean* (Washington, D.C.: The World Bank, 1996).
23. Raymond Colitt, *Financial Times*, November 13, 1997.
24. Stephen Fidler, *Financial Times*, March 17, 1997.
25. The rescue package included $20 billion for the US Treasury, $18 billion from the IMF, $10 billion from the Bank for International Settlements, and $3 billion commercial banks (Leslie Crawford, *Financial Times*, June 2, 1995).
26. Stephen Fidler, *Financial Times*, February 12, 1998.
27. Leslie Crawford, *Financial times*, June 18, 1998.
28. Jonathan Wheatly and Geoff Dyer, *Financial Times*, March 5, 1998.
29. Redclift, *The Crisis of Development of Latin America*.

7

Financing Bolivia's Urban Informal Sector

A Poor Landlocked Country

Bolivia is a big landlocked country. Its size is roughly that of the combined land areas of Japan, the United Kingdom, Sweden, and Switzerland. What is now Bolivia was part of the Inca Empire. It was conquered in 1538 by Hernando Pizarro, the younger brother of the Spanish conquistador who subjugated Peru, which was the center of the Inca Empire. More than half of Bolivia is a vast tropical forest that lies in the Amazon basin but, like Peru, Bolivia is best known for its snow-capped Andean peaks and highlands. Population density is the lowest in Latin America. There are about as many Bolivians as Swiss, but if Bolivia had the same population density as Switzerland there would be some 200 million Bolivians, instead of 7.5 million.

Like the rest of Latin America this country is highly urbanized. In 1995 almost 60 percent of all Bolivians lived in urban areas, compared with fewer than one-third twenty years earlier. La Paz is the largest city and main business center. It is located in a high valley at an altitude of 12,000 feet, where the oxygen-poor atmosphere leaves newcomers gasping for breath. The mining industry, the country's economic backbone for centuries, is also in the highlands, at more than 14,000 feet above sea level. Commercial agriculture is in the tropical lowlands—the Yungas—where there are also some oil fields. Sucre, the capital, is in the lowlands and has about one-tenth of the population of La Paz.

Four out of every five Bolivians are Indians and *mestizos*. Many of them do not speak Spanish, the country's official language. For 30 percent of Bolivians, Quechua is the first language, for 25 percent it is Aymara, and for 15 percent, Tupi Guarani. There also are innumerable indigenous dialects in the highlands and forests. The Indian majority is subjected to an egregious form of cultural apartheid by the Spanish-speaking Caucasian elite. They treat all non-whites as if they were an inferior race, and have always excluded them from political life and management positions in the private and public sectors. The 1993 election of an Amerindian Vice President, Victor Hugo Cardenas, was an unprecedented one-time event. Even so, indigenous culture and folk-lore—from music to traditional dresses—are more vibrant in Bolivia than in any other Andean country. Even in La Paz Indian women wear their tradi-tional bowler hats, shawls, and multi-layered woolen skirts, and on Sundays and holidays the city resonates with the vibrant sounds of Andean music.

Bolivia is a very poor country. With an average annual per capita income of $770—a little more than two dollars a day—it has the region's third-lowest average income after Nicaragua and Honduras. Independent estimates put more than two thirds of all Bolivians below the poverty level.[1] In 1992, a World Bank assessment of poverty in Bolivia found that the poorest are sub-sistence farmers, agricultural workers of Indian origin, and women, all of whom have few employment opportunities and no access to credit. The same report also pointed out that the poorest have benefited little, if at all, from public expenditure, and that they have virtually no access to infrastructure, health care, education, and vocational training.[2]

Rural poverty is most pronounced among Andean Indians, and in the rain forest. But there are also many urban poor, particularly among recent mi-grants from the highlands. Most of them have settled in El Alto ("the high one"), the poorest area of La Paz. It is a barren, windswept plateau that sur-rounds the city. Virtually all housing there is substandard, services are minimal, and the international airport is the only source of formal employment. Most days of the week thousands of its residents go down to La Paz, working at market stalls or as street peddlers. Others are domestic servants, janitors, and shoeshines. Most market vendors stay in the city, and sleep under their stalls to protect their wares.

A poignant testimony of the deprivation that reigns in El Alto is that many families which live there cannot even afford proper burials for their dead. Even in death the poor have no rights of tenancy; they are buried in squatter cemeteries, where graves are frequently vandalized and desecrated. In 1996 there were about fifty informal graveyards around La Paz.[3]

In contrast with the surrounding areas, the business district of La Paz is surprisingly clean. It has many new office buildings, and most old colonial mansions and monuments have been restored. There is also a relatively well-developed road and transportation infrastructure. The city is low-key and quiet. It does not have the urban glamour zones one finds in Bangkok, Jakarta, or Lima, and traffic is manageable and uncommonly disciplined. A tribute to student activism, right in the center of town, a huge mural on the campus of the national university depicts a defiant Che Guevara.

Chaos and Shock Therapy in the 1980s

As in other Latin American countries, the roots of Bolivia's economic problems during the 1980s go back to the 1970s, when it too borrowed heavily from foreign banks. In fact, Bolivia borrowed so much that it became Latin America's most heavily indebted country, relative to its income and population. In 1988 the public external debt of $5.7 billion represented $850 for every woman, man, and child, and was equivalent to 134 percent of national income.[4] Although a number of debt-for-nature swaps reduced the country's commercial debt, Bolivia's public external debt had doubled by 1995. The post-1985 increase in indebtedness resulted from stepped-up lending by the World Bank. Between 1985 and 1995 there was a six-fold increase in the volume of its lending to Bolivia, while the commercial banks managed to reduce their exposure.[5] This is typical of most low-income countries which lost access to international credit markets after 1982.

Because Bolivia was more heavily indebted (in relative terms) and is also much poorer than the other Latin American problem debtors, it fared worse than them during the first half of the 1980s. Per capita income dropped by 4.5 percent per year between 1980 and 1985[6] (a cumulative decline of 18 percent), private consumption and exports plummeted, and investment declined by close to 17 percent each year from 1982 to 1988.[7] The government nevertheless tried to service some of its commercial debt, and ran up colossal budget deficits to bail out loss-making state-owned enterprises and fund social programs, at a time falling tin prices were sapping the country's main source of export revenue.

By 1985 the economy was out of control, and went into freefall after the already-low price of tin continued to sink. Inflation soared to a staggering 24,000 percent, one of the most dramatic levels in world history and almost as much as in Germany's Weimar Republic, and the national currency, the Boliviano, became worthless. The situation was desperate. A friend of mine who was returning to La Paz when inflation was at its peak, was told that she should bring a large bag to carry her money, and a small one for her purchases. The situation became so chaotic that then-President Paz Estensoro declared: "Bolivia is dying."[8]

To bring the country back from the abyss and put an end to the chaos the government took drastic measures. In August 1985 it introduced a radical

Debt Reduction with Debt-for-Nature Swaps

In a typical debt-for-nature swap, a third party, usually a foundation, purchases debt owed by the government to foreign creditors at deep discounts, and the debtor country agrees to set aside nature reserves or national parks in exchange for the cancellation of its debt. These swaps were pioneered by an international NGO, Conservation International. In 1987 it purchased $650,000 of Bolivian commercial debt for 15 cents per dollar. In exchange for canceling a part of its debt, the government set aside 3.7 million acres in the Amazon area for environmental preservation. These swaps have since been used in other parts of the world, including Madagascar.

New Economic Policy (NEP). Oddly enough, NEP was the name Lenin had chosen in 1918, for a program that tried to revive the faltering Soviet economy with market incentives. Bolivia's program was masterminded by Harvard economist Jeffrey Sachs. The program was so draconian that it was called "shock therapy." Its centerpiece was the government's commitment not to spend more than it could collect in taxes. Public spending was reduced in one fell swoop by an equivalent of 10 percent of national income, the last remaining state-owned tin mine was closed, and all subsidies were eliminated. The Sachs program also included comprehensive tax and budgetary reforms. The tax system was overhauled and simplified to stem tax evasion and raise revenue, value-added tax replaced the cumbersome sales taxes, and the government instituted property taxes. In addition, the government liberalized finance and trade, lifted interest-rate ceilings, devalued the currency, took measures to stabilize the exchange rate, and adopted a single unified external tariff of 20 percent for all imports.[9]

A little anecdote is called for here. In 1989 Jeffrey Sachs replicated his shock therapy in Poland. In a speech to the Polish Parliament, the Sejm, Sachs allegedly said that "one cannot cut off a dog's tail one bit at a time." The budget cuts he recommended were so severe that the next day people joked that "Dr. Sachs wants to cut off the dog's tail at the neck."

After the initial shock, the rest of the program was implemented in stages. Its final component, involving the capitalization of public-sector enterprises, was announced in March 1994. Capitalization is a diluted form of privatization in which the government sells 49 percent of the equity of state-owned enterprises to private investors. In return for management control, the investors must inject new capital and technology into the enterprise. The Law on Capitalization of 1994 decreed that the telephone company, the state oil company, the national airline, the electricity board, the national railways, and the steelworks would all be capitalized. Fearing that this would result in job losses and wage cuts, the leading trade unions struck in March 1996. The Government retaliated by threatening to declare a state of emergency, and there were violent riots in La Paz.

The Vanishing Mining Industry

One of the factors that contributed to the catastrophic deterioration of Bolivia's economy was the irreversible decline of the mining industry. For several centuries mining had been Bolivia's main source of wealth. Silver mining began during the colonial period and lasted until the nineteenth century. In the early twentieth century, when silver coinage ceased to be legal tender in most countries, silver was supplanted by tin, and Bolivia became the world's largest producer of tin, a metal in great demand by canneries.

Tin mines brought fame and fortune to their owners, and were a major source of foreign earnings. Because tin mining totally dominated the economy during the first half of this century, Bolivia's economic woes were all the greater when the mines went into irreversible decline in early 1950s. The military junta that seized power in 1952, in one of the country's innumerable coups, introduced state capitalism. It made the state the sole source of new investment, and the owner of all the key industries. The Junta nationalized the largest tin mines, placing them in a state-owned holding company, the Compania Minera Boliviana (COMIBOL).[10] Under COMIBOL's mismanagement the mines began losing money. Mine closings began in the late 1970s and 23,000 miners, or more than 90 percent of the remaining mine workers, were furloughed in 1985.[11] Except for a few thousand miners who are still working in a few privately owned silver mines, a generations-old lifestyle vanished. Potosi and Oruro, the once-thriving mining towns in the western highlands, became ghost towns. Like Silverton, and other former mining towns in Colorado, they are now tourist attractions.

The collapse of the mining industry shifted economic and political activity to the lowlands. But, because transportation costs in this large landlocked country are extremely high, developing new export-oriented industries is costly, and industry never took off in the lowlands, which are essentially a source of raw materials: tropical crops, crude oil, petroleum products, and coca leaf.[12]

Shock Therapy and the Flight to Informality

The results of Sachs' shock therapy were impressive. Within one year it brought down inflation from 24,000 percent per year to 10 percent, and the budget deficit fell from 27 percent of GDP in 1984, to a more manageable 6 percent four years later. After years during which per capita income sometimes fell by as much as 30 percent, growth resumed in 1987, the first time in a decade.[13]

But unemployment and informality also surged as a result of budget cuts. By the end of the 1980s, close to two-thirds of the economically active urban population, and 90 percent of the rural population, had joined the informal economy. Many of them were former tin miners and their relatives. After the mine closings they settled in La Paz. Others went to Cochabamba, Sucre, and Santa Cruz, in the lowlands, or became farmers in the Yungas and Chaparé lowlands.

In discussing the social impact of NEP one must bear in mind that the status quo ante of runaway inflation, huge budget deficits, and impending economic implosion was sustainable, and that, as is always the case, hyperinflation harmed the poor much more than the well-off, who could keep their savings abroad. The question thus, is not whether something had to be done to stop economic chaos, but *how* it was done. In this respect there is an interesting contrast between the course and outcome of stabilization and reform in Bolivia and Peru. By 1995, when both countries had stabilized their economies, and implemented economic adjustment and reforms, the proportion of people living in absolute poverty was seven times higher in Peru than in Bolivia, even though Bolivia's per capita income was only one-third that of Peru.

One of the explanations for this is that, in Bolivia, the social effects of the shock therapy were cushioned by what remained of the social and economic programs of the populist governments of Hugo Banzer and Victor Paz Estensoro, whose presidencies spanned the period from 1971 to the mid-1980s. Both presidents had used social programs and income subsidies to gain political acceptance and legitimacy, amassing huge budget deficits and foreign debts in the process. While their actions undoubtedly contributed to the economic chaos of the early 1980s, the residual effects of their social programs softened the impact of the shock therapy on the poorest. Not only is the percentage of Bolivians who live in absolute poverty much lower than in Peru, it is also four times lower than in Brazil, one of Latin America's wealthiest countries, and, to this day, income distribution is less skewed in Bolivia than anywhere else in Latin America.

A more plausible explanation of the contrasting experiences of Bolivia and Peru is the timing of adjustment. In Bolivia, where the economy began growing again in 1987, social conditions began to improve and there was no further increase in poverty. In Peru, on the other hand, in 1990 the economy was in almost as desperate a situation as in Bolivia five years earlier. Moreover, the "Fujimori shock" of 1990, which had many similarities with Bolivia's own shock therapy, made no provisions for poverty relief, and average income continued to fall, declining by close to 2 percent per year from 1985 to 1995, even though by then Peru had (briefly) one of the highest growth rates in the world.

The Urban Informal Sector

In the urban informal economy there is a clear distinction between La Paz and smaller towns. In the metropolitan area the informal sector consists mostly of services—vending and food preparation. The smaller businesses, such as fruit and vegetable stands and fast-food stalls in street markets and public squares, usually belong to Indian women from El Alto. The larger stalls that sell clothes, imitation "designer" wear, and more expensive household goods belong to men. In contrast, in Cochabamba and other provincial towns the informal economy is more diversified. It consists mostly of small-scale artisan production and garment workshops, some of which have grown into small businesses, on the borderline between the formal and informal sectors.

As in most Latin American countries, competition and ingenuity are hallmarks of urban microentrepreneurs. For instance, Bolivia has relatively few private telephones and hardly any public ones, except in La Paz. There, virtually every second street stall in the business district offers a *servicio de teléfono*. One only has to look up, high above the stalls, to see that their telephones are hooked up to overhead telephone cables, from which the stall owners somehow manage to divert free lines, even for long-distance calls. The fact that the practice is widespread and in public view, suggests that it is "tolerated" and that money changes hands between the providers of informal telephone services and the employees of the telephone company who "protect" the stall holders.

BancoSol, the country's largest provider of financial services to informal businesses, ranks its potential clients in four categories of creditworthiness, and ability to use loans productively. These categories broadly correspond to the "tiers," outlined in Chapter 2.

- The top 10 percent are businesses that qualify for fairly large individual loans and could "graduate" to borrowing from commercial banks, provided that they become formal. These businesses mostly engage in semi-industrial production.

- A third of BancoSol's lending goes to microentrepreneurs who own small mechanical or artisan workshops, or are market vendors with fixed stalls and regular customers. These businesses use loans productively, and usually manage to earn enough to rise above the poverty line.

- The lower-middle tier, which comprises roughly half of the informal sector, consists of businesses that can benefit from small loans, but whose owners are unlikely to rise above the poverty level. They mostly belong to Indian women. The majority of BancoSol's clients in La Paz are in this category.

- The lowest tier of the informal economy, representing about 10 percent of the self-employed, consists of shoeshines and peddlers who have too few skills to manage a small business, or use loans productively. Others are women who sell goods in market, but who have no fixed stalls. BancoSol shuns people in this group. Not so Pro Mujer, an NGO that does poverty lending, and almost exclusively with Indian women who are in this tier.

The Coca Trade and the Rural Informal Economy

Much of Bolivia's rural economy consists of smallholders and peasant farmers. In the pastures of the *altiplano* (highlands), shepherds tend herds of llamas and *vicuñas* (the two are related) which are prized for their pelts and meat. In the lowlands, smallholders grow tropical crops, including coca leaf.

Coca is a native shrub with leaves that resemble tea leaves. Bolivia is one of the largest producers of coca, but only one-quarter of the production is legal, for traditional consumption. In Andean culture coca is a sacred herb. Dried leaves are mixed with lime or wood ash, and chewed, or consumed as coca tea—*maté de coca*. These potions cure altitude sickness, and stave off cold and the pangs of hunger. Their cocaine content is minimal, and consumption is beneficial and non-addictive. Coca leaves and tea are sold in stalls and shops all over the country, and one can buy coca tea in La Paz airport. As many unsuspecting Bolivians have found out, this can cause serious problems with US Customs in Miami.

Unfortunately, the rural informal economy has become criminalized because about three-quarters of the coca harvest is illegal. It is used to make cocaine and is sold to the Colombian drug cartels. The fact is that, for small farmers, who have grown coca for generations, doing more of the same is easier and more lucrative than switching to conventional cash crops, even if it means dealing with Colombian thugs. There is also an abundant supply of new growers among the former tin miners who settled in the lowlands. Moreover, because the consumption of coca leaves is so ingrained in Andean culture, the growers—*cocaléros*—claim that they have a birthright to continue growing it, and staunchly resist efforts to destroy their crops. In January 1996, several hundred *cocaléras*" (women coca farmers) marched hundreds of miles from the lowlands to La Paz. There they held a week-long series of protests and a demonstration to defend their cultivation rights. They even met with the president's wife, who wanted to make a statement that coca farmers are to be taken seriously.

Early Experiments with Village Banking

With its enormous informal sector, Bolivia is naturally in the vanguard of microfinance. In Latin America it is one of the few countries where microfinance is highly developed, and where the leading microfinance institutions are profitable and financially self-sustaining. Moreover, Peru and Bolivia are among the handful of countries where governments have taken legislative action to promote microfinance.

As mentioned in Chapter 3, Bolivia was also the birthplace of the precursors of FINCA's network of village banks. These early Bolivian village banks were launched by John Hatch, the founder of FINCA. Located in remote areas, they offered one-year loans to smallholders and subsistence farmers, mostly men. The village banks prospered until the mid-1980s, when they were decimated by hyperinflation. Surprisingly, FINCA has not resurrected its founder's experiment. The three village-banking systems that are currently active in Bolivia are managed by NGOs that have no connections with FINCA. They are all quite small. One of them, the "San Antonio Credit Association," is managed by the Bolivian affiliate of Freedom from Hunger. Located in the department of Cochabamba, it combines credit with training education. It is minuscule; in 1995 it had only twenty women members.[14] The other two are community-banking systems, operated by Save the Children and Pro Mujer.

But, beyond village banks, what has put Bolivia on the map of microfinance is the success ACCION affiliates: Banco Solidario and PRODEM.

BancoSol and PRODEM

Known as BancoSol, Banco Solidario is one of the most successful and best-managed microfinance institutions. Its achievements are remarkable: it has more clients than all of Bolivia's commercial banks put together and, for many years it was the only private commercial bank that loaned exclusively to informal businesses, doing so strictly for profit. BancoSol lost its monopoly in 1997, to two NGOs that became banks: Banco Ademi in the Dominican Republic and K-REP Bank in Kenya.

The bank was founded in late 1992 after a long gestation period that culminated in the legal metamorphosis and subsequent reincarnation of PRODEM (it means the "Foundation for the Promotion and Development of Microenterprise") a financial NGO that was founded in 1986. PRODEM used start-up funding from ACCION, USAID, the Bolivian business community, and Canada's Calmeadow Foundation to lend to the fast-growing urban informal economy. It adopted Grameen Bank's group lending with social collateral, which it called *crédito solidario*. In meeting some of the credit needs of urban microbusinesses PRODEM filled a gap in Bolivia's financial system and became an instant success. By 1992, the year of its "metamorphosis," it had close to 20,000 active clients.

Creating BancoSol involved a complicated and innovative assets-for-shares swap in which PRODEM transferred its entire loan portfolio, office equipment and premises, and virtually all its staff to BancoSol, in exchange for a 35 percent share in the capital of the new bank.[15] Since they were still dealing with the same loan officers, the transition was seamless for PRODEM's clients. The only difference was that they could open savings accounts.

BancoSol has a full banking license and is subject to prudential supervision and regulations of the Superintendency of Banks and Financial Institutions (SBFI). For its part, PRODEM remains an NGO, and there is a division of labor between it and its offspring. Keeping its predecessor's original mandate, BancoSol serves urban microentrepreneurs and leverages its capital with client deposits. PRODEM's role is to open pilot branches in smaller towns. As soon as a pilot branch reaches financial break-even—usually after about two years—it sells it to BancoSol in exchange for more shares. In addition, it has begun opening rural branches to finance farm-related businesses. Both ventures are successful.

Prudent Banking in the Service of Microentrepreneurs

As mentioned, like Grameen, BancoSol does group lending. This, and the fact that both banks share the limelight in the small world of microfinance, can lead to confusion. In reality the two institutions are quite different from one another. In Bolivia, groups are of mixed gender, and, unlike Grameen, BancoSol does not try to change the world. It does not demand strict discipline from its clients, make them recite slogans, or seek to empower women. Nor does it target the poorest of the poor, or turn banking practice on its head. BancoSol actually shuns the absolutely poor. It lends only to urban microentrepreneurs who already have a business, even if only a small one, and clients' income must be above a minimum threshold. BancoSol also lends to mixed-gender groups, and expects clients to come to its offices, rather than the other way around.

There are other differences with Grameen: BancoSol does not coach new clients on how to form solidarity groups, and it does not have a standard matrix for borrower groups or the organization of branch offices. Finally, whereas all Grameen offices are spartan, BancoSol's head office and most of its regional offices are anything but. Its main office in La Paz is one of the city's most elegant colonial buildings, restored to a high standard. Surprisingly, Indian women who are market vendors seem to feel at ease in those surroundings.

PRODEM and BancoSol have identical operating procedures. The keys to their success are prudent banking practices, careful client selection, fast turnaround in credit approval and delivery, and combining simple services with streamlined, transparent procedures.

The first step in becoming a client of BancoSol is to attend a promotional presentation at which the bank's staff present its loan and savings products, and explain the credit policies. On average, each branch office holds two presentations per week. At the end of each session, participants are invited to register with a loan officer and begin the credit-screening process. Most people are eager and ready to apply for loans, and many are fully prepared, having formed groups before attending a briefing session.

The criteria for group membership and composition, all based on common sense, are designed to provide maximum safeguards against defaults. They are similar to those of other programs that do group lending:

- Each group must have at least four members, but not more than ten. Each member must be at least twenty-one years old, or, if not, be married—this applies mostly to women.

- Groups can be of mixed gender, but BancoSol always tries to have more women than men in each group, to prevent men from dominating the proceedings. Three-quarters of all clients are women.

- To ensure mutual trust among co-guarantors, the members must know each other and be from the same neighborhood. But they may not be related to one another, and husbands and wives cannot belong to the same group.

- Those who wish to join a group must already have a business, with at least one year's track record. There are no start-up loans.

- Each group must designate a coordinator who handles all contacts between the group and BancoSol. Most coordinators are women.

- To ensure equitable burden sharing among co-guarantors, no single group member can have more than 40 percent, or less than 10 percent of his/her group's total borrowing. In groups of ten all members automatically have equal loans.

Meticulous Screening and Fast Credit Approval

The credit-approval cycle, from application to disbursement, usually takes a week. This is considerably faster than in most microfinance programs. For repeat borrowers who belong to groups with immaculate repayment records, loan approval can take as little as two days. Speedy credit processing matters for people for whom time away from their market stalls and workshops means lost business and less income. It also cuts operating costs, provided that speed does not compromise quality. Hence the need for transparent procedures and double-checks of all transactions, to minimize the risks of fraud and of approving bad credit.

Because people are eager to obtain loans, credit evaluation is always thorough, be it for group credit, or individual loans (see below). As soon as a new group is constituted, a loan officer visits each member for an in-depth evaluation of both the member's business skills and the member's ability to repay a loan from the business's cash-flow. In family-run microenterprises it is virtually impossible to separate what belongs to the business from what belongs to the household. Loan officers must, therefore, look for tell-tale signs of potentially bad credit risks—untidy workshops, neglected homesteads, stale merchandise, and poorly stocked market stalls. They also do "morality checks," looking for possible signs of excessive drinking and marital discord.

Once all members are deemed credit worthy, a group can submit a collective loan application. To ensure transparency and disclosure within groups, loan applications must be presented on a single form that lists the names of all group members, and is signed by each one. That way, nobody can claim not to know how much each member is borrowing, or for what purpose. When a group loan is approved, each member must co-sign the collective loan agreement, which mentions the amount of each member's loan, and all loan disbursement orders identify the group to which a borrower belongs. As a final safeguard, each member's spouse and her/his group's coordinator must co-sign the disbursement order. The only difference between BancoSol and PRODEM is that, in the latter, clients have "borrower booklets," which are annotated at the time each loan installment is paid. This is an easy check of clients' repayment records.

In addition to group credit, BancoSol gives individual loans to a select few long-standing clients. As is also the case in BRI's *unit desa,* some of those clients own and manage businesses that have as many as forty employees, and individual loans sometimes exceed $10,000. Although credit approval for individual loans can be faster than for group loans, BancoSol requires formal guarantees and collateral. This is time consuming and often delays disbursements.

Lending for Profit with Strict Discipline

BancoSol lends strictly for profit. Since the legacy of hyperinflation is the partial dollarization of Bolivia's economy, loans can be in Bolivianos or US dollars at a client's option. To avoid confusion, loans to the members of a group must all be in the same currency. First-time clients can only borrow for three months, in limited amounts: traders and market vendors may not borrow more than $100; working-capital loans for workshops can not exceed $150. Follow-up loans normally mature after six months, and have a ceiling of $3,000 per group member.[16]

Both institutions charge the same interest rates. In February 1996 loans in Bolivianos were at a flat 4 percent per month, plus a loan-processing fee of 2.5 percent of the loan amount. For three-month loans this translated into a nominal annual rate of 50.5 percent, and an inflation-corrected rate of 36.5 percent. Loans in US dollars were at a flat 2.5 percent per month, plus a 1 percent processing fee, or an effective annual rate of 31 percent. Although these rates are comparatively high, they are well below the 10 percent per month that moneylenders customarily charge in Bolivia. Moreover, with gross profit margins in informal trade being on the order of 100 percent, there is still ample room for profit. At the end of 1995, BancoSol's loan portfolio had a 30:70 split between Boliviano and dollar loans, with an average blended lending cost of about 33 percent.

Except for large individual loans, loan demand, income, and cash flow are cyclical: demand peaks at the end of October when market vendors begin building up their inventories, in preparation for the festive season. Loan demand tapers off after the New Year, when many traders start repaying their loans, but picks up again in February, before Carnival. The fact that many clients have no loans outstanding for parts of the year makes it difficult to smooth income, because client deposits tend to rise when loan demand falls, and vice-versa.

BancoSol imposes strict discipline in arrears management. If a group is overdue by as little as one day, the loan officer who is responsible for that group must contact all its members and put them on notice that they are overdue. The bank does not accept partial loan repayments. If a group's coordinator is unable, for whatever reason, to pay the full amount of a loan installment on the due date, the entire group receives a bad mark, which can temporarily disqualify all its members from obtaining new loans. When loans are overdue by more than sixty days, prudential banking rules require full provisioning and legal proceedings. Since 1992, lending arrears and delinquencies have consistently been lower than in commercial banks. Arrears rarely exceed 5 percent of loans outstanding, and the actual default rate is close to zero.

A Strong Emphasis on Savings

BancoSol is one of the few of microfinance institutions that stress deposit taking and client savings, both to leverage its lending capacity and to encourage thrift among its clients. It offers three types of deposits, which can be in Bolivianos or US dollars.

- *Current accounts* (*cuenta libre*) from which depositors can make withdrawals at any time, without penalty. Interest rates vary in line with conditions in the domestic money market and with the rates commercial banks offer to their clients (BancoSol always pays slightly more). There are no minimum opening balances.

- *Savings accounts* (*cuenta de capital*) from which there can be no more than two penalty-free withdrawals per semester. In January 1996 these accounts paid annual rates of 8 percent in US dollars and 18 percent in Bolivianos, compounded semi-annually.

- *Fixed-term deposits* designed to attract larger deposits from private depositors and businesses, rather than from BancoSol's client base. These accounts must have a minimum balance of $200 and interest rates vary in line with the amount deposited.

BancoSol in Perspective

BancoSol estimates that some 200,000 Bolivian microentrepreneurs have no access to financial services, other than from moneylenders and self-help groups. Its aim is to increase its outreach in this group. After growing rapidly 1994 and 1995, the bank entered a phase of consolidation in 1996. To support its future growth and even out the peaks and troughs in loan demand, it began emphasizing marketing and client-oriented services.

The bank also redefined its objectives to establish long-term relationships with clients. For this it uses a variety of techniques to improve its outreach and strengthen its image as a community bank: door-to-door promotional contacts, public-relations campaigns to ask community leaders (*listas de notables*) to refer new clients, and daily advertising on popular local radio stations. (Whereas commercial banks advertise on television, the people BancoSol tries to reach listen to the radio while working. Radio advertising is also less expensive than television.) Each year the bank's branch offices organize street festivals in their communities to increase local outreach. Prizes are raffled at these festivals, and people are encouraged to become clients.

PRODEM, for its part, is expanding its outreach in rural areas, especially among Aymara and Quechua communities in the *altiplano,* where credit needs remain largely unfulfilled.

These marketing efforts have been highly successful. At the end of 1995 the bank had a loan portfolio of more than $40 million, or about one half of all the loans outstanding in the country's entire commercial banking system. With more than 70,000 active borrowers, it had more clients than all the other banks combined. In 1995 these clients were served through twenty branch offices, by a staff of 600. In the Cochabamba region, which is representative of BancoSol as a whole, branches were covering 107 percent of their operating and financial costs in 1995. This region had a staff of seventy-eight and had already made close to 67,000 loans, averaging $750 per loan. Arrears were around 2 percent.

PRODEM has also expanded its new activities. At the end of 1995 it already had twenty-seven branch offices, serving 44,000 active clients, all of whom had received loans in 1995. In that same year it disbursed $13.3 million and made $80.3 million in cumulative disbursements. Taken together, PRODEM and BancoSol had a combined outreach of close to 120,000, and more than $50 million in loans outstanding.

To ensure its *financial sustainability* the bank has gradually diversified its funding sources. In 1996 it began raising US-dollar time deposits in the local inter-bank deposit market, was actively promoting its savings accounts to attract large individual deposits from non-borrowers, and was planning to raise funds from foreign depositors, including from a number of US money-center banks and in the Eurodollar market. To strengthen its financial performance and productivity BancoSol has installed a new computerized management-information system, with new software and faster computers, and brought all its regional and branch offices online in 1996. The new system streamlines financial management, reduces operating costs by simplifying the daily reporting of key financial ratios to the superintendency of banks, and makes credit monitoring more efficient. The system includes a set of performance indicators to track the growth and performance of the portfolio.

In 1996, managers were also taking steps to increase productivity and reduce operating costs with a campaign of "total quality," a popular concept in Latin American business circles. To improve staff performance salary increases were tied to individual performance.

Three Success Stories

In La Paz, where the informal economy consists mainly of trading and services, the majority of BancoSol clients are vendors with stalls in open air markets. Some have individual fruit and vegetable stalls. Others sell clothes and footwear, most of which are imitation designer wear and sneakers. Their turnover is high. Making "designer" wear has become an art form in Bolivia. It has spun off a cottage industry that supplies the city's garment workshops with "Made in the USA" labels, Lacoste "crocodile" symbols, and the red pocket tags for Levi jeans. What is interesting is that, by lending to manufacturers and vendors of counterfeits, BancoSol indirectly stifles creativity in the informal sector.

In the provinces the client mix is different. It includes a large proportion of garment manufacturers and mechanical workshops with loans that are generally larger than those to market traders. What follows are three examples of the socioeconomic impact of BancoSol's activities in Cochabamba.

Alfred and Elizabeth

They are a young couple still in their twenties, and both come from mining families that migrated to Cochabamba when the tin mines in Oruro stopped production in 1985. Unlike their parents, who never managed to adapt to their new lives, Alfred and Elizabeth are successful microentrepreneurs. Their parents could not afford to send them to secondary schools, but the fact that they only have primary education does not seem to have been an obstacle for them. On the contrary, still in their teens, they both began working as seamsters in local garment workshops. After they were engaged in 1991 they saved every penny, until they had enough cash to buy a second-hand sewing machine, and start their own business. They were married the following year, when Elizabeth became a client of PRODEM. She and the women in her group were among the last to borrow from PRODEM, just before BancoSol opened for business. Elizabeth received a first loan of $150, the maximum for a first working-capital loan.

After four years of hard work the young couple has already accumulated quite a bit of capital. They own a thriving garment workshop, on the outskirts of Cochabamba, where they make children's blue jeans, dungarees, and jean jackets. As a punctual payer in a group that has never missed a single loan installment, Elizabeth gradually qualified for larger loans. In 1996 she was almost in the top tier of BancoSol's group borrowers, with a loan of $2,000. The couple's bustling workshop employs a dozen young men, each with his own sewing machine. Most of them are likely to follow Alfred's example. They too will start their own businesses as soon as they have saved enough money. This makes for a high turnover. But there are enough unemployed people in Cochabamba, and finding workers is never a problem. Alfred and Elizabeth also have their own sewing machines, and work with their crew when they are not doing other things.

Production is in twelve-hour shifts, six days a week. In a normal week they produce about 1,000 pairs of diminutive jeans and dungarees, which are piled high on every bit of empty floor space. When demand peaks in the spring and early summer, the pace of activity becomes hectic. Then the workshop gears up to produce more than 2,500 dozen pairs of jeans per week, and work continues around the clock in two shifts, on alternate days.

This business is so successful that it is making garments with its own designer label, "ALFRED NEW DESIGN." The entire team is conscious of the fierce competition in the garment trade, and is constantly producing new styles. Alfred designs the clothes and cuts the patterns. Elizabeth chooses the materials and checks the quality of all products. Using middlemen, they import denim cloth from Brazil, and export most of their production to Peru and Argentina.

The couple lives frugally, but their life is not totally devoid of comfort. They rarely take a break and never go on vacation. The results speak for themselves: with hard work they have achieved a much higher standard of living than their parents and siblings, and their income is well above the country's average. But their comfort is relative. Elizabeth and her husband live and sleep in one of the two interconnecting rooms that constitute their workshop, store room, and living quarters. The only signs of affluence are a big refrigerator (at the time of my visit it was still in its packing carton) and electric stove, a hi-fi system, a VCR, and a big-screen color television set.

What makes this young couple stand out is that, rather than opting for the easy way of producing imitation designer labels, they have created their own brand name. For them and their workers this is a source of pride, and an incentive to be quality conscious. Although this small business has "big" brands to compete with, it has created a niche for itself, and the quality and design of its products are on a par with those of genuine brand labels.

Denisio and Maria

A middle-aged couple, Denisio and Maria live three blocks away from Alfred and Elizabeth and both have their own business. Denisio owns a backyard body-repair shop. Working in the open air, in a muddy yard, he and two young apprentices try hard to give a new lease on life to trucks and buses that are well past their prime. The yard is always littered with engine and body parts, partly assembled trucks, welding equipment, and paint sprayers. In January 1996 the three men were working on a bus that had seen better days. They were planing its battered flanks, replacing doors and windows, and welding new body parts on its rusting chassis. Fetching tools involved wiggling around old trucks and other vehicles that were awaiting their care, clambering over acetylene torches, welding equipment, jacks, and other tools, and treading gingerly through puddles of greasy water.

Denisio dreams of owning a proper garage, with walls, windows, a solid roof, and a store room for parts and materials, where he can build new buses from scratch. Like Alfred and Elizabeth, he became a client of PRODEM in 1992. By 1995, he too had qualified for a $2,000 loan. He told me that the six-month maturity of his loans was too short for his type of business. Rebuilding a bus takes several months, and he only gets paid on delivery. In the meantime, he must pay his workers, buy paint and body parts, and pay the electricity bills. Because of this he can never accumulate enough capital to expand his workshop and hire more apprentices.

Maria, his wife, runs a small general store, across the street from the body shop. She mostly sells fruit, vegetables, soft drinks, and candy. She received her first loan of $100 from BancoSol in September 1995. Neither the store nor the body shop are registered, and there are no proper deeds or titles for the land they occupy. Yet, the couple owns the body shop, the store, and the house they have built behind the store. It is a solid brick house with glass windows and tiled floors. It has electricity, but no plumbing.

Denisio and Maria are unique because of the extraordinary upward social mobility of their family. When I asked Maria if she had children, her wrinkled face lit up with a big smile. She said that she had two grown sons, both students at the University of La Paz. The eldest was studying architecture, the younger computer science. Barring unforeseen events, these young men will become professionals in the formal economy.

Doña Avelina

Avelina works by herself. She is an example of adaptability and imagination. A widow since 1990, she has raised her six children by herself. In 1996 the eldest was twenty, the youngest six. She and five of her children were living in a small, ramshackle house in a poor neighborhood of La Paz. Her house is also her workshop. At Christmas, Easter, and before other religious festivals, Avelina makes colorful religious artifacts and statuettes out of papier-mâché, which she sells in local markets and through a wholesaler. As soon as she finishes her Christmas production, she switches gears to prepare for Carnival. For this, she has another set of molds and various pots of bright paint to make cheerful masks. The rest of the time, during the slack period, she makes souvenirs for the tourist trade. Avelina's children help her during periods of peak demand.

She and four of her neighbors formed a borrower group and became members of BancoSol in 1994. The other members of her group are market vendors. Each one began with a loan of less than $100, but they have been inching up with higher amounts in each loan cycle. Avelina said that she was thankful for BancoSol's financial support, which had helped her and the members of her group expand their businesses. She and her sons could eat more often, and were healthier than before she joined BancoSol. Most of all, Avelina has learned to survive by her wits and imagination—more than bringing food to her table, becoming a member of BancoSol and having access to credit had made it possible for her to use her talents, enjoy her work, and feel empowered.

Government Initiatives to Promote Microfinance

Aware of the social role and economic potential of the informal sector, the government used its General Plan of Economic and Social Development to take legislative action to stimulate lending to informal and small businesses. A legislative decree of October 22, 1994, allows unregistered lenders, financial NGOs, and other non-bank financial intermediaries to become private finance companies—Fondos Financieros Privados (FFP).[17] These are specialized financial institutions, whose sole purpose is to lend to microenterprises and small businesses. They may not call themselves banks, or offer checking and current accounts to their clients, but can make pawn loans, and accept savings deposits. They are subject to the Banking Law, are regulated and supervised by the SBFI, and must observe prudential standards, and capital and reserve requirements. These requirements are supposedly adapted to the special risks of microfinance: like BancoSol, the FFP have more stringent prudential criteria than commercial banks. This reflects the bank supervisors' difficulties in understanding the business of institutions that work exclusively with "unbankable" clients: when in doubt they err on the side of caution.

Following PRODEM's Example: Procredito and Los Andes

The first financial NGO that took advantage of the new legislation was Procredito. This NGO was founded in June 1991. Like Peru's municipal savings banks, Procredito was established with the help of Germany's GTZ. GTZ and its consulting arm,IPC[18], are also assisting the Bolivian government with reforms of the financial sector.

In July 1995, after four years of successful lending to informal businesses in La Paz, Procredito was reincorporated as Caja Los Andes, after the superintendency authorized it to become an FFP. Procredito, from which it emanated, is no longer lending. Its sole legal purpose is as principal shareholder of Los Andes. To effect the change, Procredito used the assets-for-capital swap pioneered by PRODEM. It too transferred its entire loan portfolio, clients, office premises, and equipment to the new institutions, which has $1.2 million in equity capital, owned by Bolivian and foreign shareholders.[19] GTZ continues to offer technical and managerial support to Los Andes to improve data collection systems, incentive structures and portfolio-management criteria.

In early 1996 Los Andes was the country's only FFP. It had just begun accepting savings and term deposits from the public, in dollars and Bolivianos, offering the same interest rates as BancoSol. It has two types of individual, fully guaranteed loans.

- *Pawn loans* for which clients pledge their gold or gold jewelry. Disbursement is immediate, for a maximum of two-thirds of the assessed value of the gold, which is kept in custody in its vaults. Almost all users of pawn credit are women.

- *Individual loans* in bolivianos or US dollars for urban and rural microenterprises, most of which are former clients of Procredito. Even though SBIF guidelines only require collateral for loans in excess of $20,000, Los Andes demands adequate guarantees or collateral.

Depending on the size and maturity of loans, repayments are weekly, bi-weekly or monthly. At the end of 1995, about one-tenth of all loans outstanding had maturities between three and six months, one-third matured in nine months, and one-sixth in eighteen months. Only the last category had monthly repayments. Lending rates are the same as in BancoSol—2.5 percent per month in US dollars, and 4 percent monthly in Bolivianos—but there are no additional charges or loan processing fees, which reduces borrowing costs.

In 1995, lending was equally divided between pawn loans and individual loans. By activity, about one tenth of all loans to microenterprises were for service activities (market vendors and food preparation), two-thirds for trade, and the remainder for garment workshops. Fewer than one-half percent of loans were guaranteed by mortgages. By type of use, about 90 percent of individual loans were for working capital, the rest for investment in plant and equipment. Most loans are to women and women-owned microenterprises.

After including pawn lending, two-thirds of all loans were for less than $500, and they represented only one-fifth of all loans disbursed and outstanding. This points to a skewed distribution in loan demand, and to a concentration of risk in Los Andes's portfolio. Procredito had been profitable since its inception, and Los Andes managed to make a small profit in its first half year of operations. In November 1995, it had a total loan portfolio of $9.2 million. Less than 1 percent of loans were in arrears by more than thirty days.

Pro Mujer and the Women of El Alto

Pro Mujer is a small NGO that began working in La Paz in 1990, with a small grant from USAID. Its founder and general manager is an American woman. Pro Mujer organizes urban and peri-urban community banks in poor neighborhoods and targets women. Its activities are concentrated in El Alto and in the marginal neighborhoods of Cochabamba and Sucre. It has a hybrid legal status: although Pro Mujer works in Bolivia, it is incorporated in the United States as a private voluntary NGO, which qualifies for tax-deductible donations from US-based tax payers.[20] By 1995 it had forty-five active community banks, with 1,500 active members, most of them in El Alto.

Pro Mujer's community banks (bancos comunales) make small loans, and offer basic business training and family counseling to their members. Most are Indian women who have recently migrated from rural areas and from the former mining communities in Potosi and Ororu. The community banks are for and by women, who manage the banks they belong to—more than 98 percent of the banks' members are women who are also the main, if not sole, breadwinners in households where husbands and sons are unemployed former miners and farm laborers.

A Social Philosophy Inspired by Grameen and FINCA

This NGO's social philosophy is inspired by Grameen. Its founding manager spent time at Grameen's training center in Dhaka, and, like Yunus (Grameen's president), uses small loans to empower poor women. But it differs from its role model in many ways, and its community banks replicate the structure and organization of FINCA's village banks. The reason for this is that the village-bank model is better adapted to the social and cultural environment in Bolivia.

Each credit cycle follows a two-stage process: Pro Mujer lends donor funds to its community banks, which then on-lend to their own members. Pro Mujer is also and apex. It supervises the banks' activities, and keeps central, computerized records of all its financial transactions with the banks, and of the banks' loans to their members.

Each bank has about fifty members. They are divided into sub-groups of five people who are jointly responsible for their borrowings from the communal bank to which they belong. As soon as the members of a new bank are trained, and have elected a secretary and treasurer, and appointed a credit committee, their bank becomes a self-managed entity.

As with FINCA village banks, all loans are for sixteen weeks, repayable in equal weekly installments. Loans start at $50, and rise to a maximum of $400 in increments of 20 percent per loan cycle. Depending on members' preferences, the banks hold weekly or bi-weekly meetings to discuss new business, disburse new loans, and collect loan repayments. In the latter case, loan repayments are also bi-weekly, a departure from the FINCA model.

Members must set aside 20 percent of each loan as forced savings, and can only borrow the amount of a previous loan, plus the 20 percent she has saved, subject to the $400 ceiling. The forced savings thus become the bank's capital. The women are also encouraged to make personal savings. As with FINCA, each bank must have *two separate accounts, to avoid mingling the cash flow on loans and the members' savings.* The weekly *principal and interest payments* which are owed to Pro Mujer flow through *each bank's external account* are deposited with a commercial bank. The women's forced and voluntary savings are deposited in their internal account, in their bank's savings account at a commercial bank. Funds from an internal account can be used as a rotating loan fund, from which members can borrow.

Pro Mujer charges a flat monthly interest rate of 4 percent on its loans to the community banks. All loans are in local currency, and there are no commissions or loan-processing charges. The interest the banks charge to their members is discretionary. As is the case with peer groups composed mostly of women borrowers, arrears and delinquencies are extremely low—below 1 percent in 1994. For loan arrears and late payments members pay a penalty of Bs.5 (about $1).

A Strong Emphasis on Group Dynamics and Training

Pro Mujer uses the community banks for social intermediation by arranging group-based training by qualified instructors. They use colorful charts, diagrams, and picture books that are designed for people with rudimentary education.

- *Induction training* for the members of newly established banks is in two two-hour sessions. It teaches unskilled women how to manage a community bank, and what it means to belong to a peer group. This training serves to instill group identity.

- *On-going training* takes place during the banks' first two sixteen-week loan cycles. It teaches basic business skills. During this period Pro Mujer's in-house instructors attend the banks' weekly meetings. They supervise their activities, and help with tallying loan repayments and discussing loan proposals. Training during this interim period covers basic business practices, basic arithmetic, price setting, and financial discipline, to ensure that members select profitable activities, and become dependable borrowers. The instructors also show people how to set up and run a small store, serve clients, and manage a retail inventory.

- *Social training* offers advice on child and family care and family planning, and links its members with local family-planning services and clinics. Instructors also accompany interested women to family-planning clinics. During each loan cycle PM's instructors reserve a number of days for social training.

Formal training stops after two loan cycles. Then, the women must assume responsibility for the day-to-day management of their banks. They become responsible for loan collection, balancing their books, and depositing loan repayments in Pro Mujer's bank account. The apex nevertheless continues to supervise the banks' activities, by sending its instructors on random spot checks of meetings. They spend most of their time with the weakest and most recent communal banks. Each instructor is responsible for up to five communal banks, and 200 to 250 members. The instructors are all professionally trained. Many began as members of community banks, and are still active in their original groups. They are paid by Pro Mujer.

Pro Mujer's Financial and Social Impact

Typical clients are middle-aged women with several children. Most are recent migrants from their native highlands and mining communities. Their weekly meetings are casual. Many women bring their children, who play hide-and-seek games under the tables and chairs while their mothers talk business. Sometimes the women come with their husbands to show them what they are doing. Over time, the weekly meetings become gatherings of friends. Attending their banks' meetings also instills strong group identity among members, and the meetings become support groups where the women can talk freely about family problems. Belonging to a group, away from domineering husbands, gives shy and reserved women greater confidence. Social training and counseling on health and family planning also gives women greater awareness of the importance of personal hygiene, helps prevent illness, and helps them control their fertility—they have fewer children than non-members.

Although Pro Mujer's outreach is limited in comparison with that of most other microfinance programs, it has a very strong social and economic impact in the four communities where it has helped establish active groups. One indicator of this is that, while more than half of its members had no business experience and were unemployed at the time they joined a communal bank, after three loan cycles they had become street and market vendors, and were able to improve their families' living standards with what they earned in their businesses. The women who already had their own businesses before joining a community also benefited by being able to turn unprofitable activities into profitable ones. In either case, they had gained confidence and self-respect, and their status in their families had improved. Community bank members are expected to graduate after six loan cycles—that is, in two years—and become clients of BancoSol or Los Andes. As for Pro Mujer's own institutional and financial viability and sustainability, it is clear that this small NGO will only survive by relying on the support of USAID and other foreign sponsors.

Lessons From Bolivia

This overview of the evolution of microfinance in Bolivia is revealing for a number of reasons.

- ACCION's bold experiment with PRODEM and BancoSol has created a successful private commercial bank that is dedicated solely to microfinance. BancoSol is also one of the few institutions in this field that attaches equal importance to lending and deposit mobilization, and one whose management is constantly trying to improve efficiency by adopting the latest forms of information technology and specialized software.

- BancoSol's credit policy of restricting loans to six-month maturities is an example of the limitations of standardized programs that are not always adapted to the needs of clients who, like Denisio's body shop, have an irregular income stream and need longer maturities. For him and other clients, repaying loans within six months limits the potential to accumulate working capital.

- Despite these limitations, Bolivia offers examples of how small loans and microfinance can generate enormous upward social mobility. If it were not for the lack of title to their dwellings and workshops, people like Alfred and Elizabeth, and Denisio and his wife, could hope to graduate into the formal economy, and obtain credit from commercial banks. In that sense, BancoSol meets the ultimate test of the social and economic impact of microfinance: helping people rise above poverty.

- Working on a smaller scale, Pro Mujer is helping Indian women integrate into urban society and become independently active. In this respect it exemplifies Grameen's philosophy of empowerment through self employment.

- Bolivia is one of the few countries where the government has taken the initiative to promote new forms of microfinancing that are adapted to local needs. Among other things, it has introduced legislation to transform NGOs and other non-bank financial intermediaries into special-purpose finance companies that must comply with banking laws, and are subject to formal supervision. Procredito was among the first to take advantage of the new legal framework. In establishing the Caja Los Andes under the terms of the new law it is likely to become a model of financial "formalization" in Bolivia, and in other countries and continents.

- Because the only legal and acceptable collateral is real estate—plant and equipment cannot be used as collateral for loans—the possibilities of graduating the informal businesses into the formal sector will remain limited, as long as there is no large-scale effort to legalize informal land ownership.

- A final lesson is that, because this is one of Latin America's poorest countries, Bolivia became a fertile testing ground for new initiatives in microfinance. FINCA's early experiments with Andean village banks were as innovative in their own time as the early phases of Grameen. They have become the model for a worldwide network of replicators, from the highlands in Northern Thailand, to the poorest countries of Africa, and, most recently, to the West Bank. Although FINCA is no longer active in Bolivia, it has found a worthy, if small, successor in Pro Mujer, which is doing ground-breaking work with unskilled native women from the poorest communities.

Notes

1. Maurice Lemoine, "Réformes sous Etat de Siège," in *Le Monde Diplomatique*, October 1995.
2. *Poverty Reduction Handbook*, (Washington, D.C.: The World Bank, 1992), A-1.
3. See Gabriel Escobar, *The Washington Post*, May 14, 1996.
4. *World Debt Tables 1988–89*, Box 1, xviii, and *WDR 89*, 164.
5. In 1994, Bolivia's external debt was still 90 percent of GNP (*World Debt Tables 1996*, Table A1.4, 45).
6. Juan Antonio Morales and Jeffrey Sachs, "Bolivia's Economic Crisis," in *Developing Country Debt*, NBER Conference Report, 1987.
7. *World Debt Tables 1988–89*, Box 1, xviii.
8. John Williamson, *The Progress of Policy Reform in Latin America* (Washington, D.C.: Institute for International Economics, 1990), 4–6.
9. Williamson, *The Progress of Policy Reform in Latin America*, various pages.
10. Juan Antonio Morales and Jeffrey Sachs, "Bolivia's Economic Crisis," in *Developing Country Debt*, NBER Conference Report, 1987, 37.
11. Maurice Lemoine, "Coca Répression chez les Paysans Boliviens," *Le Monde Diplomatique*, October 1996.
12. Juan Antonio Morales and Jeffrey Sachs, *NBER Conference Report*, 1987, 37.
13. Eduardo Gamarra, *Democracía, Reformas Económicas y Gobernabilidad en Bolivia* (Santiago de Chile: ECLA, United Nations, 1995), 19–20.
14. *Village Banking*, FINCA, 19–20.
15. The other shareholders include the Interamerican Investment Corporation, Bolivian commercial banks, the Calmeadow Foundation, Canada, ACCION, FUNDES (of Switzerland), and the Compania Minera del Sur.
16. At the time of my visit, that loan ceiling was under review by BancoSol's management.

17. The legal status and scope of the FFP is further defined in Supreme Decree 24000 of April 1995, which defines their powers to lend and engage in leasing.
18. The acronym stands for *Interdisziplinare Projekt Consult* (interdisciplinary project consulting).
19. The shareholders of Los Andes include Procredito, IADB, the Andean Development Corporation, and private Bolivian shareholders.
20. In 1998 Pro Mujer also began working with community groups in the United States.

8

Rising Informality and Microfinance in Peru

Peru has a population of twenty-four million, in a land area that is about the same as that of South Africa. It shares borders with Ecuador and Colombia to the north, Brazil and Bolivia to the east, and Chile to the south. Its Pacific coast stretches for more than 1,500 miles. Lake Titicaca, at an altitude of more than 12,000 feet the highest navigable lake in the world, is located between southeastern Peru and western Bolivia. The area surrounding the lake was one of the seats of pre-Colombian civilization.

Like Bolivia, Peru is best known for its Andean peaks and arid *altiplano*, but much of the country consists of lowlands. The endless coastal plain is parched and normally has little or no rainfall. Beyond the Andes, most of Peru's northeast is a vast rain forest that is part of the Amazon basin. Forests and woodland cover more than half the country.

With a 1995 average per capita income of $2,310, almost three times that of Bolivia, Peru is in the upper range of the World Bank's "lower-middle-income countries." Like most of Latin America it is highly urbanized: three out of every four Peruvians live in urban areas. Indians and mestizos make up more than 80 percent of the population. Quechua, the principal Indian tongue, is one of the two official languages, an exception in Latin America where official unilingualism predominates.

Mining, agriculture, and fisheries are the main economic activities and export sectors. The mining and petroleum industries thrive on rich deposits of copper, iron, precious metals, petroleum, coal, phosphate, and potash.

Agriculture is concentrated in the coastal plain, accounting for 12 percent of national income and a third of the active labor force. The main cash crops are coffee, cotton, sugarcane, potatoes, rice, and plantains. As in Bolivia, Andean highland farmers breed llamas and *vicuñas* for their milk, pelts, and meat, and rain-forest logging is a source of tropical hardwoods. Deforestation and overgrazing have reached critical levels in many parts of the country.

The fisheries are highly industrialized. They depend on a single catch, anchovy, a protein-rich fish that is processed into an animal-fodder additive.

For many years Peru had the world's largest fishing fleet, with thousands of coastal trawlers delivering their daily catches to fishmeal factories, and the integrated anchovy industry became a major player in the agro-industrial and export sectors. Surging exports of fishmeal to Europe and the United States boosted export earnings and brought prosperity to coastal areas. The fisheries' "Achilles' heel" are their vulnerability to periodic climatic changes that raise the temperature of coastal waters. Known as El Niño ("the Christmas child"), ocean warming happens on average every five to seven years, when the southeasterly trade winds stop. This makes the heavy, cold waters of the Humboldt Current, which normally hugs the west coast of South America, sink below the surface. Warmer coastal waters then drive the anchovies far offshore, in search of colder waters, and out of reach of the coastal fishing fleet. Since the mid-1980s the fisheries have suffered a series of devastating blows from unusually severe El Niño effects, and much of the industry is in irreversible decline.

In 1997 and 1998 El Niño was so ferocious and prolonged that its effects were felt worldwide. On Peru's Pacific rim intense ocean warming caused the worst natural disaster in fifty years. Hundreds lost their lives in raging floods that turned the coastal desert into an immense wetland, creating the surreal sight of pink flamingoes wading in newly formed lakes, in the middle of the desert. The floods also inundated towns and cities, destroyed crops and shantytowns along the entire coast, and caused mud slides that cut the Pan-American highway. By February 1998 crop losses already exceeded $500 million, and total losses capped $1 billion, not counting the lost lives and the cost of repairing the devastated infrastructure.[1] This national calamity caused a slowdown of the economy, and widened the trade gap as exports slumped.

Early Decline Leading to Chaos and Terrorism

As in all of Latin America, income distribution is highly skewed, and ethnicity and poverty are closely correlated. More than 60 percent of Quechua speakers are poor and one-third of them live in absolute poverty. Extreme poverty is most pronounced among Andean Indian communities and in the rain forest, where two-thirds of all people are indigent, and in Lima's sprawling slum belt of *pueblos jovenes*.

Peru was caught in a vicious circle of slow growth and mismanagement well before the rest of Latin America, and its economy was already headed downhill in the 1960s.[2] Later on, during the 1970s, Peru became severely indebted and suffered the full effects of the debt crisis. In 1985 the newly elected president, Allan Garcia, tried to buck the trend. To boost growth, he suspended debt-service payments to foreign creditors, including the World Bank and IMF, and used public-works programs, deficit spending, and imports to reflate the economy and create jobs. This worked for a while and there was a brief flurry of import-led growth. But Garcia's unorthodox populism was doomed from day one. By breaking relations with the multilateral agencies he made Peru a pariah in the international financial community. Cut off from all funding, growth stalled in 1988, and the economy went from boom to bust in a matter of months. Runaway inflation surged to 4,000 percent in 1989; national income declined by more than 12 percent;[3] government finances were in disarray; and the budget and current-account deficits were out of control. The central bank tried to stop the downward slide with price controls and by manipulating the exchange rate of the inti, the national currency. In 1990, at the end of Garcia's term, there were more than ten "official" exchange rates, not counting the curb market. Attempts to slow down imports by rationing import permits and US dollars failed, and became a rich source of graft for officials who "sold" currency and import permits to the highest bidders.

By 1990 the economy was distorted by hyperinflation and an overvalued exchange rate. In the meantime, cumulative arrears of $14 billion on the external public debt, two-thirds of which was owed to commercial banks, had made the debt rise to well over $21 billion—three-and-a-half times more than in 1985.[4] Meanwhile, Alan Garcia and the governor of the central bank had become embroiled in a financial scandal with the Bank for Credit and Commerce International (BCCI), a Middle-Eastern bank of ill repute, to which they had pledged a large chunk of Peru's treasury bullion as security for a loan. When BCCI declared bankruptcy, Peru lost most of its gold reserves. Adding to the scandal, the governor of the central bank fled the country after pocketing some of what remained of the currency reserves.

The country's economic woes were made worse by terrorism, fueled by inequality and poverty. At their peak, in the late 1980s and early 1990s, the terror campaigns and indiscriminate slaughter of civilians by the Shining Path and *Túpac Amaru* guerrillas were paralyzing the country, bringing investment to a halt. Desperate to flee poverty and guerrilla terror, Andean villagers migrated en masse to the slums of Lima and other cities. This was to no avail. By the late 1980s the guerrillas had infiltrated Lima's shantytowns, whence they waged a mass terror campaign of assassinations, kidnappings, and random car bombs in the metropolitan area. On each of my trips to Peru during those years I could see that Lima was paralyzed by fear. A mere car backfiring would make people duck, fearing for their lives, restaurants and parks were deserted, stores shuttered, and the historical center of downtown Lima was all but abandoned by the middle classes who sought refuge in safer suburbs.

The Fujimori Shock

In 1990 President Alberto Fujimori succeeded Alan Garcia. He inherited a hopeless situation. Annual inflation exceeded 7,600 percent. Even the smallest-denomination bank notes had many zeroes but were worth only a few US cents. Fujimori immediately sprung into action. He restored relations with the World Bank and IMF; resumed debt service to foreign banks; undertook stabilization and structural-adjustment programs; and adopted sweeping market reforms, including price deregulation and a market-based determination of the exchange rate. His program followed the orthodox path of sweeping spending cuts and "induced" deflation to restore order in public finances, curb inflation, and reestablish macroeconomic stability. The effects were brusque. With price deregulation the cost of gasoline soared overnight from 17.5 intis a gallon to 21,000, in August 1990; economic activity virtually came to a halt; and, much like in Indonesia in 1998, companies defaulted on their dollar debts.[5]

The measures were so draconian that they were nicknamed "Fujimori shock." But, as in Bolivia, shock therapy brought the country back from the brink. Annual inflation dropped in stages, leveling off at less than 60 percent in 1992, and the budget deficit fell to 1.5 percent of GDP.[6] Growth also returned after more than a decade of decline and GDP, which had fallen by close to 29 percent between 1981 and 1990, grew by 19 percent during the following five years.[7] The return to stability was accompanied by trade liberalization and the privatization of state-owned enterprises. The telephone company was sold to the Spanish state telephone company, and Aeroperu (the national airline), most utility companies and fishing port authorities, and all pension funds were privatized. The president also managed to curb guerrilla violence, capturing Abimael Guzmán and senior cadres of the Shining Path in a spectacular coup in September 1992.

By the mid-1990s the economy was growing at an annual rate of 13 percent, one of the highest in the world,[8] bringing signs of renewed prosperity: a building boom with new luxury hotels, smart new shopping centers, and office buildings; a thriving emerging stock market that attracted large amounts of foreign portfolio investment; scores of foreign bankers and businessmen rushing to Lima to negotiate trade deals and privatizations; and an import boom. Most of all, city life returned to normal. Lima's streets and squares, deserted at the height of the guerrilla terror a few years earlier, were once again teeming with pedestrians. Parents felt safe taking their children and pets to parks, playgrounds, and beaches. Peace also boosted business. Shops and restaurants were no longer shuttered, and people, no longer afraid to sit outside, were again frequenting pavement cafés and restaurants.

A Heavy Social Debt

The flip side of the Fujimori reforms is that, for most people, the benefits of price stability and renewed growth were offset by a high quotient of inequity. In 1994, the year in which the economy briefly achieved record growth, the lowest decile earned less than 2 percent of national income, and the shock therapy had done nothing to curb underemployment and unemployment, on the contrary. The share of wages in GDP had fallen from 51 percent in 1985, to 40 percent in 1993. By 1996, more than four out every five workers had no full-time jobs.[9] Also, instead of boosting exports and creating new jobs for those who had none, trade liberalization and lower import duties spurred imports of luxuries and low-priced consumer goods and clothes from China,

Taiwan, Korea, and other low-wage countries. By 1995, the current-account deficit had swelled to 6.64 percent of GDP, and was three-and-a-half times greater than in 1990.[10]

Even the informal sector was not spared the adverse effects of trade liberalization. Scores of local craftsmen lost their livelihood because their handmade products could not compete with imports of low-price, mass-produced goods. The precipitous decline of living conditions at the bottom of the income scale can be judged from the fact that in Lima real wages for manual laborers declined by more than 60 percent between 1980 and 1995, and that more people were living in poverty in the 1990s than a decade earlier.[11] Put differently, the purchasing power of wages was only 40 percent of what it had been fifteen years earlier.

To make matters worse, instead of focusing on education, poverty, and social programs, after the border conflict of 1995 with Ecuador, the government squandered hundreds of millions of dollars on fighter planes and weapon systems. But there was not enough money to buy school books for the 90 percent of children who did not have any. For all the therapy, by 1997 the level of poverty had risen sharply: one out of every two Peruvians was living below the poverty line, and more than 20 percent of the population were in absolute poverty.

In 1998, in Lima's fast-growing belt of *pueblos jovenes* more than half of all households still had no access to drinking water, and two-thirds had no flush toilets, using outhouses instead. Most housing is marginal, on untitled land. The few dwellings that have electricity usually get it by tapping overhead power cables and, for lack of communal standpipes, people must buy water from private distributors who deliver it by tanker truck. This leaves them at the mercy of unscrupulous "pirate" truckers who sell polluted water, spreading infection and disease in poor communities, where children are most at risk. There are no sewers, and sewage run-offs from the slums along the coast pollute beaches and in-shore fishing grounds, causing periodic outbreaks of cholera. In the early 1990s a health advisory went unheeded and people continued to eat their favorite delicacy—ceviche of marinated raw fish. The result was a massive cholera epidemic that left scores dead. In many rural areas living conditions and housing are even worse, on a par with what one finds in the most poverty-stricken parts of Africa and Asia.

But the government did not budge one inch, ignoring the needs of the poorest. Indeed, the socially regressive reforms and policies of the early 1990s were the product of an authoritarian regime that brooked no criticism. When there were signs of opposition in April 1992, Fujimori simply suspended civil rights with his *auto golpe* (self coup), sending tanks to close down congress and the courts. Since then the government has done little to restore civil liberties, or create democratic and representative institutions, giving instead a free rein to security services that have committed widespread human-rights abuses, murdering and torturing anyone suspected of sympathizing with the guerrilla movement. Even so, Fujimori enjoys spectacular popular support because he is Japanese, which sets him apart from the white "establishment"—the populace affectionately calls him *Chino* ("little Chinaman"). To his credit, the president is neither venal nor corrupt, and is a stern hands-on leader who takes personal charge of critical situations, such as rescuing hostages during the siege of the Japanese embassy in Lima in 1997, or directing flood control in the coastal plain after the latest El Niño onslaught.

Multi-tiered Informality and Microfinance

In 1995, the informal economy accounted for close to 50 percent of national income, and had estimated financing needs of $5 billion to fulfill its economic potential.[12] Given Peru's high level of urbanization, informal activities are predominantly urban. Also, whereas in Bolivia a single institution, BancoSol, dominates microfinance, in Peru the field is highly segmented. Different institutions have carved out market niches, specializing in serving specific sections of the informal sector.

- CREDINPET is a newly created financial institution, dedicated to financing small businesses. Its preferred clients are workshops and businesses with credit needs ranging from $5,000 to $20,000, well above the "micro" level.

- The Cajas Municipales de Ahorro y Credito (Municipal Savings and Loans Banks), lend primarily to individuals and businesses in the fast-growing middle tier of the informal sector. Others that work in this segment are credit cooperatives, such as IMPULSO and IDESI Nacional. The latter was launched in 1996 with the support of UNDP. Its network of nineteen branches provides finance, training, and technical assistance to microentrepreneurs.

- The lowest-tier microenterprises mostly belong to women who migrated from the Andean highlands—like elsewhere, there is feminization of poverty. They rarely borrow more than $100 at a time. Because urban poverty is so extensive, financing these businesses offers a considerable potential for poverty reduction. Major northern NGOs, CARE and Christian Action among them, dominate poverty lending and have managed to tap the boundless creativity and resourcefulness of the poorest women. Local NGOs, such as Candela ("the candle") and Mujer y Sociedad ("woman and society") work in the same sectors, and there also are ROSCA-type *tanamoshi* in ethnic Japanese communities (see Chapter 3).

As in Bolivia, the government—that is, the president—has taken legislative action to promote microfinance and soften some of the consequences of the free-market policies. There are grants for grassroots initiatives, such as the mothers' clubs and communal kitchens of Lima's slums. There has also been action on the legislative front, with the enactment of a 1994 law for the promotion and development of small and micro enterprises by dedicated non-bank financial institutions—EDPYMES.[13] President Fujimori was also one of the least expected "distinguished guests" at the February 1997 Microfinance Summit in Washington, D.C., where he announced additional government support for the informal sector, acting through COFIDE.[14] These initiatives have helped defuse some of the social discontent about poverty and inequality.

CREDINPET: From NGO to Formal Intermediary

Like Bolivia's BancoSol and Los Andes savings bank, CREDINPET began life as an NGO: the Instituto de Promoción de Desarrollo Solidario (Institute for the Promotion of Solidary Development)—INPET. It was founded in 1979 with the financial support of Oxfam International, and Dutch and German foundations. At first, it only offered free legal advice to self-employed microentrepreneurs. Over time, services were expanded to include business advice and management-training courses. INPET began lending in 1982 at highly subsidized rates. That, and hyperinflation eroded its capital and, from 1993 onwards, the principal amount and debt service of all loans was indexed to the US dollar. By 1994 INPET had $3.5 million outstanding in 2,900 loans to about 1,500 clients. Roughly one-third of its clients were women, with 23 percent of loans outstanding.

Responding to shifts in the urban labor force, rising unemployment, and the growing number of informal businesses, INPET decided to reorient its lending and work selectively by focusing on larger urban microenterprises in the top tier of the informal sector. In 1994 it applied for an operating license as a non-bank financial intermediary, working under the supervision of the Superintendency of Banks and Insurance (SBI). To that end, it reorganized its management structure to cope with higher-volume lending; appointed supervisory and management boards; trained its staff in credit-evaluation techniques and loan management; and hired foreign consultants.

Those efforts have borne fruit. In January 1996 INPET became the first NGO to received a license from the central bank, and was reincorporated as CREDINPET, with a share capital of $555,000. Its foreign sources of funding include the European Union, USAID, and Canadian funds. CREDINPET also has a $1.5 million line of credit from the government. At the time of my visit, in February 1996, it had just installed cashiers' booths in its main office, and had applied for permission to accept deposits from the public.

In early 1996 CREDINPET had three branch offices in Lima, and was preparing to open three more and to begin lending outside Lima. The long-term goal is to work nationwide with a break-even target per office of $500,000 in loans.

It lends only to businesses that have the potential of becoming formal, and client selection emphasizes "bankability," the very opposite of the ground rules of microfinance. All new clients must:

- have a proven business track record and have good credit, meaning that they have no arrears on rent or utility bills

- have a stable family environment (each borrower's spouse must co-sign all loan documents)

- have begun the process of "formalizing" their businesses and have submitted all the necessary applications for business licenses and permits

- use loans only to finance purchases of machinery and equipment, which become loan collateral (the value of the collateral must be at least double that of a loan)

By signing a loan agreement, the borrower automatically assigns title to the equipment to CREDINPET, which reserves the right to repossess it in the event of loan arrears, which it does: the branch office I visited in Lima's garment district was jammed with several sewing machines that had recently been recovered from delinquent borrowers. Clients only qualify for a second loan if they have completed the process of formalization; their businesses must be in the formal economy from the second loan cycle onwards, at which point they are ready to obtain loans from commercial banks.

A Sample of CREDINPET Clients

Most clients are in central Lima, many of them in the garment business. They make women's apparel, children's clothes, socks, and stockings. Some of these businesses combine workshops with small retail outlets. Others sell their products through wholesale distributors.

Clients in the garment district in the center of Lima are all located within a few city blocks of one another. Many have workshops in what used to be the warehouses and office buildings of companies that moved to safer havens during the guerrilla campaign. In some of these multi-story buildings each floor accommodates up to a dozen busy workshops.

The owner of one of the workshops I visited had used his loan to purchase a special sewing machine to make buttonholes. It cost $8,000. He and his wife were taking turns, doing contract work for the other garment workshops in the building, sewing thousands of buttonholes each week, on trousers, jackets, shirts, and coats. The other four workers, all young women, were making children's clothes.

What struck me was that all the garment workshops in the building were using up-to-date technology. Each had at least one high-speed mechanical cloth cutter that can cut intricate patterns, in up to one hundred layers of cloth. Such machines cost more than $2,000. They also had high-speed electrical sewing machines. In the building next door, a distributor of industrial sewing machines was doing extremely good business: in one month alone he had sold sixty new sewing machines to CREDINPET clients.

Other clients I visited made cotton and woolen socks on high-speed electrical sock-knitting machines. Beneath deceptively modest appearances—a back room in a unpretentious row house in a quiet back street—one of the sock makers was using five state-of-the-art, numerically controlled sock-knitting machines, each of which had cost him more than $50,000. The owner said that he had been in business for ten years, and that he had gradually built up his business, starting with a single old knitting machine. He sold his socks to department stores and wholesalers, netting 25 percent. The value of his equipment, with a replacement cost of $300,000, was an indicator of "bankability," the epitome of this institution's lending philosophy.

By carving out a niche at the upper end of Lima's growing small-business sector and encouraging its clients to make the difficult and costly transition from the informal to the formal sector, CREDINPET is a catalyst for change. Though its approach differs from that of all the microfinance programs that are described in this book, helping informal businesses become formal can be a positive step. It eliminates the hidden costs of informality, broadens the scope for business growth, graduates former microenterprises to commercial bank credit, and increases the government's tax base. Taking its commitment to formalization to its logical end, CREDINPET had already begun working with some of its larger clients to promote garment exports to Argentina and Brazil. It was also urging its clients to form a garment manufacturers' union, and was encouraging them to make goods under their own brand labels, rather than copying foreign designer labels. That too encourages creativity.

It is too early to assess this lender's financial health and sustainability. One positive indicator is that it strictly implements a zero tolerance for defaults and repossesses loan collateral in case of default.

Emulating Germany's Municipal Savings Banks

Peru's municipal savings and credit banks are modeled on their German counterparts. They are Germany's largest Latin American financial project, managed by GTZ with a long-term technical-support contract, as part of the Peru-Germany Cooperation Treaty. The banks also receive technical assistance from the German Savings Banks' and Giro Association, and have financial support from the government and from the European Union Cooperation Fund.

As their name indicates, the banks attach equal importance to savings mobilization and lending. Each bank is incorporated under public law and is supervised by the SBI, which sets minimum capital requirements and supervises all lending and deposit-taking activities.

The first savings bank was established in 1982 in Piura, a busy market town of 300,000 inhabitants in Northern Peru. Piura is also the country's oldest colonial settlement. It was founded in 1532 by Francisco Pizarro, the Spanish conquistador who conquered Peru and subjugated the Incas by having Atahualpa, their last Emperor, strangled in 1533. Today it is a peaceful town, and the commercial center of the Piura valley, where cotton, rice, and sugarcane are cultivated.

The savings banks' system has grown rapidly. A second bank was founded in 1984 in Trujillo, a city of 500,000 inhabitants in the coastal desert of northwestern Peru, which is a major business and industrial center, with textile and food-processing industries. Thereafter, the involvement of GTZ and the enactment of a revised Law on Savings Banks in 1986[15] gave new impetus to the savings banks, and ten new ones were founded between 1986 and 1995.[16] The resulting twelve autonomous savings banks vary greatly in size. Piura has close to one-third of the system's total assets and close to two-fifths of all its deposits. In contrast, the smallest and most recent bank, in Pisco, had less than 2 percent of all assets and zero deposits in October 1995.

Municipal Ownership

As in Germany, each savings bank's sole owner is the municipality in which it is located, acting through the Municipal Council (Consejo Provincial). Each bank has a seven-member supervisory board, three of whom are members of the Council, and one of these three must belong to the opposition party. This provision is a bit odd, since there are no independent political parties or actual "opposition" in Peru. The remaining four board members are "notables" who represent civil society—the local chamber of commerce, the Roman Catholic Church, and the local association of small businesses.

Following the German tradition, the governance structure of each bank is bicameral, and the members of the supervisory board may not influence the decisions of the banks' management, or involve themselves in day-to-day operations. The Law on Savings Banks guarantees the banks' political and economic autonomy and protects them from political interference and manipulation. The law also stipulates that each bank must cover its operating costs and use appropriate banking technology, and that all lending must support local and regional businesses—the banks may not lend outside their province.

Like all other financial institutions in Peru, the savings banks experienced enormous difficulties during the crisis years of 1988 to 1990, when clients' savings dwindled and hyperinflation eroded the value of their loans and capital. Piura's savings bank came close to becoming insolvent in 1989 and narrowly avoided having to declare bankruptcy.

Since then, the municipal banking system has benefited from new banking legislation in 1990 and 1993[17] that integrates it in the formal banking system. The new laws also allow the savings banks to open branch offices in provinces that do not have their own savings banks, and make it possible for smaller provinces that have limited resources to pool their funds to establish a single bank of which they are joint shareholders. In addition, the laws allows the savings banks to establish a special fund that gives them access to national and international funding sources. In January 1996 I witnessed the implications of the new law first hand, when I joined the managers of the Sullana savings bank, one the system's largest, in their preliminary negotiations with

the municipal council of Tumbes to establish a branch office in that municipality. Tumbes is a small coastal town on the border with Ecuador, whose
merchants do a lot of cross-border trade, and sell their wares in market towns
across the border. This will assure ample demand for credit. (Tumbes is also
one of the coastal towns that was ravaged by El Niño in 1983 and 1998.)

Supervision by an Apex

The savings banks are required by law to work under the umbrella of a
national federation, the Federación Peruana de Cajas Municipales de Ahorro
y Crédito (FEPCMAC) which is incorporated under public law. The federation's
board is comprised of the mayors of each of the municipalities that have a
savings bank and of the presidents of the banks' supervisory boards.

As the system's apex, it coordinates and supervises the savings banks'
lending and deposit-taking activities, and no new bank or branch office of an
existing bank can be established without its permission. The federation must
also audit member banks at regular intervals, offer technical support on matters such as staff training and information technology, and represent them in
their dealings with other institutions. In addition, the federation does public
relations on the banks' behalf.

These centralized functions occasionally result in wasteful duplication of
efforts, and can create tension between the system's apex and the operational
units. One case in point is the development of software and systems for a
uniform computerized accounting and management-information system for
all the savings banks. The federation went ahead with this project even though
Piura had already developed and perfected software for cash management,
record keeping, and management information that could have been adopted
by the other banks.

The Savings Banks as Pawnbrokers

As soon as a new savings bank opens for business, it normally starts off
with the simplest, most profitable activity, pawn lending (*crédito prendario*)
that is fully secured by the borrowers' gold or gold jewelry. There is considerable demand for pawn credit as it offers cash-strapped households virtually
instant cash when it is most needed. All loans are for one week but can be
rolled over from week to week provided there are no arrears on the weekly
interest payments. This is far more preferable to going to curb pawnbrokers
who appropriate the collateral instead of extending maturities. The savings
banks have made pawning a way of life in many communities, where people
use their jewels as working assets, rather than luxuries. This may explain why
many households in municipalities that have savings banks invest much of
their spare cash in jewels, instead of depositing money in savings accounts.

Pawn lending is also good business. It has low overhead, is virtually risk
free, and provides high returns. Instead of having to analyze credit proposals
and visit prospective clients at home, all that is needed is someone who can

assay gold to determine the value of the collateral. People can walk in with their jewels and obtain instant cash. Because pawn loans are short-term and fully collateralized they were the only form of credit that remained viable during the period of hyperinflation. This became habit forming and pawn lending is still, by far, the savings banks' principal form of lending, in terms of the number of clients and loan turnover. During the first ten months of 1995 the twelve savings banks had made more than 200,000 individual pawn loans. But, because pawn loans are for small amounts, they represented only 11 percent of all loans outstanding.

In 1995 the Piura savings bank, the pioneer of pawn lending, made more than 93,000 pawn loans, or more then 300 loans per working day, and has perfected pawn lending into an assembly-line business. There are two large waiting rooms in its basement: one for the clients who are awaiting their turn to pawn their jewels, and one for those who wish to repay their loans and reclaim their pawns. Beyond the waiting rooms the entire operation is heavily protected by armed guards, and all transactions take place in a small purpose-built room where clients enter one at a time. On an average day there are about 750 pounds of pawn gold in the bank's vaults. Loan demand peaks toward the end of the week, on Fridays and Saturdays (the banks are open on Saturdays), and repayments peak on Tuesday and Wednesdays. Most borrowers are women.

Other Credit Programs

Aside from pawn lending the savings banks offer personal loans and microfinance. There is no group lending. Since Peru's economy is partially dollarized, loans can be denominated in US dollars or in the new national currency, the Sol, at the client's option. Interest rates vary according to the currency. In each case, there is only one lending rate, regardless of the type, amount, or maturity of a loan. In January 1996, these rates were 3.5 percent per month in soles, and 22 percent per year in US dollars.

Personal loans are for salaried workers with stable jobs in the private and public sectors. They can be for up to ten months. As guarantee the banks garnish the borrowers' monthly paychecks. In the first ten months of 1995 they had made more than 55,000 personal loans and the balance outstanding at the end of October of that year represented one-fifth of their loan assets.

Loans to microenterprises and small businesses were only introduced in 1990. Demand is strong and the volume of lending has grown rapidly, recording a thirty-six-fold increase from 1990 to 1995. By then, the ten largest savings banks had made close to 54,000 such loans, totaling US$48 million, for an average of $890 per loan. In October 1995 these loans represented about 60 percent of the banks' loans outstanding. Working-capital loans to microenterprises and small businesses range from one to twelve months. Investment loans can have maturities of up to two years. Repayments are weekly or monthly, depending on amounts and maturities. Instead of requiring formal collateral, such as mortgages, the savings banks rely on personal guarantees and careful credit analysis. Typical business loans are for service activities—many clients are taxi and minibus operators—and handicrafts. A good example of this is a handicraft center in a small town some twenty miles from Piura. The center was built with a grant from UNESCO. The potters, weavers, woodcarvers, jewelers, and graphic designers who have their studios in the center are all clients of the Piura bank.

The volume of business lending varies greatly among the banks and bears no immediate relationship to a bank's size. In 1995, for example, loans to microenterprises and small businesses represented close to one-third of total assets in Piura, and about half in Trujillo, the system's second-largest bank. In Arequipa and Sullana (which are respectively the third- and fifth-largest banks in terms of balance-sheet total) this type of lending was much higher, accounting for respectively two-thirds and three-quarters of all loans. The greatest demand for working capital and investment financing is from shopkeepers and market vendors who buy new equipment or build up their inventories.

Savings banks that have offices in fishing ports and farming communities have broadened the range of their business lending activities to include farm credit and financing for commercial coastal fishing vessels, to promote small-scale enterprises in rural and coastal areas. *Farm credit* is for staple cash crops such as rice, plantains, cotton, mango, papayas, and lemons, and for livestock fattening. Piura is the most active in rural lending. Its professional staff includes four agronomists. They assist loan officers in evaluating farm-credit proposals, and offer advice to clients on crop rotation and new farming technology.

Fisheries' lending is a more recent development. It was pioneered by the municipal bank in Paita, a small coastal town, where the mainstays of the local economy are anchovy fishing and fishmeal processing, both in sharp decline as a result of El Niño's vagaries. Paita's harbor is a big old grimy dock. In the middle of it several old vessels are rusting at anchor. They have been retired from the fishing fleet and are waiting to be scrapped. Nearby are the rusting hulks of three enormous Russian trawlers that have been impounded for non-payment of fuel and docking fees. They have been there for years. Fearing lawsuits, nobody knows what to do with them. What is certain is that they are no longer seaworthy, and will never make it back to Vladivostok, the port from which they hail. The local fishmeal factory is a smelly, smoke-belching monster, built in the late 1950s.

The clients of the Paita savings bank include several artisan fishermen who are retooling for non-traditional catches after too many lean years during prolonged spells of El Niño. Because maritime mortgages on small coastal vessels are cumbersome and costly to register, the fishermen assign title to their boats' marine diesel engines as collateral.

One of Paita's main clients is a fisherman who owns and operates two coastal trawlers, with an estimated market value of US$100,000. As security for a $5,000 loan he had assigned title to the reconditioned engine of one of his trawlers. The drawback of this type of security is that if the borrower defaults, the bank must impound the vessel to repossess the engine. Another client was in a totally different line of business; a neighborhood pharmacist, who had borrowed $1,000 to buy materials so that he could build living quarters on the floor above his shop. At the time of my visit the second floor was still but a scaffold, and stacks of bricks and bags of mortar were piled in front of the bright yellow storefront of the pharmacy.

Tapping Local Savings

As financial institutions that are subject to prudential supervision and regulation, the savings banks can accept deposits from the public. They offer passbook savings accounts and term deposits. The latter are for larger deposits. Like the bank's loans, savings accounts can be in US dollars and soles (the national currency). In both cases interest rates are slightly higher than in commercial banks. By 1995 only the larger savings banks had been able to tap enough savings to leverage their capital. For instance, in Piura client deposits represented just under 60 percent of total liabilities and were equivalent to 95 percent of loans outstanding. In the system as a whole deposits represented 47 percent of total liabilities and 68 percent of loans outstanding in October 1995. The banks supplement deposits from the public with deposits from commercial banks.

Evaluating the Municipal Savings Banks

Given the nature of their shareholders, the extensive support from the government and international agencies, and the banks' own management structures, the savings banks are institutionally viable as a group. They are also examples of good governance that have avoided the weaknesses one normally associates with public ownership of financial institutions. As regards individual savings banks, by the end of 1995, only the four largest had reached self-sustainability, and Piura was large enough to absorb some of the smaller operations. The fact that each savings bank is supervised by the Superintendency of Banks, is bound by prudential capital ratios, and is supported by an apex adds to their institutional viability.

Financial sustainability has to be evaluated on a case-by-case basis. In 1995 all but the smallest and most recent bank—in Pisco—were covering their operating and financial expenses, and making enough profits to accumulate capital. The largest banks had also achieved solid *outreach* in their communities. They had supported new family-owned microenterprises, and shown initiative in branching out into non-traditional activities, such as farm and fishery lending. Last but not least, through active promotion of pawn credit and personal loans, the savings banks are providing a valuable community service, and bringing activities that are traditionally part of informal lending into the realm of formal financing. This has driven moneylenders and pawnbrokers out of business.

Inching Out of Poverty in CARE's Mothers' Clubs

CARE-Peru is part of CARE International. In Latin America it has programs in Bolivia, Costa Rica, Ecuador, El Salvador, and Peru. In each of these countries it works exclusively with the poorest segments of society and targets women. Their work exemplifies poverty focus. CARE-Peru has four microfinance programs, which are among the most progressive in the field of microfinance.

A *machines and tools for development program* assists individual microenterprises and local associations of microentrepreneurs. As part of this program, it leases second-hand machines and tools, donated by Canadian companies, to individuals and producer cooperatives. The cash flow from the leases is reinvested in new machines. In 1996, seven hundred microentrepreneurs had already leased equipment and tools from CARE. This helped create new jobs: close to half of the program's participants had hired two to three helpers since acquiring their new equipment.

An *urban microenterprise program* promotes self-employment in marginal urban areas. It is managed in cooperation with community leaders. CARE staff do all the credit appraisals and follow-up visits to clients, and give them basic technical and business training. Whereas CARE's microfinance programs in Thailand involve group lending, in Peru all loans are to individuals. This is an example of replication with adaptation: there isn't a single case of group lending in Peru, and CARE follows local custom. Loans range from US$250 to $1,000. In 1996 this program had already made close to 10,000 loans totalling $6.9 million. Although late payments are frequent, defaults are minimal and overall recovery rates are close to 97 percent. This is a high-cost program in which interest charges cover only about a quarter of the operating expenses.

CARE-Peru's other two programs are the rotating loan funds of the Proyecto Mujer, and the Nutrition and Income Generation program. Both are managed by women's groups, organized as "mothers' clubs"(*clubes de madres*). The nutrition program is a lifeline for marginal communities. It works with the women's clubs to help them organize and manage community kitchens (*comedores populares*) that sell nutritious meals to women and children. This ensures that they have at least one nourishing meal a day. In communities where there are such kitchens health and nutrition are improving.

The Mothers' Clubs

All the clubs are located in marginal neighborhoods, such as the shantytowns that form a broad semi-circle in the foothills that surround Lima. These are homegrown communal initiatives that are unique to Peru. They use collective training and social intermediation for the self-empowerment of their members, all of whom are women who are among the country's poorest. Their role is particularly important in deprived communities where machismo is still deeply ingrained, and where domestic violence is commonplace.

The clubs give their members advice on basic hygiene, family planning, breast feeding, and child care. This helps women control their fertility, and reduces infant mortality, when young mothers stop mixing baby formula with contaminated water and begin breast feeding their babies. The clubs also offer counseling and moral support to battered women. Most of all, they are catalysts for communal activities in group kitchens and rotating loan funds. The success of these groups shows the enormous potential of grassroots initiatives and of programs that involve their members in all aspects of decision making. In this sense women's empowerment in the mothers' clubs is much more powerful and direct than in Grameen's centers. The clubs also have the advantage of working with women who have not internalized a culture of oppression and religious conservatism.

Some clubs have been in existence for several years. Each one is organized and managed by its members and is, in many ways, the focal point of their daily lives. Working together has created strong bonds among the women, and anchors some of the most destitute squatter communities, establishing a base for social progress. During the 1980s and early 1990s, when the guerrillas' urban terror campaigns were at their peak, the clubs also taught people in the slums how to organize self-defense groups.

The Rotating Loan Funds of the "Mujer" Program

These self-managed rotating funds are similar to ROSCAs. Like the latter, the Mujer funds are too small to accommodate all the members' credit needs at the same time, and people take turns at borrowing the kitty. The main difference with ROSCAs, in which members make pre-agreed weekly contributions, is that CARE's loan funds represent the accumulated profits of each club's community kitchen. The net cash flow from loan repayments and interest charges is also pooled and used to make new loans.

The funds are open-ended and can remain active as long as their members wish to remain involved. Each year a club's members must elect a president and credit committee that manages the loan fund. Without exceptions, these small loan funds are vital for widows and women whose husbands are away from home, looking for work. Borrowing from the funds gives them a chance to become self-employed and be more independent from menfolk.

Like Pro Mujer in La Paz, CARE's Proyecto Mujer is funded by a USAID grant, which CARE on-lends to the clubs at 4 percent per month, in amounts of $500 to $1,500, as start-up money for their loan funds. CARE also assists the clubs in organizing credit committees, and offers advice on keeping loan records and accounts for the loan funds. Between 1989 and 1995, CARE helped organize more than 550 loan funds in Lima and six other cities. In 1995 those funds had 8,200 women members and made close to $550,000 in loans. The impact of these loans, which can be for as little as $40, can be judged from the fact that the income of women who participate in the program had more than doubled. Although they are still poor, they are no longer destitute and have regained their dignity.

The Club de Madres Santa Teresita

Santa Teresita is in one of Lima's poorest slums on Lima's barren eastern flank. It was founded in 1993 with a start-up loan of $1,000 from CARE's Mujer project. It had also received a grant of $1,200 from the government. In 1996 it had twenty-five members. CARE's staff assist them with advice and basic training on managing their small loan fund.

Every day of the week, including Sundays, the members of Santa Teresita take turns working in their communal kitchen. They cook nourishing meals, which they sell for a few cents to their members, and to women and children in the neighborhood. Their kitchen is large and open-air. All cooking is done with wood. On an average day they prepare and sell more than two hundred meals. They buy their supplies from local merchants and, when transport is available, from the wholesale markets in Lima. They also receive occasional food donations from businesses and charities. The women are especially proud of their new propane bread oven, and they bake and sell fresh bread daily. The oven has pride of place in an alcove at the side of the club's meeting room. For the people in the community having fresh bread every day is an unheard-of luxury that has won the club great praise.

The club house is a modest one-story red-brick building of about 1,000 square feet. What is remarkable, and shows how much the women identify with their club, is that they bought all the building materials for the club house with their own savings, and persuaded their husbands and sons to build the club house for them. The land is untitled and cannot be purchased. But this does not bother them. After all, who would wish—or dare—to evict them? Besides serving as eatery, kitchen and neighborhood bakery, the club house is also the members' meeting place, and the home of the credit committee and rotating loan fund.

Doña Nelida Palomino, the newly elected club president for 1996, told me that the club encourages her and the other women to become self-employed. The club pools the earnings from the bakery and eatery, and the cash flow of loan repayments to replenish its rotating credit fund. In January 1996 the fund had a cash balance of more than $2,500. The loans ranged from 100 soles ($43) to 500 soles ($215 equivalent). Club members pay a flat 8 percent interest per month, and non-members up to 15 percent. Although these rates are high, they are a bargain, compared with the local moneylenders' rates of 10 percent per day. All loans must be guaranteed by another club member. They must be repaid over three or six months, depending on the amount. Any member who wants a loan must tell the credit committee how much money she needs, what she will do with it, and how she will repay her loan.

As in Bangladesh, Bolivia, or Guinea, receiving a small loan to become independent and self-employed is a real achievement for any poor, uneducated woman. Nelida Palomino explained how proud she felt when the credit committee agreed to give her a loan of 200 soles that helped her become a fruit-and-vegetable vendor with her own stall. What she felt then is the same as the pride and joy of first-time borrowers at Grameen Bank, or of Indian women who join a Pro Mujer communal bank in La Paz. Besides granting small loans to women who are so marginal that they could not borrow from any other source, belonging to a rotating loan fund has also taught them to make regular savings.

The Club de Madres Santa Angela

The Santa Angela club is in one of the newest and poorest shantytowns, in the Eastern Sierra, about fifteen miles from the center of Lima. The newly surfaced road from downtown ends at the bottom of a barren hill. From there it is a long uphill trek to the club house, on a dusty, rocky trail. For several years the Shining Path controlled this district. It blocked the road to Lima until 1994, and held the residents captive. Many of those who tried to flee paid with their lives.

On a bright sunny morning in February 1996 the club house was a hive of activity. Several women in aprons and head scarves were busy in the open-air kitchen. They were laughing and talking while preparing the day's meal, a rich stew of meat, potatoes, and vegetables. They had already peeled dozens of pounds of potatoes, and were cutting big hunks of beef into cubes. A first batch of stew was already simmering in two twenty-gallon cauldrons.

Amidst all the activity in the kitchen, several men were coming and going, carrying roof tiles and planks. Doña Irma Manrique, the club's president, said that they were members' husbands who had volunteered to build a roof over the kitchen. They had also begun building the brick walls for a new meeting room, and had already erected a rudimentary scaffold to begin work on a second floor. The tiles, bricks and mortar, and other building materials had been purchased with a $1,200 loan from CARE. The fact that the men were volunteering to do hard work with much enthusiasm and good humor, to help their wives make a head start, spoke volumes of the community spirit the mothers' clubs had achieved.

The Community Swimming Pool

A few yards from the club house there is a small neighborhood swimming pool. It too was built with the members' communal savings, and weeks of hard work. The women had taken some of their savings from the loan fund to buy bricks and cement for the pool, and bamboo for the fence that surrounds it. Their husbands had spent weeks digging a five-foot-deep hole, some twenty feet by forty, carting tons of soil downhill in wheelbarrows. Because they could not afford to rent a concrete mixer, the men had mixed hundreds of pounds of cement and sand with shovels, and used wooden trowels to line the sides of the pool with concrete. The result is somewhat rudimentary, but pleasant nonetheless. There are no shiny tiles, water chutes or diving boards, and every few days tens of gallons water have to be fetched in buckets from the stand pipe at the bottom of the hill to top up the pool. But who cares? What matters is that weeks of hard labor have brought laughter and happiness to kids in one of the poorest parts of Lima. This is a great achievement for the women and men who have made this possible, and was well worth the effort and sacrifice it involved.

Making a Living in the Shantytowns

What follows are two examples of what some of the members of the mothers' clubs did with the money they borrowed from their loan funds.

Doña Maria's Children's Clothes

Doña Maria's modest dwelling is not far from the Santa Angela club house. She has two young children. Her husband, a car mechanic, lost his job and became a street vendor in Lima. Maria was among the first to borrow from her club's rotating fund, which had begun lending in May 1995. In January 1996 she received her third loan of $90, and used it to buy denim and other cloth to make children's pants and jackets. With an old electrical Singer sewing machine, which she bought with her first loan, Maria can make two dozen pairs of pants or a dozen suits, working seven days a week. She sells the suits to a wholesaler for $50 per dozen. With a third loan, and more material to work with, she hoped to gross around $2,600 per year. After repaying the loan over six months and buying cloth and yarn, she expected to earn about $20 net per week—less than half the national average—to feed her family and even save a bit.

Maria and her family have been living and working in the same one-room "house" for four years. The accommodations are modest to say the least: an earthen floor, a tin roof, and walls made of cardboard, reed matting, and plastic. There are no windows and the door has no lock. There is no stove or heating, even though it gets bitterly cold in the hills during the winter months, and there is no running water or flush toilet. Maria does all her cooking with wood and keeps water in big buckets at the back of the house. Her only luxury is (intermittent) electricity from a neighborhood generator, without which she cannot use her sewing machine, or make a living. Like Denisio in La Paz, Maria's dream is to have brick walls and a solid roof over her head. But after feeding her family and paying for electricity she and her husband never manage to save enough money to even *think* of buying building materials.

Lidia and Juan's Brassiere Business

Lidia Quispe Alfrado and her husband belong to one of CARE's longest-running clubs, the Club de Madres "Antonia Moreno de Caceres." Over the years this couple has built a thriving business making brassieres. Working from dawn to dusk, six days a week, they can sew and embroider thirty-six dozen brassieres. They own three sewing machines. The third one is for their teenage son who helps out after school, sewing the shoulder straps on the brassieres. Lidia is in charge of marketing. Twice a week she goes by bus to Lima's main street market, laden with a big bundle of new white brassieres, which she sells to local merchants. Juan stays at home to make more bras.

Juan is also a talented folk musician. He plays the fiddle. On Saturday and Sunday evenings, he and a friend who plays the Andean harp, do gigs in the mothers' club, and at weddings and local celebrations. Both play by ear and, even though they cannot read music, compose their own tunes. In 1996, Juan and his friend had already recorded three cassettes. (I bought one of each and am still enjoying their music two years later.)

Before they began making brassieres Lidia and Juan sought advice from the club. They had to learn how to cut and sew brassiere cups and straps, and embroider delicate patterns with an electric sewing machine. By 1996, they had already borrowed $1,000, in two loans from government agencies that support small businesses, and also had a small loan from Lidia's club. Their one-room house-cum- workshop is more spacious and solid than most others in their community. It has brick walls and a roof made of reed matting and plastic. It also has two windows, a small enclosed courtyard, electricity, and a water well.

The Impulso Credit Cooperative

Impulso is a small savings and loan cooperative that specializes in microenterprise financing.[18] It opened for business in 1989, and works almost exclusively in marginal areas that have a high concentration of microenterprises. It is particularly active in La Victoria, one of Lima's largest and most deprived communities where there are more than 6,000 informal clothing workshops.

During its first two years of operations Impulso had difficulty attracting deposits in the hyperinflation environment and its capital was severely eroded. Later on, during the first stages of market liberalization, it found that artisans and traditional microenterprises among its clients were driven out of business by low-priced imports, and the quality of its loan portfolio began to deteriorate.

To deal with these difficulties and generate new business and fee income, Impulso began working with ROSCAs, to mobilize funds and make loans. Impulso calls its ROSCAs *tanamoshi,* the Japanese word for "trust." The *tanamoshi* were introduced in Peru at the beginning of the twentieth century by Japanese immigrants. They used these savings and loan clubs to mobilize funds to start various types of businesses. Impulso's *tanamoshi* have ten members each. As in ROSCAs, members pledge to save a fixed weekly or monthly amount, of the order of $200 to $300, and take turns at borrowing the entire monthly kitty. Turns are allocated by bidding, which involves offering to pay a premium over one's pledged amount. The highest bidder receives the entire amount, which can be as high as $3,000. Repayment is normally within ten months. Impulso guarantees the credit risk on all loans.

This initiative has a number of interesting aspects. First, by managing *tanamoshi* on behalf of their members, Impulso has commercialized what has traditionally been an informal source of credit. It also offers its members a broader range of deposit and lending options and has made it possible for them to earn higher rates of interest on their savings. Second, Impulso's intervention gives protection and added assurance to savers. Thirdly, the bidding process is a way of encouraging thrift and accumulating larger communal savings, since each successful bidder is obliged to save the original amount pledged, plus the premium. Finally, managing the ROSCAs is profitable business: Impulso receives a fee of 2 percent of each rotating fund to administer it and guarantee loan repayments. In mid-1996 it was handling about $50,000 per month in *tanamoshi* funds, and had plans to raise it to about $80,000.

In addition to managing these ROSCAs, Impulso offers other services to the local community, including short-term working-capital credit for microenterprises. Because of the scarcity of loan funds, it can rarely satisfy more than one-fifth of total loan demand, and only lends for three to six months. Impulso also provides basic training on financing and management to microentrepreneurs.

The Rural Savings and Credit Associations

Peru also has a network of Rural Savings and Credit Associations (Cajas Rurales de Ahorro y Credito) that were founded in 1980 to fill the vacuum in the rural financial sector that had been caused by the liquidation of Banco Agrario, the State Agricultural Development Bank.

The mandate of these small rural banks is to serve rural microentrepreneurs. In this they are supported by the Ministry of Agriculture and COFIDE. In 1994 there were nine rural associations with total loans outstanding of $12 million. These savings associations, each of which is controlled by a small group of private shareholders, have suffered from poor management and a lack of governance, and most of them had problems with releasing their paid-up capital. In addition, rather than helping develop rural microenterprises, several rural associations had the same problems as US S&Ls in the 1980s, and made loans to their own shareholders. As is always the case with these types of "insider" loans, arrears and delinquencies are high. The Superintendency of Banks intervened in 1995 in an attempt to deal with these various problems.

Evaluating Peru's Experience

Peru's experience with microfinance is interesting for several reasons. First, the Municipal Savings Banks are unique examples of public-sector financial intermediaries that have successfully adapted to the growing informalization of economic activities and reoriented their lending to accommodate the needs of the informal economy. Second, these institutions have also shown how pawn credit can be a way of turning microfinance into household finance. Third, CARE's programs with women in the poorest shantytowns are edifying examples of empowerment through self-management, and make an interesting contrast with Grameen's method of empowering women through quasi-military discipline—Grameen's regimental methods could never succeed in Latin America.

But Peru also stands out for its authoritarian regime that has enforced market liberalization and fiscal austerity, regardless of the immediate social cost. Yet, the government has rallied to the cause—or, perhaps jumped on the bandwagon—of microenterprise development in a deliberate effort to defuse social discontent over growing inequality of income and widespread poverty. As a first step, it took legislative action to allow financial NGOs to become specialized financial service institutions—EDPYMES—that are dedicated to financing micro and small enterprises. This initiative, which formalizes microfinance programs, and subjects them to the banking law and supervision by the Superintendency of Banks, may help raise the volume of microfinance by leveraging the lenders' resources with deposits.

A second government initiative supports the launch of a new microfinance program, MIBANCO, a dedicated source of credit and financial extension services for low-income microentrepreneurs. MIBANCO's capital will be subscribed by commercial banks and corporations. Third, policy makers are aware that there is a large volume of unusable collateral in the country's marginal communities and shantytowns where informal housing is built on untitled land. This means that some of the businesses that are theoretically "bankable" cannot borrow from commercial banks because untitled and unregistered real estate cannot be used as collateral. The Ministry of Housing estimates the value of the housing stock on untitled land at $20 billion, and has launched a program to regularize and register the property titles of one million households by the year 2000.[19]

Finally, in Lima the mayor is working with the leaders of market vendors and ambulantes to reclaim the capital's historic downtown by relocating all informal traders to a new market complex, close to the center. This marks a break with past practice, when the government used police harassment to expel vendors and stall holders from the center. Moreover, by negotiating with the representatives of the informal sector, the city administration gives them de facto legitimacy.

Notes

1. *La Republica*, Lima, February 11, 1998.
2. *Challenges for Peace, Towards Sustainable Social Development in Peru* (Washington D.C.: Inter-American Development Bank, April 1995), 5.
3. *The Economist*, August 5, 1995.
4. *World Debt Tables 1991–92*, Vol. I, Box 1.5, 25.
5. *Challenges for Peace*, 21.
6. *Challenges for Peace*, 21.
7. *Peru, Land of Opportunities for Micro-Loans* (Lima: ANC-COPEME, 1996), 26.

8. Calvin Sims, *The New York Times*, December 29, 1996. Note: in 1995, after the costly war with Ecuador, growth declined to 7 percent (Marie Arana-Ward, *The Washington Post*, March 19, 1995).

9. Calvin Sims, *The New York Times*, December 29, 1996.

10. Burki and Edwards, *Dismantling the Populist State* (Washington, D.C.: The World Bank, 1996), Table 3, p. 4.

11. Burki and Edwards, *Dismantling the Populist State*, Table 6, p. 8, and Table 8, p. 11.

12. CREDINPET data.

13. The acronym stands for *Entidad de Desarrollo de Pequeñas y Medianas Empresas*. The statute of EPYDMES was defined by a resolution of the central bank of December 23, 1994 (Lima: *El Peruano*, December 24, 1994, page 128173).

14. The acronym stands for *Corporación Financiera para el Desarrollo* (Development Finance Corporation).

15. Decree 191-86 EF, of 1986.

16. There are also savings banks in Lima and Callao. These predate the CMAC, and are not part of it. They are governed by separate laws and decrees.

17. Supreme Decree D.S. 157-90-EF of May 1990, and Legislative Decree 770 of October 30, 1993, which defines the new legal framework for financial institutions and insurance companies.

18. This section is based on information received from Impulso.

19. Data cited by President Fujimori at the Microfinance Summit, in Washington D.C., on February 2, 1997.

Part IV

Experimenting with Microfinance in West Africa

The two chapters in this section review microfinance in West Africa, and analyze it in the context of Guinea.

Chapter 9 begins with an overview of the social and economic environment in West Africa, followed by a general discussion of recent developments in microfinance. As this chapter points out, in rural communities the custom of sharing income in extended families and kinship groups means that microfinance institutions that are already working in a difficult physical environment face the additional burden of dealing with people who are averse to change and experimentation.

Chapter 10 describes the activities of Guinea's two leading microfinance institutions—PRIDE and Crédit Rural de Guinée—both Grameen "adaptations" that belong to the maximalist school of microfinance and are among West Africa's foremost microfinance programs.

9

West Africa: A Region Mired in Poverty

West Africa has a total population of more than 200 million in twenty countries. Nine of them are former French colonies, and, except for Guinea, are also members of the "franc zone."[1] Despite immense mineral wealth and abundant natural resources, all West African countries fall in the World Bank's category of low-income countries with annual per capita income of less than $730. Social indicators are low everywhere, and the social infrastructure is dismal. Illiteracy is almost universal in villages, and health standards are among the worst in the world. African women give birth to more children than women in other parts of the world, and have so little prenatal care that they are more likely to die during childbirth than women in Asia or Latin America. When their children survive, life expectancy at birth remains among the lowest in the world, and more than one-third of the children who live past their first birthday are likely to suffer from malnutrition.[2]

Tuberculosis, malaria, and water-borne diseases are rampant, and, in some countries, AIDS is reaching epidemic proportions—acute malaria causes anemia and often requires blood transfusions that spread AIDS through HIV-contaminated blood.[3]

Poverty is extreme and shows no signs of abating—by the year 2000 more than half of sub-Sahara's population will most likely be living in absolute poverty.[4] In Sierra Leone, West Africa's poorest, war-ravaged country, average daily income is less than 50 US cents, and in Ghana, one of the rare examples of relatively sound economic management, close to two-thirds of the population is living in absolute poverty.[5] Even in Senegal and the Ivory Coast, where average income is the highest, average daily income is still less than $2 and more than half of all people live in absolute poverty.

For sub-Saharan Africa as a whole, average income actually fell by 15 percent between 1975 and 1995, and the combined national incomes of all the countries south of the Sahara, whose population is more that ten times that of France, was just *one-fifth* of France's national income.[6] In the few African countries where income actually grow, the gains are so minimal, and

195

the expanding population grows so rapidly, that there is no perceptible influence on living conditions, except for the elites. Although there are signs of social and political improvement—regional conflicts are slowly coming to an end, and democracy is taking a tentative hold—the region's near-term economic prospects remain grim.

Many of Africa's problems are the legacy of nineteenth-century colonialism, which partitioned the continent with total disregard for ethnic and tribal boundaries. Sporadic outbreaks of tribal fighting, episodes of genocide in Rwanda and Burundi (both former Belgian protectorates), and devastating civil wars often begin as disputes over land rights, and over ethnic and land boundaries that were drawn by treaty between warring colonial powers, or settled by committees in Berlin and Paris. When the colonies finally gained independence during the 1960s, decades of colonial exploitation left them ill-prepared for the tasks ahead. The new nations lacked strong institutions and trained cadres, and had no democratic traditions.

But not all of West Africa's problems and misfortunes can be blamed on colonialism. Excessive population growth, rudimentary infrastructures, and a host of natural calamities add to the general misery, weaken already frail economies, and exacerbate poverty. After independence the former colonies faced an uncertain future, without cadres. They were ruled by ruthless leaders who had fought hard for their people's freedom, but established despotic regimes after independence. These regimes repressed civic movements, violated human rights, implemented misguided economic policies, and wasted public funds on armaments and extravagant projects and monuments of limited economic value.

Africa's new leaders institutionalized corruption, using their power and privilege to enrich themselves and their allies. Corruption is so widespread that it affects people's daily lives at all levels, be it by venal police officers who extract bribes by threatening drivers with hefty fines for imaginary traffic violations, or in state and provincial bureaucracies where one cannot obtain permits of any kind without *dash* (bribes). In extreme cases, such as Zaire's Mobutu (who stole tens of billions of dollars from public enterprises and state coffers and simply arrogated the proceeds of the sales of minerals and diamonds), countries were mired in poverty, while dictators enriched themselves beyond the dreams of avarice.

Overloading Weak Institutional Structures

West Africa's economies are predominantly rural—on average about three-quarters of the economically active population work in agriculture, which accounts for a third or more of national income. Most rural dwellers eke out a livelihood from subsistence crops, petty trading, and handicraft. Farmers' lives are regularly beset by inclement weather—monsoons in the south and west, and desertification on the rim of the Sahara desert—that reduce crop yields and make living conditions precarious. In villages, most people live in reed huts that have no electricity, water, indoor lavatories, or other amenities.

Prolonged neglect of infrastructure makes living conditions in cities even more desolate. Electricity is scarce, and its supply unpredictable, punctuated by frequent brown-outs and black-outs; most roads are garbage-strewn tracks with crater-like potholes that make driving perilous; housing is substandard; there are no sewers; drinking water is of doubtful quality; most street markets are fetid; and crime is rampant.

Outside cities, telephones are rarities—in Guinea, for instance, there is only one telephone for every 433 people. That, and too few surfaced roads, makes communications difficult. Distances between towns and villages are magnified by the time it takes to travel on bush tracks, through forests, or across sand dunes. In tropical coastal zones, the bush tracks that make up most of the road network become dangerous quagmires during the rainy season, and trips that normally take a few hours can stretch into days of slogging through mud. In more arid regions, at the peak of the dry season strong winds and dust storms reduce visibility, and make road conditions equally hazardous.

Like the region as a whole, West Africa has a large external debt. Most of it is owed to the World Bank and bilateral creditors, its sole sources of long-term financing. In 1994, sub-Saharan Africa's debt of $313 billion to bilateral and multilateral agencies amounted to two-and-a-half times the value of exports, and annual debt-servicing payments of $13 billion surpassed the combined budgets for health and primary education.[7] Debt and debt service of that magnitude drain economies that already have little to spare. They also stifle the paltry growth potential because funds that *could* go to infrastructure and poverty reduction are used instead to repay official creditors, at a time those same creditors are cutting their overseas-aid budgets.

Africa's current predicament—lagging development, ever worsening living standards, and rising poverty—is deplorable. It is also difficult to comprehend, given the immense amounts of development assistance that have been siphoned into this continent. Between 1982 and 1995, some thirty sub-Saharan African countries received close to $200 billion in bilateral and multilateral development aid, in more than 160 loans and stabilization programs from the World Bank and IMF.[8]

The debt burden is all the higher because West Africa's poorly educated labor force and hopelessly inadequate infrastructure put it at a considerable disadvantage in the global economy. It is so costly to do business there that it discourages foreign investors and makes African products uncompetitive in world markets. To make matters worse still, most exports consist of low added-value products—mostly tropical fruits, cash crops, and minerals—that have unfavorable terms of exchange with manufactured goods. For their part, the members of the franc zone have the added problem of an overvalued currency—the CFA franc—that makes their exports even less competitive than those of neighboring countries.

Under the circumstances, it is somewhat surprising that the World Bank's 1994 report *Adjustment in Africa* declared that Africa had turned the corner, and that adjustment policies and programs are working and gradually restoring growth.[9] This is at odds with the World Bank's own income statistics for sub-Saharan Africa, and with deteriorating welfare indicators.[10] As one of the critics of the Bank's 1994 report points out:

> The development crisis in Africa is, first and foremost, a crisis of the African state, and through its adjustment programs, the World Bank has overloaded the weak institutional systems in Africa with too many reforms in an inappropriate sequence, further weakening the African state. . . . Growth rates in even the best-performing country, Ghana, are still too low to reduce mass poverty in the medium term.[11]

The failure of development aid in Africa does indeed suggest that aid programs were poorly designed and implemented, and that much of the funding was probably not used as specified. The point is that African countries will only succeed in developing their economies and societies if the initiative comes from within, through good governance, investment in education, less corruption and civil strife, and more open and democratic societies. Foreign development aid can assist this process, but no amount of dollars can make up for a lack of commitment to democracy, and efficient and transparent governance. But, not confident that Africa would find a way out of its predicament, in 1996 the World Bank and IMF announced a joint, ten-year initiative of $25 billion to revive development in Africa.[12] What is certain is that it will add $25 billion to the $313 billion that sub-Saharan Africa already owes to official creditors. But, judging by past experience, unless multilateral development aid is better focused and better adapted to local needs than in the past—and used to promote governance and social priorities—the next decade may be as disappointing as the last two. In the meantime, the IMF's and World Bank's initiative to forgive a part of Africa's external debt, bringing debt service to more sustainable levels, should be pursued, and debt reduction should be conditional on social change and investment in education.

The Perverse Currency Effects of the Franc Zone

The franc zone is a single-currency system that includes all the former French colonies in West and Central Africa, except Guinea—twelve countries in total.[13] Their currency, the CFA franc, is tied to the French franc. From 1956 to 1994 its parity remained unchanged, at one French franc for every 50 CFA francs. For poor African nations, belonging to a stable, multi-country currency zone offers certain advantages, and having a convertible currency is something they could not normally aspire to. Because the CFA franc is a de facto French franc it is fully convertible, can be traded in international currency markets, and has a comparatively stable exchange rate with other European currencies. Maintaining a single currency for several countries also reduces the costs of intra-regional trade by eliminating exchange-rate costs and risks. Finally, a stable exchange rate keeps inflation at bay: until the CFA franc was devalued in 1994, the franc zone enjoyed low inflation that made it the envy of the developing world.

However, belonging to the franc zone carries considerable negative externalities that vastly outweigh those benefits. First of all, maintaining a fixed exchange rate among twelve different countries that are all commodity producers and exporters, some of whose products compete against each other in the same export markets, is an artificial construct. Second, zone countries surrender all control over their monetary policy, which amounts to a loss of sovereignty. West Africa's monetary policy is defined by the Banque de France in Paris, and implemented by the two regional central banks of the franc zone.[14] This means that the exchange rate of the CFA franc against the major international trading and reserve currencies—the US dollar, Japanese yen, and German deutsche mark—is dictated by the monetary and exchange-rate priorities of the French treasury. These are guided by the imperative of keeping the French franc in the European Monetary System, with little regard for the needs of underdeveloped African economies. To wit, during the early 1980s, when the US dollar was weak, and the French franc, Deutsche mark, and other European currencies gained strength, the CFA franc automatically did the same. The problem was that, unlike the French franc, the CFA franc became vastly *over*valued relative to the currencies of other developing countries.

Overvaluation is a relative concept. In mature economies, such as Japan, Germany, and the United States, the appreciation of the national currency against other currencies has little effect on export prices and competitiveness if it is offset by productivity gains. Not so in the commodity-based economies of the franc zone, where the potential for productivity gains is virtually nil. Thus, the prolonged appreciation of the CFA franc distorted relative prices, undermined the competitiveness of exports, and resulted in mounting trade deficits. During the 1980s and early 1990s exports from franc-zone countries to the rest of the world declined. At the same time, the "strong" CFA franc made imports of manufactured goods and luxuries comparatively inexpensive. This created an absurd situation: until 1994 camembert and champagne cost about the same (in French francs) in Abidjan and Dakar as in Paris. This meant that the elite could gorge themselves on fine foods and wines, oblivious to the rising trade deficits. In this Kafka-esque situation the only way West Africa could gain a toehold in the global economy was by importing.

The Parity Adjustment of 1994

By 1994 currency stress was evident and the countries' current-account deficits had become unmanageable. Taking unilateral action, the French central bank and the regional central banks cut the value of the CFA franc by half. While a parity adjustment was necessary and long overdue, cutting the value of the CFA franc by 50 percent in one fell swoop (rather than doing so gradually) had catastrophic results for the majority of the population and did little to improve economic conditions, at least in the short term. The devaluation doubled the price of imports overnight, and cut the value of exports by half. This had an immediate inflationary effect and worsened the terms of trade of member countries: from one day to the next, it took twice as much in exports to pay for a given amount of imports.

The parity adjustment also unleashed fierce competition among countries which were all trying to maximize the short-term gains from their new-found competitiveness. But gaining a competitive edge within the franc zone was not easy. For Senegal, among others, it meant undertaking a radical World Bank adjustment program, and "liberalizing" the labor code, thereby depriving workers in the formal economy of security of employment—so that exporters could reduce wages and make their good more competitive. This unleashed a race to the bottom in the wage economy. Those who lost their jobs turned to the informal sector, while many who still had jobs were forced to moonlight, doing informal work to supplement their meager wages.

Because the franc zone imports many staples, including food, the parity realignment also provoked hardship, impoverishing people who had little to spare and whose purchasing power had dwindled almost overnight, and there were angry mass protests against the devaluation in Senegal, Mali, and other countries.

Even so, nothing had been done to eliminate artificial constraints on the franc zone countries' ability to conduct their economic policies, and let their exchange rates fluctuate in line with internal conditions and export potential. Even after the devaluation of the CFA franc, twelve low-income countries *still* had a single currency tied to the French franc. As pressure mounts on France to meet the Maastricht Treaty conditions for the inclusion of the French franc in the European Union's single currency—the euro—in 1999, the CFA franc will again become overvalued and, sooner or later, another devaluation will repeat what happened in 1994.

Informal Credit: A Challenge for Microfinance

Most West African microfinance institutions work in sparsely populated rural areas, where the terrain is difficult, the climate inclement, and the crumbling infrastructure makes travel hazardous and communications a logistical nightmare. In addition to having to cope with an inhospitable physical environment, microfinance institutions face social obstacles when they work in rural communities where people are reluctant to experiment with new ideas. One of the reasons many people are loath to experiment with formal credit and borrow from financial institutions is that they are accustomed to informal arrangements.

In Africa family groups are the principal sources of credit in rural areas. Family and kinship ties are strong, and, in countries that have no other safety nets, the custom of sharing income and wealth in extended families and kinship groups is an essential support mechanism for the needy. Depending on a family's or an individual's position in society, sharing is a burden or a blessing.

People who have a steady income are duty-bound to share their income with less fortunate kinfolk. When extended families become very large, sharing is crippling. This happens in predominantly Muslim countries, such as Guinea, Mali, or Senegal, where polygamy is still widely practiced, and extended families include the relatives of two, and sometimes three wives. This can add up to a lot of people, and extended families of thirty or more are not uncommon. Sharing one's income with so many others makes it impossible to save and accumulate capital. It constrains people's ability to invest in their own businesses, is an obstacle to job creation in the informal sector, and limits the economic potential of self-employment.

But sharing also conveys social status and prestige. In Conakry, Guinea, a driver for a foreign development agency told me that, because he had a reasonably good income, he and his wife were supporting and feeding twelve relatives and their ten children—twenty-two people in total, some of whom had actually moved in on a semi-permanent basis. This involved a great sacrifice because he already had four young children, but gave him, and his wife, a special place in their village. In other words, the social status which success imparts, more than offsets the "cost" of sharing.[15] There is also a deterrent: reneging on one's duty to provide for less fortunate relatives brings scorn and opprobrium.

For people at the receiving end, belonging to a kinship network offers protection and security during hard times, if better-off relatives can give them a job or lend them a little money at favorable terms to start a small business. But noblesse oblige: as soon as poverty-stricken recipients are out of the rut, it is their turn to become benefactors to others.

Beyond sharing in family groups, there is also a tradition of self-help credit and savings associations: the *tontines* and *susus*, Francophone Africa's equivalents of ROSCAs, and logical extensions of kinship networks. While sharing within families is essentially a rural custom, *tontines* are more developed in cities and towns than in villages. But, ever-increasing rural poverty and an unstoppable tide of urban migration are spreading the rural custom of sharing and providing to urban areas, and impoverished rural migrants impose on relatives who migrated before them.

Belonging to a *tontine* is a useful fallback for those in need of credit. They can postpone borrowing from friends and relatives, and keep kinship support as a last resort—it will always be there when in dire need. An added advantage is that *tontines* make it possible to accumulate savings, out of reach of needy friends and kin. In Western Africa it is not uncommon for people to belong to more than one *tontine* so that they can leverage their borrowing power, and informal credit channels commonly outperform urban and rural microfinance programs. In Senegal, with $125 million in loans outstanding, the volume of *tontine* lending in 1993 was almost *thirty times larger* than that of the country's leading microfinance program.[16]

Microfinance in West Africa

In 1996 there were around 130 active microfinance programs, or about one-third the number of Latin American programs.[17] Most are of recent vintage and rooted in village tradition, relying on the support and approval of village elders and local elites to gain credibility and the confidence of rural communities. This makes microfinance build on consensus, maintaining the social status quo in villages.

What is striking is that group credit and peer-group guarantees fit well in the African custom of sharing within kinship networks. It also blends well into village traditions. Hence the appeal of village banks that follow FINCA's model. The largest village-bank network is Mali's Caisses Villageoises du Pays Dogon. FONGS in Senegal, a grouping of farmers' associations, combines some of the features of village banks with those of *tontines* and has some 40,000 active borrowers. There also are a few Grameen replicators, such as Sahel Action in Burkina Faso, and Crédit Rural and PRIDE in Guinea. Sahel Action, which follows the Grameen model most closely, was established in 1988 with the help of the French Government. Like its model, it lends exclusively to groups of impoverished rural women and does poverty lending, its loans averaging $48. In 1995 it was active in two hundred villages and had close to 30,000 active clients. After FECECAM (see below) and FONGS it has the largest outreach in West Africa.[18]

One general observation is that virtually all rural programs work in inhospitable environments, sparsely populated areas, with high operating costs and limited outreach. In extreme cases it can cost one dollar to lend a dollar. In such circumstances, programs can only survive with donor support. In 1996, only a handful of West African rural microfinance programs had more than 10,000 clients, and only a few institutions—including Benin's Federation of Rural Savings Banks (FECECAM), a federation of credit unions with a combined membership of close to 200,000—could reasonably hope to become financially and institutionally sustainable.

Donor grants and external funding cover the programs' operating costs and supplement clients' limited savings capacity. Major "northern" agencies that support microfinance in West Africa include USAID, the European Union, and the governments of Canada, Germany, and France. Several major northern NGOs, such as CARE, OXFAM, Christian Aid, Save the Children, and CRS are also involved, managing and providing funding for local microfinance programs.

Some donors also finance basic training for the clients of the microenterprise programs that they support. For instance, in PRIDE, which offers advanced courses to its best clients, course fees are more than they can afford and are partly covered by USAID. Other microlenders use donor funds to cover the cost of social, non-financial programs. Donors can justify doing so on social grounds since health standards, literacy, and school enrollment are usually higher in households of people who belong to microfinance programs that offer business training and emphasize social intermediation, than in households belonging to minimalist programs.

The biggest urban microfinance programs are ACEP, a Senegalese credit union, and PRIDE in Guinea. Both have the advantage of working in an environment with better infrastructure, and can be more selective in deciding to whom to lend, since NGOs and informal sources cover the financing needs of the poorest in urban settings.

What is striking is that, like in Latin America, credit unions are widely represented in West Africa. In many countries they are the principal sources of formal rural credit and financial intermediation between rural borrowers and savers—about two-thirds of all rural lending is done by credit unions.[19] The reason this corporate and legal structure is so prevalent in Francophone Africa is that it was introduced there by French and French-Canadian credit unions. France's Crédit Agricole and Canada's Caisse Desjardins provide financial and technical support to their counterparts in West Africa. Crédit Mutuel of Senegal and Guinea (the institutions are not related) are among the region's largest credit unions.

Following the principle of mutuality, credit unions are either occupation-based, or gender-based. There are credit unions for fishermen, school teachers, public servants, and farmers. Benin has a Women's Urban Savings Association, and Gambia a Women's Finance Association. As was shown in Chapter 3, the main drawbacks of the credit-union model are that it emphasizes savings over credit, offers only short-term loans, and lends only to members in limited multiples of their savings. This constrains the volume of lending, and makes credit unions uncompetitive and ill-suited for all but grassroots support to the smallest microenterprises. Furthermore, mutuality can create governance problems. On the other hand, through their voting power, members control their credit unions, and the emphasis on savings encourages thrift and makes credit unions less dependent on external funding.

In 1996, West Africa's regional central bank, BCEAO, drafted new guidelines to regulate the activities of credit unions in the franc zone. They include criteria for the accreditation, supervision and recognition of credit unions as specialized financial institutions, governed by the banking law. If these guidelines become a template for microfinance programs throughout the franc zone, imposing the credit-union model will stifle financial innovation and competition by making it more difficult to operate outside the prescribed model. Moreover, if franc-zone countries are forced to comply with interest-rate ceilings under the laws on usury (an annual rate of 16 percent in 1996), microfinance programs will be obliged to introduce hidden fees and forced savings in order to cover their operating costs.

Benin's FECECAM is an interesting example of a national network of rural credit unions. It began in 1975, and by 1986 there were close to one hundred local credit unions in Benin. In 1987, the system's first apex—CNCA

(Caisse Nationale de Crédit Agricole)—went into liquidation after making heavy losses. In 1998, the system completed a ten-year rehabilitation program. FECECAM is the new apex and technical secretariat for all the affiliated credit unions. It works through a middle tier of seven regional unions, each of which offers support services to between nine and ten local rural credit unions. By 1998, the FECECAM network consisted of sixty-two local credit unions, each with its own staff and management. The apex and the regional unions are funded by donors. The local unions accept deposits from members and non-members, from which loans are funded.

The affiliated credit unions have close to 190,000 members—the largest membership of any financial institution in Africa—and more than 200,000 depositors. Loans outstanding in 1996 exceeded $18 million, compared with deposits of about $27 million, with non-member deposits representing 20 percent of all deposits. Except for a program of small loans to groups of women, FECECAM credit unions do not lend to the poorest.

Notes

1. West Africa is comprised of Benin, Burkina Faso, Cameroon, Cape Verde, Cote d'Ivoire, Gabon, Gambia, Ghana, Guinea, Guinea-Bissau, Equatorial Guinea, Liberia, Mali, Mauritania, Niger, Nigeria, Sao Tome & Principe, Senegal, Sierra Leone, and Togo.
2. OXFAM International Position Paper, 11.
3. Robert D. Kaplan, *The Ends of the Earth* (New York: Vintage Books, 1996), 18.
4. OXFAM International Position Paper, *Multilateral Debt, the Human Cost*, 1996, 11.
5. *World Bank News,* April 20, 1995.
6. Nicholas Woodsworth, "Black Man's Burden," *Financial Times*, February 14–15, 1998.
7. Barbara Crossette, *The New York Times,* March 17, 1996.
8. *The Oxfam Poverty Report*, OXFAM, Oxford, 1995, Introduction.
9. *Adjustment in Africa, Reforms, Results and the Road Ahead* (Washington, D.C.: The World Bank, 1994).
10. *WDR 96,* pp. 188 and 196, and *African Development Indicators, 1996* (Washington, D.C.: The World Bank, 1996), 6.
11. Nguyuru H. I. Lipumba, *Africa Beyond Adjustment*, Policy Essay No. 15 (Washington D.C.: Overseas Development Council, 1994), 13 and 17.
12. Barbara Crosette, *The New York Times*, March 17, 1996.
13. The franc zone is divided into two groups of former French colonies, in West and Central Africa respectively, each of which has its own regional central bank. Notionally there are two distinct CFA francs, with separate coinage and bank notes, but identical exchange rates.
14. In West Africa it is called the Banque Centrale des Etats d'Afrique Occidentale (BCEAO).
15. Graeme Buckley "Microfinance in Africa: Is It Either the Problem or the Solution?" in *World Development 25*, no. 7 (1997), 1089.
16. See Leila Webster and Peter Fidler, *The Informal Sector and Microfinance Institutions in West Africa* (Washington, D.C.: The World Bank, 1995), 162–

63.
17. *An Inventory of Microfinance Institutions in Western and West Central Africa* (Washington, D.C.: The World Bank, January 1997), 15–18, and *A Worldwide Inventory of Microfinance Institutions* (Washington, D.C.: The World Bank, July 1996).
18. Webster and Fidler, 191 et seq.
19. *An Inventory of Microfinance Institutions*, 10.

10

Blending Microfinance with Training:
Lessons from Guinea

With a population of 6.5 million, Guinea is slightly smaller than Oregon. It is located on the Atlantic coast between Guinea-Bissau and Senegal to the north, and Sierra Leone and the Ivory Coast to the south. There are four distinct geographical regions: maritime Guinea, the coastal plain where most people live; middle Guinea, which consists of a huge semi-arid savanna; high Guinea in the mountainous interior; and *Guinée forestière* (forest Guinea), which has what remains of the fast-shrinking tropical rain forest.

The tropical climate has two seasons—a dry season from December to May, and a monsoon-like rainy season from June to November. During the monsoon torrential downpours cause frequent and extensive flooding in the coastal plain. In the dry season, gusting winds whip up dust clouds, making travel on bush tracks hazardous.

The capital, Conakry, is the country's main ocean port and economic hub. The city is on a long, narrow peninsula that juts out into the Atlantic. The small downtown has the usual cluster of modern office buildings, embassies, and hotels, and a small residential area with heavily guarded private villas. The rest of Conakry is a sprawling shantytown where endless road works wreak havoc with traffic. Guinea generates its power from hydro-energy. This means that there is virtually no electricity during the dry season, but there are frequent brownouts and blackouts, even during the rainy season. For people whose dwellings have no electricity this is a moot point. At night only the hotels, private residences, and the airport are lit, and use generators as back up. From dusk to dawn the rest of the city is shrouded in darkness, punctuated only by the flickering lights of the candles, wood fires, and oil lamps that people use to illuminate their houses and businesses. This creates an eerie atmosphere. It also makes driving unsafe because people dart back and forth across roads in the smoke-filled nights, totally oblivious to the oncoming traffic.

But Conakry is not devoid of charm. There is a refreshing ocean breeze, and by day the city is a riot of colors, with streets and alleys lined with tropical hardwood trees, fruit trees, and flowering shrubs. As one longtime resident puts it:

> Conakry's ugliness is still punctuated by flashes of intense beauty, unexpected encounters with nature, and glimpses of African tradition: the mountains of Grecariah seen across the ocean on a clear day, fruit bats descending on the mango trees, like the flying monkeys of the Wizard of Oz; the subtleties of this melting pot of cultures. But it's going fast, turning into a cheap imitation of every other big city. I'm told that in the fifties deer and even big cats would stray into Minière (a Conakry neighborhood) where I now live. Now, almost every square inch is walled, right onto the streets, which we are impatient to have paved. Conakry, not a town that can afford to lose much more charm, is doing its best to modernize away all that is interesting and beautiful.[1]

A Mineral-Rich, but Poor Country

This is a poor country where most people live in villages. As in other parts of Africa, their dwellings are simple huts. Firewood is their only domestic fuel. Deforestation, soil erosion, and creeping desertification are reaching critical levels and, in many parts of the country, gathering a day's supply of firewood is becoming increasingly difficult and time consuming. Most days women must walk miles to garner wood, which they carry on their heads in big bundles.

Social indicators are dismal: life expectancy at birth—about forty-four years—is one of world's lowest, while the rate of illiteracy is among the highest. This is not surprising in a country where school enrollment is low, and actually declined in secondary education during the 1980s. In 1980, enrollment rates were 10 percent for girls, and 24 percent for boys. By 1993, only 6 percent of girls and 17 percent of boys were attending secondary schools. In 1998, close to 80 percent of all women and 50 percent of men aged fifteen and over could not read or write, and in most villages everyone was illiterate.

Rapid population growth (2.7 percent) and low life expectancy make for a young country: close to half of all Guineans are less than fifteen years old. Population growth has also been fueled by more than half a million refugees who fled bloody civil wars in neighboring Liberia and Sierra Leone, and by the practice of polygamy in this country where 85 percent of the population are Muslims. Polygamy is legal and still widely practiced, particularly in villages, where more than one-third of all households are polygamous. It is not uncommon for men to have three or four wives and twenty or so children, and even the country's President has three wives.

French is the official language, but most older people only speak their native tongues, mainly Peuhl, Malinké, and Soussou. This makes for an extremely low-skilled labor force since few workers have enough skills and education to work in modern industrial and commercial enterprises.

Guinea is a typical case of poor physical and social infrastructure that marginalizes the country in the global economy and hinders its growth potential. Even at the best of times the rudimentary road network makes internal travel cumbersome. For most people, traveling involves taking a ride in a *taxi de brousse* (bush taxi). These are mostly battered Peugeot station wagons that are well into their ninth lives. Heavily laden with far too many passengers and roof racks piled high with suitcases, crates, live chickens, and goats, these jalopies ply the pot-holed roads and tracks at break-neck speed, with total disregard for road conditions or their passengers' comfort.

The economy is still predominantly rural. Agriculture accounts for 40 percent of national income and agro-industrial plantations are the sole sources of wage labor in rural areas. The main export cash crops are bananas, oranges, other tropical fruits, coffee, palm products, and fish.

But, given its abundant mineral resources and considerable agricultural and hydroelectric potential, Guinea should not be poor. It has more than a quarter of the world's known bauxite deposits; is one of the largest producers and exporters of processed bauxite (alumina); and has substantial diamond, gold, uranium, and iron ore deposits. Exports of minerals and alumina account for roughly one-quarter of national income and 85 percent of export revenues. The country's industrial base consists mostly of mining. The huge bauxite mines in Fria, about fifty miles from Conakry, were developed by the former USSR, as part of a Guinean-Soviet trade agreement that involved bartering Guinea's bauxite for third-rate Soviet machine tools and industrial equipment. The mines and the alumina processing plants, which are now operated by French and US companies, are a modern enclave with a small labor aristocracy of skilled workers and expatriate managers, in an otherwise backward economy.

Most industrial and service enterprises—the bauxite industry, Conakry's international airport, the telephone company, the handful of factories that produce processed foods and metal products, and the hotel industry—are controlled or managed by foreign, mostly French, corporations. This is a source of resentment and the dominant presence of the country's former colonial rulers in industry, commerce, and services, as well as through countless advisers and consultants, is eliciting the snide, but not totally unwarranted, comment that "the whites are back."[2] In fact, France's neo-colonial influence in Guinea is fairly recent. It only resumed after the government abandoned central planning in the late 1980s. Before that Guinea had Soviet advisors and consultants.

Naturally, the French cannot be blamed for the country's lagging performance during the era of Soviet-style central planning. The return of the French actually had a positive impact, filling the vacuum in bilateral aid after the collapse of the Soviet Union abrogated Guinean-Soviet cooperation. What is to be blamed is that French and other foreign companies repatriate most of their profits and make few new investments in Guinea.

This creates a paradox: despite its vast mineral wealth and exports, Guinea is a highly indebted low-income country that spends an inordinate proportion of its export earnings to service an external debt that almost trebled from 1980 to 1994. By 1995, when average daily per capita income was a paltry $1.50, the external debt amounted to $491 for every man, woman, and child.[3] Growth is also insignificant. From 1985 to 1994 the economy grew by a mere 1.3 percent per year, less than half of what is needed to prevent a steady erosion of living standards and create jobs for new entrants in the labor market. Surprisingly, income distribution is less skewed than elsewhere in Africa. For instance, in Senegal, where per capita income is considerably higher than in Guinea, twice as many people (54 percent) live in absolute poverty as in Guinea (26 percent).[4]

There are no reliable employment data. But, judging by the large numbers of idle men of working age one sees at any time of the day, milling around, doing nothing, the level of urban unemployment is staggering. While this gives the impression that even the informal sector is saturated and cannot absorb the idle men, there is a more plausible explanation, namely that, in cities, unemployed men simply squander their time, letting the women earn a living, selling goods in open-air markets, or running small informal businesses. Indeed, there are no idle women anywhere.

For those who have jobs, wages are low, particularly in the public sector. As is to be expected, corruption is rife and has reached epidemic proportions among petty officials who try to supplement their pitiful incomes with baksheesh (bribes). Bribe taking is commonplace in the customs service and among the "forces of law and order." Most days, private cars, taxis, and buses must run a gauntlet of police officers who routinely stop the traffic in cities and on main roads, demanding "presents." One day, while riding in a private car in Conakry, I rolled down the window, pointing my camera at two burly policemen who were "talking" to a taxi driver. Noticing what I was up to, the driver became quite agitated, and warned me of the distressing consequences of my actions if the policemen saw me taking their photograph. When in Rome . . . , I immediately tucked away my camera.

The Informal Economy and Microfinance

Informal activities hold a virtual monopoly on small-scale production, trade and services. Unofficial estimates are that four out of every five economically active people do informal work, either full time, or as a secondary occupation. The total output of the informal sector is estimated at close to two-thirds of national income, growing at almost twice the rate of the rest of the economy. Like almost everywhere, informal work is highly feminized. In villages men are often away from home for long spells, working on plantations and in mines, or hustling for casual work in Conakry, and women are the main bread winners. They work the land in subsistence farms, and look after children and the elderly. In cities some women find work as maids for the urban elites and expatriates. But most others have low-productivity "feminine" activities, selling food and dry goods in open-air markets and on the

streets; making clothes; weaving baskets; and cooking in neighborhood eateries. While their presence in the informal sector is overwhelming, women's
participation in the wage economy is negligible, except in the lowest-paying
jobs in the public sector, or as hotel chambermaids and office cleaners.

The World Bank ascribes the preponderance of informal activities to the
legacy of central planning.[5] While it is true that black markets have always
been an inherent feature of centrally planned economies, this does not explain
why the informal economy is still expanding, accounting for the bulk of job
creation and for the largest share of economic activity, more than ten years
after central planning was abandoned. Moreover, today's informal sector is a
far cry from what one expects to finds under central planning: it is legal and
supported by donor-funded microfinance programs. The actual causes of the
predominant place of informality in the economy are high population growth;
a labor force that is largely unskilled and mostly illiterate; and a "modern"
sector that consists almost exclusively of capital-intensive extractive industries and agro-industry that do not reinvest their profits or create new jobs.

Given the huge size of its informal sector Guinea has surprisingly few
active microfinance programs. Two of these are NGOs—the African
Development Foundation and Opportunities Industrialization Centers
International"; two are credit unions—Crédit Mutuel de Guinée and Crédit
Rural; and one is a PRIDE, a USAID-sponsored NGO.[6] All five have their
headquarters in Conakry, and all but PRIDE and Crédit Rural are active in
the capital. The rest of this chapter is devoted to reviewing the activities of the
last two institutions.

PRIDE: A Successful Program Built on an Experiment

PRIDE[7] was launched in 1991 as an experimental microfinance program
with a $6 million grant from USAID. Volunteers in Technical Assistance (VITA),
an NGO that is based in Arlington, Virginia, was the implementing agency. As
a donor-funded program PRIDE is a de facto NGO. This means that it is not
a licensed financial institution, and that it cannot accept deposits from its
clients. The first office was opened in 1992 in Mamou, a busy market town
and business center in the interior, about 120 miles southwest of Conakry. By
1996, PRIDE had branches and agencies in Guinea's four geographic regions.

This program works with urban microentrepreneurs. It incorporates some
of the features of the Grameen Bank, which it has adapted to Guinea's social
structures. PRIDE adopted peer-group lending from Crédit Rural, the country's
other major microfinance institution—and part-replicator of Grameen's group
credit—with which it cooperates closely. All clients are organized into groups
of five members. The groups are self-standing, and there are no multi-group
centers. Moreover, the groups can be of mixed gender, and, unlike Grameen
or Crédit Rural, PRIDE works exclusively in urban and peri-urban zones.
Contacts with clients always take place in branch offices, and, except for training courses, are conducted on an individual basis.

Credit screening and client selection are based on sound, common-sense prudential principles. Before a loan can be approved there must be an appraisal visit to each prospective borrower. As soon as a loan has been disbursed the credit officer must check that the funds have been utilized as agreed. Thereafter, all credit officers and branch managers maintain close relations with their clients, with at least one visit per month to all active clients.

PRIDE lends only to Guinean citizens who are at least eighteen years old. The citizenship condition serves to screen out applicants who are refugees from Sierra Leone and Liberia, who could be tempted to take the money and run after receiving a loan. All the members of a group must live in the same neighborhood, but may not be related to each other. They must be able to understand and sign simple loan documents. The client and credit mix are representative of the urban informal sector. Two-thirds of PRIDE's clients are women. The bulk of lending is for petty trading and market vending, followed by food processing and traditional crafts.

The key stage in the credit-screening sequence is that each new client must be declared creditworthy and honorable by a member of his or her "neighborhood supervisory committee" (*conseil de surveillance*). Each committee has five members who are elected by PRIDE's active clients in their neighborhood. Committee members, who can also be PRIDE clients, are usually established merchants, school teachers, and police officers, and are the neighborhood elite. As regards PRIDE, their tasks consist in referring and recommending new clients (they receive no commission), and co-signing the loan documents of each client they have referred or vetted. Doing so does not imply co-guaranteeing, but is a way of exerting moral suasion on borrowers.

PRIDE has zero tolerance for late payments—any loan repayment that is overdue by even as little as twenty-four hours is considered in arrears—and is one of the handful of programs that can claim genuine zero arrears. On the other hand, insistence on favorable recommendations from neighborhood committees has tinges of social control, and detracts from the poverty focus. Indeed, unlike Grameen's Muhammad Yunus, who often says that people who own the least need loans the most, PRIDE's management has a more conservative stance: to qualify for a loan people must already own a business, no matter how small.

Credit and Savings Services

Loan maturities range from six to twelve months, depending on a borrower's income. First-time borrowers qualify only for six-month loans, a sensible precaution that is also used by other microfinance programs. All loans are repaid in equal monthly installments after one month's grace period. Monthly installments have the advantage of giving borrowers more time to accumulate cash, but loan performance is more difficult to monitor than in the weekly repayment schedules of Grameen and other programs.

All loans are at an annual interest rate of 24 percent. After including the "cost" of forced savings, an initiation fee of FG2,000 (about $40), and training fees (see below), the actual cost to borrowers is more than 40 percent. This is high, but less than it costs to borrow from Crédit Rural and Crédit Mutuel. Long-term clients with spotless repayment records and good business potential can graduate from group credit to individual loans. These loans have two-year maturities, and can be for up to $5,000—nine times the average per capita income. Personal loans require formal guarantees and collateral. At the end of March 1996 all but two branch offices had made such loans.

PRIDE uses forced savings of 4 percent of loan amounts, both as a form of loan guarantee, and to encourage its clients to save. The savings are placed in guaranteed funds that are pooled among borrower groups by neighborhood or locality. The funds offer safeguards against defections and arrears by other group members. Withdrawals are permitted only if people opt out of the program, or move to another town or neighborhood. As an additional precaution, 1 percent of each loan is placed in a group solidarity fund that strengthens ties within groups and gives co-guarantors protection against the financial consequences of other members' deaths, serious injuries, or other events that impair their loan repayment capacity. Both funds must be placed on deposit with a commercial bank, and carry interest at below-market rates.

In 1996, PRIDE had plans to become a licensed financial institution so that it could accept client deposits. It had begun training branch personnel on deposit taking and accounting, and was getting ready to launch a pilot program of passbook savings in its four main branches. The intention was to set the interest rate on passbook savings below that on savings accounts at commercial banks, on the assumption that small depositors are more concerned with safety and liquidity than yield. On this point, PRIDE's reasoning is the same as that of BRI's village units, which pay lower interest rates on deposits from rural clients than on those from urban clients.

Teaching Clients How to Succeed in Business

One of the keys of PRIDE's success is that it integrates credit with training. Because so many Guineans are illiterate, people must take a basic training course (*formation de base*) to qualify for a loan. This coaches them on loan procedures and conditions; assists in group formation; teaches the rudiments of group discipline and responsibilities; and explains what it means to borrow for self-employment—all loans must be repaid. Basic training is in two two-hour training sessions, and is free of charge. At the end of the course there is a simple test. People who do not attend the course or pass the test are automatically disqualified.

All active borrowers, regardless of the number of loans they have received, must enroll in follow-up training (*formation continue*) during each loan cycle. This training is designed to improve their business skills, productivity, and earning power. At first, this too was free. In 1995, PRIDE began charging a fee of $4 per six-month loan cycle, and clients must pay the fee regardless of their attendance. The reasoning being that, if a course is a "free good," people will attend, but not necessarily be attentive. But if they must part company with money they develop a sense of ownership: the course becomes "theirs." There is another incentive to attend: clients who consistently fail to show up run the risk of becoming ineligible for further loans and of being forced out of the program. The result: participation, which was sporadic when training was free, has been close to 100 percent since 1995.

Finally, there is an optional advanced business training (*ateliers sur l'esprit d'entreprise*) to hone the entrepreneurial skills of upper-tier clients who qualify for medium-term individual loans. The advanced courses were designed by North American consultants, who prepared the course material. They also ran the first workshops in Conakry and trained PRIDE's in-house instructors. Advanced training lasts twelve days—which is a lot for microentrepreneurs—in groups of twenty to thirty-five participants.

Clients can apply directly. Others are nominated by their credit officers. All are screened at pre-enrollment registration interviews to make sure that they will benefit from participating. The hefty course fees—they range from $95 to $240, depending on whether workshops are held in a regional language or in French—and time-commitment involved in attending these workshops are additional self-screening devices. Because people who elect to join a French-language course are literate by definition, they receive written course material. (The higher fees for these courses cover the cost of the course material.) Since the fees do not recover the full cost of organizing the workshops, these advanced courses are partly funded with a grant from USAID. On the whole, communication is better, and the participants' enthusiasm greater in ethnic-language workshops.

By May 1996, more than 1,000 clients had already graduated from advanced workshops. Credit officers do post-training interviews to find out if their clients have benefited from the training. Participants' comments are taken into account to fine-tune course content. The general feedback is that the courses give participants the confidence to expand their businesses and become more productive. Some of the people I talked with in branch offices said that they were making more money than before, and that their businesses had expanded to the point that they had hired more helpers. Some graduates of advanced training even said that their businesses had become so large that they had become small enterprises in the formal sector, and had begun paying taxes—the ultimate accolade for someone who began at the bottom of the ladder. Although these conversations took place in the presence of branch credit officers, I had no reason to doubt that those clients were telling anything but the truth.

A Day in a Branch Office

PRIDE's offices are busy places on any day of the week. The atmosphere is always casual, more that of a community center or social club than a mini-bank. Oftentimes, people mill around in the street in front of the building, chatting and exchanging notes about their businesses. It is much the same inside, where staff always greet their clients effusively like old friends, and call everybody by their first names. The training courses I observed all had much jollity and enthusiastic participation by men and women. The general atmosphere is totally different from the restrained and disciplined tone of Grameen's center meetings. Indeed, one could not begin to imagine that Guinean women should stand at attention, make military-style greetings, or recite slogan. If they had to, it would become yet another excuse for merriment.

Because there is no, or, at best, unreliable electricity, office technology is rudimentary. Bookkeeping is done by hand in old-fashioned ledgers, and the weekly activity reports for head offices are typed on manual typewriters. Only a handful of branches have electricity generators and telephones, and only Conakry has desktop computers. To communicate with each other, and with Conakry, the branches use battery-powered short-wave radios. When distances are beyond a radio's range, other intermediate offices relay the messages.

In Mamou I visited PRIDE's oldest branch. At that time it had close to seven hundred clients, many of whom were long-standing borrowers who had taken advanced training. Loans averaged $200 per client. During my visit a follow-up training workshop was in full progress. As it happened, the course was in French, and I could sit in and ask questions form the twenty-odd participants, some of whom were already in their third loan cycle. Later on, I went to their market stalls and workshops, most of which were located in the nearby central market. Many of the clients I called on were women who owned tiny garment workshops, sidewalk eateries, and market stalls.

One of them owned a restaurant in the central market. She used bottled gas to cook and had a gas-powered refrigerator, which she had bought with a $500 loan. It was market day and she was doing a brisk business selling cold drinks and rice-and-meat dishes to an early lunchtime crowd. The restaurant was immaculately clean, its wall painted in cheerful colors. There were about a dozen Formica tables, each with a random selection of chairs. The shiny new refrigerator took pride of place in this small establishment, and the customers were complimenting the owner on her recent acquisition.

Most of the women I visited were working by themselves; only the restaurant owner had a young helper. She was one of PRIDE's first clients, and, after repaying her current loan, was about to graduate to a medium-term individual loan. She had been told that she would have to assign title to her gas stove, refrigerator, and restaurant furniture, as collateral for the loan. Other clients I saw in Mamou were barbers, and owners of mechanical repair shops. They all spoke highly of the local branch office.

The next day, I accompanied PRIDE's general manager, Paul Rippey, to the newest branch, in Dalaba. Unlike Mamou, this was a one-man agency, a sub-branch of a larger office in nearby Labé. Dalaba is a charming provincial hill town. Because it is much cooler than Conakry it was the favorite summer retreat of the French during the colonial era, and the town has many handsome French-style villas, one of which had become the home of PRIDE's office.

In mid-1996, six months after it had begun lending, it already had 220 clients. Loans averaged $100 per client. All but a few of its clients were first-time borrowers, some of whom had loans of as little as $25.

When we arrived in Dalaba, the office was a hive of activity, on the last day of an advanced workshop. Three instructors were working with a group of about thirty-five local men and women, using flip charts and graphics to sum up the key points of the course and "test" the participants. The workshop was conducted in Peuhl, the region's language. I could not understand what was being said but, judging by the convivial atmosphere and the participants' enthusiasm, it had been a great success. The lead instructor, a former manager of Crédit Rural, was an agricultural engineer with a Ph.D. from the University of Leningrad. (When Guinea had close ties with the USSR many students received scholarships to study in the Soviet Union.) He was also a graduate of the Grameen Trust "replicator training program" in Dhaka.

In keeping with Guinea's high level of informal activities, the workshop had created a temporary business opportunity for some local women. Five of them were waiting outside the building with pots of steaming rice, meat and vegetables, and a huge pile of plates. As soon as the course broke up for lunch, the participants gathered on the patio outside the office and bought their lunches from the impromptu caterers.

Judging PRIDE by Its Results

Given its short history this program has achieved a lot. In 1996 it had eight full branch offices and four sub-branches, and was active in Guinea's four regions. Loan disbursements and the number of clients had grown by 80 percent during 1995, after doubling in 1994. In 1995, cumulative loan disbursements reached $6 million, in 25,000 loans to 16,000 clients, and there was $1.1 million in loans outstanding, making it one of the largest microfinance programs in West Africa. The median loan size was $240—roughly 40 percent of per capita income—with individual loans ranging from $25 to $600.

• *Institutional sustainability*: VITA, the implementing agency, has vast experience, managing microfinance programs in several African countries—it has programs in Benin, Chad, Guinea, Madagascar, and South Africa, and launched a new USAID-financed program in Morocco in 1996. This has contributed to this project's success. VITA had trained a strong and capable Guinean management team, and in 1997 the expatriate general manager, Paul Rippey, handed over his functions the Guinean deputy general manager. All senior staff are university graduates. Following Grameen's example, they receive on-the-job training in field offices before beginning their field assignments. Salaries compare favorably with those in the private sector. This fosters loyalty and dedication and reduces staff turnover.

As in all decentralized credit programs there is a risk of fraud, and PRIDE has not been immune to it. In 1995 one of its branch managers had colluded with the manager of a local bank to embezzle close to $50,000 by booking phantom loans. As soon as this was discovered, PRIDE took the matter to court, and the two men were awaiting trial in June 1996. The manner in which this was dealt with, and the fact that PRIDE had taken both culprits to court shows institutional maturity.

In 1996 PRIDE was exploring a number of alternatives to anchor its sustainability through a process of "institutionalization." One approach, which was subsequently rejected, was to turn each branch into an independent, legally autonomous credit cooperative, based on the French mutualist model, and make the Conakry head office the system's apex. There was also work in progress to begin lending to clients in Conakry. By the turn of the century PRIDE expects to have a total of seventeen branches, including at least two in Conakry, and to triple the amount of loans outstanding. This is an ambitious target.

• *Financial sustainability*: There is a shadow cost of capital of 15 percent for all operations, and PRIDE has developed an efficient internal accounting and management-information system to track its operating costs and financial results. By 1996, full cost recovery was within reach, and the program was already recovering more than 90 percent of its operating costs, excluding the salaries of expatriate staff and the cost of capital. Moreover, while most other West African microfinance programs have low staff productivity, this program's average client load of about 180 per credit officer puts it well within the norms of microfinance. Zero tolerance for arrears and remarkable repayment rates are other solid indicators of financial maturity. The target is that all the branch offices should at least break even, and that the larger ones become profitable by the turn of the century, with increased outreach, more efficient procedures, and lower operating costs.

Crédit Rural de Guinée:
A Bank Rooted in Village Tradition

Crédit Rural is an adaptation of the Grameen model, and all its senior staff are graduates of Grameen's training institute in Dhaka. They have adapted their mentor's group loans and social collateral to conditions in rural Guinea. All loans are to single-gender groups of five, but there are no centers. The groups are self-selecting, organized by the villagers themselves, and the bank's highly decentralized management structure is rooted in the traditions and social structures of village life. Each local office has a staff of two—a manager and a credit office. Each branch is supervised by a five-member supervisory committee (*conseil de surveillance*). Each village committee is chaired by the village chief. The other members are elected by the villagers. The committees make recommendations on loan amounts and must vouch for the creditworthiness of new clients.

During its start-up phase this institution received technical assistance from IRAM, a French NGO that promotes alternative development strategies. It began lending in 1989 as an IRAM pilot project. Since the early 1990s it has worked under the auspices of the Ministry of Agriculture, extending credit to the rural poor, and promoting rural development adapted to village culture. It is a pillar of village life. In early 1996 it had fifty-two offices, in some of the most remote villages of Guinea's four regions. Its 40,000 clients affectionately call it *la banque de la brousse* ("the bush bank"). In 1996 Crédit Rural had more than $3 million in loans outstanding. Its business targets for the end of 1997 were 60,000 clients, and sixty village offices.

Market Day in Banguya

On a hot, busy market day in June 1996, I visited the newest and smallest cooperative, in Banguya, a small village in the coastal zone. Banguya is at the end of a thirty-mile long bumpy bush track. On market days, men and women from far-away villages and hamlets come to Banguya to sell their wares. Most set out before dawn, sometimes walking more than ten miles, carrying bundles of vegetables and other goods they hope to sell. Others come to the weekly markets to buy cows, chickens, goats, household wares, and clothes.

The "market square" is a clearing in the center of the village, where the vendors display their wares and animals. They are clustered around an enormous, hundred-year old baobab tree.

The Banguya office is on the edge of the market, where most clients have their businesses. It is a modest, spotless two-room office. By mid-1996 it had 155 clients in thirty-one groups of five members. The Banguya office has a small grant from a Belgian NGO, which it uses to teach villagers the basics of joint-liability borrowing and give them basic skills' training. The office has no electricity or telephone, but like in many other rural microfinance programs, the credit officer had an all-terrain motorbike to visit clients.

Like PRIDE, Crédit Rural uses short-wave radios for inter-office communications, with a relay system between distant points. But its system is more ingenious: Crédit Rural has designed a "low-tech" system of car batteries with solar-panel chargers to power its radios. This efficient, low-cost, renewable-technology communication system could become a model for rural microfinance programs and communities in other low-income countries where electricity is scarce. It is certainly better adapted to the needs—and potential—of a poor country than Grameen's ambitious plan to install cellular phones in villages.

Lending, Management Structure, and Social Impact

There are four loan programs that are adapted to the needs of small traders and subsistence farmers. To select their clients the local village branches rely on the advice of village chiefs. This gives them considerable credibility in poor rural communities where people have always used informal credit and loans from village moneylenders, and would otherwise have been reticent to change their habits. In 1996, all loans were at the same annual rate of 30 percent—until December 1995, the lending rate had been 36 percent.

- Rural solidarity credit for local artisans and traders. Loans are repayable in monthly installments with one month's grace. First-time borrowers cannot borrow more than $150. Longtime members can borrow twice that amount.

- Agricultural credit which bridges the price cycles of agricultural commodities. All loans are to individuals. These are disbursed in June, at the beginning of the rainy season, when prices are low, and must be repaid in three installments during the dry season, when prices rise.

- Off-season credit which finances off-farm activities during the dry season, when agriculture comes to a halt. Loans are repayable in two installments during the following rainy season.

- Commercial credit for farming. Loans can be for up to $1,000.

The bank accepts savings deposits from its members. Like PRIDE it also relies on forced savings. All borrowers, regardless of the type of credit, must put 10 percent of their loan amount in a guarantee fund, which covers loan repayments in the event of a client's death or permanent incapacity. A further 4 percent of each loan is placed in a solidarity fund. These funds are not remunerated, which raises the actual interest rate to 35 percent per annum. As in PRIDE, each borrower must also purchase a $40 share of his or her cooperative.

Operations are highly decentralized, and in early 1996, each of the fifty-two cooperatives (*caisses*) was already operating as de facto autonomous credit cooperatives. The Conakry head office is the apex. It serves as an intermediary with the central bank and foreign donors. In 1996, treasury and cash management had already been centralized in anticipation of obtaining full banking licenses for the individual cooperatives. The head office collects excess liquidity from individual offices, and uses a transfer price of 17 percent for internal lending to offices that require cash for loan disbursements. Centralized cash management and the use of transfer pricing for internal lending are comparable to those of BRI's village banking units.

The fact is that Crédit Rural is regarded as a bush bank, with strong roots in rural communities and village culture which are strong elements for institutional sustainability. As with PRIDE, there is a core of loyal repeat borrowers who are helping to raise local outreach by word of mouth. Financial self-sufficiency, however, is a more distant goal. Although its operating costs are lower than PRIDE's, in 1996, Crédit Rural was not yet covering these costs.

Notes

1. Paul Rippey, *Notes from the Interior* 2 (1995), mimeo.
2. The same is happening in other parts of Africa, where virtually all foreign direct investment is by former colonial powers. See Michel Galy, "La Guinée en Survie," in *Le Monde Diplomatique*, June 1995.
3. *African Development Indicators* (Washington, D.C.: The World Bank, 1994); *WDR 96*, 220 and *WDR 97* 214 and 246.
4. *WDR 97*, 214.
5. *The Informal Sector and Micro-Finance in West Africa* (Washington, D.C.: The World Bank, 1995), 104.
6. *An Inventory of Microfinance in Western and West Central Africa*, 16.
7. The acronym stands for *Projet Intégré pour le Developpement des Entreprises* (integrated project for enterprise development).

Part V

Microfinance in Perspective

The chapter that follows concludes the book with a summary of the lessons learned from the experiences of the microfinance programs that were described in Parts II through IV. It also looks at how the achievements of the most successful programs are helping refocus the programs of bilateral and multilateral development agencies, and at how microfinance is being used to bring jobs and skills to impoverished inner-city neighborhoods in North America. The chapter ends with some remarks about the future of microfinance.

11

Learning from Microfinance

Lessons Learned

Parts II through IV of the book yield several conclusions about the socio-economic impact of self-employment and savings programs, and about the structure, management, and client groups of microfinance.

Microfinance: A Product of Its Environment

The importance of adapting to local social—and cultural—conditions is demonstrated by Grameen replicators in various countries: to succeed, each one must adapt to the social environment in which it is working. Thus, replication means "adapting" the Grameen model to local conditions, not "cloning" it. Take the case of two replicators, Pro Mujer in Bolivia and Crédit Rural de Guinée. The first one works with Andean Indian women, recently arrived in urban areas. Its borrower groups are organized in community banks that are much larger and more flexible than Grameen's groups. They are, in many ways, closer to FINCA's village-banking model than to Grameen's social collateral concept. Crédit Rural also deviates from Grameen's model by working with mixed-gender groups, and relying on the judgment of village chiefs to select group members. Moreover, neither program has even attempted to replicate Grameen's disciplinarian approach, which is alien to their cultures.

Naturally, cloning *does* work in small, semi-formal grassroots institutions that work in local communities, such as in village banks and credit unions, that can be replicated in different countries and continents. Full replication also works *within* countries. If this were not the case, microfinance institutions could not open new branches.

Social customs too can be adopted—and adapted—in the organization of microfinance, as in the case of self-help groups, such as ROSCAs and African kinship groups. These homogeneous affinity groups consist of people who are of the same caste or locality, or who do the same type of work. One should note that the "group" concept is socially and culturally specific. It does not exist in all societies and, when it does, is most prevalent among the poor. Formal education usually inculcates individualism, and the concept of self-help and group work is alien to elites. Most NGOs use self-help groups as the nuclei of their microfinance programs to achieve a better use of funds by their clients and improve the social impact of their activities. Take the case of CARE, one of the world's leading international NGOs. In Thailand it manages credit programs for artisans, and works with groups of villagers who share the same handicraft skills and tradition. In Lima's slums it has helped organize microfinance programs that build on pre-existing women's self-help groups—the mothers' clubs.

Working with existing affinity groups presents many advantages. The groups are self-selecting and are based on mutual trust; coaching for group formation can be kept to a minimum; starting costs are negligible; and the social collateral of peer pressure improves loan recovery and reduces arrears.

Microfinance and Poverty

In countries where the formal economy accounts for only a small share of the economically active population, engaging the poor and unemployed in productive activities and giving them the wherewithal to leverage their resources is a major source of job creation. Then credit for self-employment can yield substantial productivity gains at minimal cost: with a small loan to purchase a sewing machine a seamstress can increase her productivity exponentially and make many more dresses than with thread and needle. Small loans for income-generating activities also raise household income, improve nutrition, and raise the probability that children from poor families will go to school. In most cases the people who belong to microfinance programs are able to accumulate working capital and savings.

For their part, microfinance institutions such as BancoSol, BRI, and PRIDE, some of whose clients belong to the middle and upper tiers of the informal sector, often achieve astonishing upward social mobility for those clients, to the point that they rise above poverty and can offer work to others. But these are isolated cases, and it is essential to bear in mind that credit for self-employment is not a cure-all panacea.

Microfinance cannot *eliminate* poverty by itself, and the outreach of most programs is still far too limited to rid the world of the curse of hunger. Though it is tempting to present microfinance as a "magic bullet," it is unrealistic to expect easy solutions to complex problems, if only for the fact that self-employment is constrained by working in small-scale, low-productivity activities, which use rudimentary technology, and generate no economies of scale. Reducing poverty on a *large and lasting scale*—that is, creating an environment in which everybody has an income above the poverty level—demands a holistic, multi-faceted approach, to achieve economically and socially sustainable development, and reduce income inequality and disparities in the use and allocation of physical and financial resources, within and between countries.

Put differently, microfinance and self-employment can be used to reduce *some* aspects of poverty and improve the quality of life for people in marginal communities. In that sense, microfinance should be an integral part of sustainable development—that is, development that meets the needs of the present generation without prejudicing those of future ones.

In any event, banking for the poor cannot be a surrogate social safety net for the deserving poor. The aged, infirm, and totally indigent who are unemployable do not belong in microfinance programs, regardless of circumstances, because they would never be able to use loans productively, and would be burdened with debts.

Microfinance and Empowerment

By promoting self-help and productive activities in marginal areas, microfinance has a profound psychological and economic impact. The impact is greatest in programs that target the most vulnerable groups in society—women and indigenous people, and those who live and work in the most marginalized communities.

When discussing credit as a tool for empowerment and social change, the first example that comes to mind is the Grameen Bank. It has taught landless unskilled women to fend for themselves, and is using its social constitution of Sixteen Decisions and group discipline to encourage its members to abandon the practice of dowry, control their fertility, and send their daughters to school. Grameen also challenges the social and religious foundations of women's oppression and inferior status. But it has no monopoly on empowerment. BRAC, for one, has taken women's empowerment quite a bit further by helping village women defend their basic rights and offering legal advice.

Other programs empower their members in different ways but with similar results, through village banks and urban community banks that rapidly become community support groups, as well as sources of credit. An Indian woman, recently uprooted from a small Andean village can make friends in a Pro Mujer community bank, and feel less isolated in an alien urban environment. She also has a tremendous sense of self-esteem when she receives a small loan to set up a market stall in La Paz. The same is true for the women in Lima's communal kitchens. With financial and moral support from CARE, the women are restoring dignity to the inhabitants of impoverished communities in some of Lima's worst slums, ravaged by Shining Path guerrillas and years of neglect.

Encouraging People to Save

People who belong to microfinance programs have strong incentives to make money, and usually manage to accumulate some savings, even if they do so a few pennies at a time. In FINCA village banks borrowers manage to save about $50 per loan cycle. In general all but the poorest can save most of the time, but need loans only some of the time.

Naturally, it is *always* better to save than to accumulate debts and, when providing financial services to the unbankable, encouraging them to save is more important than giving them loans. Yet, only a minority of microfinance programs offer their clients safe, reliable, and liquid savings instruments, such as passbooks and certificates of deposit. In this respect BRI's *unit desa* stand out for their success in attracting rural savings. Until the financial crisis of 1997–98, the units' savings deposits outnumbered loans by a factor of six-to-one, and the amounts on deposit are twice as large as their loans outstanding. But these are exceptions. All too often the clients of microfinance programs are faced with the paradox of having to place their savings in the very commercial banks that deny them credit—in most countries the lion's share of rural savings is in commercial banks, which use the funds to make loans to large businesses. In fact, even BRI uses the surplus savings from its rural clients in its commercial-lending activities.

The fact that the savings of the informal sector are placed, and recycled, in other parts of the economy limits the ability of microfinance institutions to leverage their loanable funds. It also means that they cannot perform financial intermediation in local communities by using their clients' savings to make loans. In this respect NGOs are at a particular disadvantage. Since they are not licensed financial intermediaries, they are obliged by banking laws to place their clients' money in commercial banks. Although this protects small savers, it perpetuates the NGOs' dependence on grants and loans from domestic and foreign sources.

Banking on People

The innovation that made microfinance on a large scale possible and relatively risk free was the introduction of group credit and collective responsibility, as an alternative to formal guarantees. Whereas commercial banks are not structured to be profitable providing small loans that meet the needs of microenterprises and always need formal guarantees, group credit has made it possible—and sometimes even lucrative—to lend to people who have no assets and cannot offer collateral. Group credit is widespread, and almost the norm in microfinance programs for the poorest. The Grameen Bank has standardized group lending and perfected it into a form of social collateral through peer group pressure in small, socially homogeneous, single-gender groups and centers. BRAC and Grameen also "bank on people" by taking banking to villages, instead of asking villagers to come to their branch offices.

As explained in Chapter 7, in BancoSol the sole function of mixed-gender borrower groups is to make people guarantee each other's loans. Because the groups' social role is perfunctory, creating a new group is a formality. Oftentimes, prospective borrowers who attend the bank's regular promotional meetings can form, and be recognized as, a group there and then, without further ado.

A third variation of group credit is in village banks and urban community banks, whose main function is as intermediaries for the on-lending of donor funds. In village banks in Surin Province, northern Thailand, that are sponsored by Catholic Relief Services (CRS), Pro Mujer community banks in Bolivia, and FINCA village banks in Latin America, the sponsoring agency acts as an apex umbrella institution that coordinates all the contacts with donors, supervises the activities of its village banks, and gives them technical and logistical support.

At the opposite end of the scale one finds institutions such as BRI and CREDINPET in Peru, that follow conventional banking practice and put no emphasis whatsoever on banking on people. They lend only to individuals, require formal collateral, and prefer lending to the middle and upper brackets of the small and microenterprise sector. This restricts their poverty impact, but leverages individual upward mobility with large loans.

Credit Delivery

Regardless of the structure of lending, prompt credit delivery and thorough credit screening are essential for the success and sustainability of microfinance. The appraisal of loan requests must be always simple and straightforward, loan documents should be easy to understand, and clients should have quick, simple, and convenient access to credit when they need it. Loan repayments should also be kept simple, preferably with frequent equal installments. In this respect, PRIDE, BancoSol, Grameen, BRI, and BRAC have all set high standards. They have perfected loan appraisal techniques and credit delivery, and are examples of attention to psychological factors. Each one has recognized that bank offices are alien places in which poor people feel ill at ease and makes a point of having simple office premises.

Loan Pricing

Lenders must charge interest rates that cover the full cost of *efficient* credit delivery. Inefficiency on the part of a credit program should never be an excuse to charge high interest rates. Interest rates on loans should nevertheless be sufficiently high to leave an adequate margin that covers operating expenses, and the cost of capital and loan-loss reserves, so as to ensure the financial sustainability of microfinance programs. But profitability and financial self-sufficiency (in the sense of being fully independent of external funding), should never be ends in themselves, only desirable goals.

All loan charges, fees, and forced savings should be explicit and transparent. While it is in the interest of borrowers to receive cheap loans, the importance of cost should not be exaggerated. Access to credit matters more than cost when people need money to start a small business; absent microfinance, their only alternative is to pay usurious rates to moneylenders and pawnbrokers.

Microfinance and Subsidies

One of the most difficult problems in loan pricing is the question of whether or not to use subsidies. There are two kinds of subsidies. The first, interest-rate subsidies, can be justified on economic and social grounds in rural credit programs that work in extremely poor, isolated areas. When used, such subsidies must be transparent and carefully targeted, bearing in mind that lending at below-market lending rates makes it impossible to offer competitive rates on savings accounts, and undermines financial sustainability. This means that interest-rate subsidies should preferably be funded by donors. Moreover, there is always a risk that borrowers will treat "cheap" loans as gifts, thus creating high delinquencies that could undermine the lenders' viability; loan repayment rates are invariably better in programs that lend at market rates than in those that offer low-cost credit.

Subsidies of the second type are operational. They are designed for microfinance institutions that have high operating costs which they cannot fully recover. While this creates "subsidy dependence" on foreign donors, such subsidies are warranted for programs that work in difficult environments, such as in sparsely populated regions in sub-Saharan Africa. Without donor support these programs could not survive. Moreover, the social benefits of bringing financial services for productive use to such areas far outweigh the cost to donors.

But there are many examples of operating subsidies that cannot be justified on any ground. One is to be found in the World Bank, which has considered offering transaction-cost subsidies for commercial banks. The point was to give the banks grants that would reduce the cost of making small loans, and entice the them to open "windows" that offer low-cost loans to small and micro businesses. Initiatives of this kind are illogical and socially inequitable; they subsidize wealthy banks and their owners. Because money is fungible the use of such subsidies is also difficult to monitor.

Loan Recovery

Microfinance is not charity, and loan recovery is the single most important aspect for the survival of microfinance institutions. The surest way to achieve good loan recovery is zero tolerance for arrears, meaning that any loan repayment that is overdue by even as little as twenty-four hours is considered in arrears, and that loan officers must immediately get in touch with clients whose loan payments are not punctual. When it is enforced strictly, collective group responsibility is an effective means of minimizing loan arrears.

Zero tolerance is justified if the lending institution has made a full and careful assessment of prospective clients' (or groups') ability and willingness to repay loans. But if credit appraisal is sloppy, it is difficult to enforce rigid repayment rules. The key to loan recovery is to monitor the use of loans by borrowers. Loan use can be enhanced by involving borrowers in program design, ensuring that borrowers "own" the programs in which they participate, and financing activities in which clients have a comparative advantage. For example, in regions where agriculture and the rural economy account for a large share of household income, microfinance for on-farm activities can generate considerable productivity and income gains. A final caveat is that microfinance is not for household consumption, except in emergencies such as deaths and illness, when people have no alternatives.

Women and Microfinance

There is considerable feminization of work in the informal sector. In villages women work the land on subsistence farms and take care of a great deal of farm-related work. In urban settings they usually engage in so-called feminine activities—preparing meals, selling goods in markets, making clothes, and weaving. Women also work longer hours than men, and the poorer the household, the longer women work.

It follows that credit programs that target women have a greater poverty-reduction impact than programs that lend mostly to men. In programs that work predominantly or exclusively with women, households derive greater benefits from credit programs than when men are the borrowers. When women can develop their own earning power, children's enrollment in schools rises (especially that of girls who are often denied formal education), families begin to save, and the men's attitudes towards their wives and daughters usually improve. Moreover, in NGO-managed microfinance programs that combine lending with social intermediation, fertility rates and pregnancy-related deaths and injuries tend to decline among women who receive advice on birth control.

Because microfinance too is highly feminized, women should be equal participants and decision makers in the use and allocation of credit. This is already the case in FINCA's village banks, where membership consists only of women: they are run for women and by women. Similarly, in Pro Mujer community banks involve women in collective decision making, teaching them to assume financial responsibilities. Moreover, as Grameen has shown, in programs whose clients include women and men, it is preferable to have single-gender groups since men tend to dominate mixed-gender groups.

There is also abundant empirical evidence that loan recovery is higher in microfinance programs that target women—women always have better repayment records than men, and programs that work with women consistently have repayment rates in excess of 90 percent.

Dealing with Fraud

All microfinance programs face a risk of fraud, and the risk is greatest in highly decentralized programs, such as PRIDE, where a branch manager colluded with the manager of a local bank to embezzle close to $50,000 by booking phantom loans.

Accountability, governance, and transparency are the most effective safe-guards against fraud. An excellent example is BancoSol's credit delivery to client groups, in which each group member is involved in all the stages of the credit process, from application to delivery, and must cosign their collective loan agreements. In other programs, from Grameen to PRIDE, all loan disbursements are made in public, in the presence of other people. Efficient and accurate management-information systems and internal audits of branch offices and key staff also help minimize fraud.

Training and Capacity Building

Capacity building covers staff, as well as clients. Client capacity building provides basic training to people who do not have business skills or proven repayment capacity. Its purpose is to improve borrowers' ability to manage a microenterprise and improve repayment levels. Training can also be used to raise people's social awareness. For example, BRAC uses legal support to make women aware of their constitutional rights, and Grameen uses group discipline and a simple social code of sixteen key principles to empower landless women, engage them in the economy and society, and challenge the social and cultural traditions that confine rural women to the private sphere of village life. It also organizes regular training workshops for its members' husbands to explain its activities and help them understand that they should not feel threatened by their wives' greater independence. PRIDE, for its part, uses training courses at different levels to coach clients and improve their performance in business.

As a rule, instead of adopting a dogmatic "minimalist" approach, it is always better to be pragmatic and, if training is offered, adhere to a few basic principles:

- Training is not a free good—experience at PRIDE in Guinea and in other programs shows that people only take training seriously if they pay a fee, even if only a nominal one

- Fees can be waived for basic training on credit procedures and group formation, and when dealing with people who are too poor to pay a fee

- There should be a clear link between content of training and the objectives of credit programs—the purpose of training is to make microentrepreneurs more efficient and improve the utilization of loans

- Social objectives and programs, such as advice on health care, family planning, basic hygiene, and nutrition should be dealt with separately, rather than be included in financial programs

Capacity building in the form of *institution building* for the microfinance programs themselves is equally important, and essential for good credit delivery and efficient client targeting. The guiding principle of institution building is to have institutional arrangements that reflect the borrowers' needs and characteristics, and a clear commitment to provide the necessary financial services.[1]

The core of institution building is to train bank workers and loan officers. Courses range from induction training for newly hired staff, regular refresher courses for existing staff, and management courses for promotions and career-track building. Not surprisingly, institution building is most advanced at BRI, Grameen, BancoSol, and other mature microfinance institutions that have sufficient resources to allocate funds to training and also recruit high-quality field staff. In Bangladesh, where employment opportunities for university graduates are few, all Grameen bank officers have master's degrees and undergo rigorous training before receiving field assignments. In that sense institution building is a key element of institutional sustainability.

But institution building can also be externally oriented. Grameen Trust, for example, is Grameen's vehicle for the creation of replicators; key management staff at PRIDE and Crédit Rural in Guinea and Pro Mujer all attended training programs at Grameen in Dhaka. Similarly Canada's Caisses Desjardins and Germany's GTZ offer assistance on capacity building to microfinance programs worldwide.

The last level of capacity building involves strengthening *community capacity*. This is particularly important for community-based organizations, such as village banks and cooperative societies.[2] The larger microfinance programs rarely focus on community capacity. In contrast, NGOs, such as FINCA, CARE, and ACCION, that work in several countries and whose individual programs are quite small, place great emphasis on community capacity building.

Non-Governmental Organizations

As financial intermediaries, NGOs face considerable obstacles, not least the fact that they are not licensed financial institutions which have no endogenous financing capacity through deposit taking. Many NGOs also have serious governance problems, lack proper management information systems, and they seldom have clear guidelines on loan classification. Another problem is that many NGOs operate on a relatively small scale, which raises costs and makes sustainability unattainable. As a result, they tend to depend on donor funding to supply loanable funds and subsidies to cover a part of their overhead costs. Using "other people's money" to make loans limits accountability and often undermines the financial discipline of NGOs.

Donor grants also present the problem of being in US dollars, which must be converted into the local currency of the country where an NGO is operating. In conditions of high inflation and/or devaluations of local currencies this can cause rapid decapitalization.

But there are many examples of NGOs with outstanding records as financial intermediaries. They use the advantage of being at the grassroots level to work more closely with the poor and local communities. Some NGOs have also made successful, seamless transitions to become fully fledged financial intermediaries. The PRODEM-BancoSol and Procredito-Los Andes metamorphoses from NGO to financial institutions are excellent examples.

Governance and Supervision

Regulation and prudential supervision of financial institutions serve to promote efficient capital accumulation and resource allocation, and maintain the soundness of institutions that take deposits from the public.[3] This provides safeguards against the risk of fraud and mismanagement in the allocation of loans. It is essential for the conduct of fiduciary functions involving clients' savings and the on-lending of donor funds. Thus, microfinance institutions that accept deposits from their clients should be held to the same prudential and fiduciary standards as any other financial institution. To be effective, prudential norms must be realistic and should not become a vehicle for financial repression. There is financial repression when regulations prevent financial institutions from working efficiently, for instance by setting interest-rate ceilings—if lending-rate ceilings are such that microfinance institutions cannot recover their intermediation costs, the supply of credit rapidly dries up and results in rationing credit.

In all cases, prudential supervision should be flexible and adapted to each institution's legal foundation. In the case of multi-entity operations, such as networks of village banks, supervision can be delegated to an apex. In other instances, such as in BRI, a supervisory system is built into the management structure. BRI also assumes de facto responsibility for the supervision of small BKD village cooperatives in Java. However, the ideal is formal supervision by a specialized regulatory agency, such as superintendency of banks and financial institutions. This is already the case in a number of countries, particularly in Latin America. The problem, however, is that here is the lack of appropriate technology and know-how to draw formerly unregulated financial intermediaries into a regulated market, and it may be necessary to create new regulatory entities.

Good governance also depends on professional, dedicated management, and on the use of appropriate management-information systems, financial technology and tools, such as banking software for accounting and record-keeping. FAO's Microbanker Project is a pioneer in this field. It has developed a flexible software program that is adapted to the needs of small village banks, and can be customized to fit the requirements of individual institutions. The Microbanker software is already being used by village banks in Jamaica, Sri Lanka, Thailand, Nepal, and East Africa.

Microfinance and the Macroeconomic Environment

In principle, an unstable macroeconomic environment that affects factor productivity and the demand for credit should also undermine the effectiveness of microfinance. But, because much of the demand for microfinance stems from macroeconomic policies that ignore (and often violate) the needs of the poorest segment of society, and because the delivery of microfinance takes place in specific environments and communities, macroeconomic stability is not a determining factor in banking for the poor. Small loans can improve income and productivity in the informal sector, regardless of the macroeconomic environment, except in situations where hyperinflation or severe recessions undermine *all* economic activities. Then microfinance is also affected. As discussed in Chapter 5, Indonesia in 1998 illustrates that situation.

Reaching Beyond Developing Countries

Small-scale lending for income-generating activities and empowerment is already reaching far beyond individual countries and communities. It has grown into a worldwide movement where new institutions and programs are being established in ever increasing numbers. At the time of writing there were more than 7,000 active microfinance programs and some 500 million people—or more than twice the entire population of the United States—were engaged in profitable micro- and small-business activities, but only a minority of them had access to financial services, other than from moneylenders.[4] Building on the success of the existing microfinance programs, there now are active microfinance and microenterprise development programs in Russia, many former Soviet republics, Bosnia, Albania, Poland, South Africa, most sub-Saharan African countries, Nepal, Laos, and Vietnam, to name but a few.

The achievements and positive social impact of the largest microfinance programs are also making multilateral and bilateral agencies re-focus their poverty reduction programs and strategies. The World Bank, for one, has begun earmarking some of its lending for financial and institutional support to enterprise development, and to increase the availability of financial services to women. The Bank's most recent loans include microfinance components. For its part, the Inter-American Development Bank is a major source of financial and technical support for microfinance institutions in Latin America with a regionwide "Initiative 2001."

USAID also supports microenterprise development, and most of its overseas missions manage sizable microfinance portfolios. Most of the microfinance programs it supports target women in marginalized communities. To ensure effective targeting the agency has set a ceiling of $300 per loan for its poverty lending. In 1995, USAID's Office of Microenterprise Development had $150 million in microenterprise loans. It also manages a special fund to promote lending to NGOs. GEMINI, one of the agency's earlier microenterprise initiatives, served to provide non-financial support for informal activities, including linking up microenterprises with larger firms to improve management skills, and promoting technological innovation in informal sectors. To strengthen the effectiveness of its microfinance programs, and remain at the cutting edge, the agency is funding a multi-year research program on "best practices" in microfinance.

Several international NGOs are also involved in microfinance. The activities of some of the leading ones—FINCA, ACCION, and CARE—are reviewed in this book. Others, whose programs are not reviewed here, are OXFAM and Freedom from Hunger. One would also be remiss in not mentioning Women's World Banking, a global financial NGO, established in 1979 to promote the participation of women in productive activities as equal partners with men. Its fifty affiliates in forty countries support women microentrepreneurs by giving them access to finance, and offering technical information and advice on marketing their products.

The achievements of microfinance in some of the world's poorest countries, and the fact that the poor and those who live in marginalized communities in developed countries also lack access to financial services, have spurred new initiatives in microfinance in the United States and other industrialized countries. These initiatives are gradually loosening the stranglehold of the traditional bankers of the poor, the moneylenders and pawn shops of impoverished inner-city boroughs.

Here too, USAID is spearheading action, applying its experience of microfinance and self-help groups in developing countries to support community initiatives in inner cities in the United States. Because the agency's charter prohibits it from lending in all but developing countries, it can only offer technical support and training to local communities. For instance, in Washington, D.C., it is supporting community housing programs and health clinics. In Baltimore it is working with groups of women microentrepreneurs.[5]

FINCA is assisting self-employment associations in the United States through a number of pilot projects. It does so by forming partnerships with community-based organizations in disadvantaged communities. In 1995 it had pilot programs with seven member associations in Minnesota and the greater Washington, D.C., area. These programs had forty-four members, most of whom were women.[6] ACCION is also active, with programs in Chicago, New Mexico, New York, California, and Texas.[7] For its part, Freedom from Hunger is applying its experience from developing countries in community health programs in the United States Deep South. There also are community-based microfinance programs in Washington, D.C., North Carolina, and Arkansas that are managed by other NGOs. One of them is the Community First Bank of D.C., which is offering microfinance to revitalize some of the US capital's most deprived neighborhoods.[8]

Another active microfinance program in the United States is ShoreTrust Bank. This Chicago-based financial institution works in inner cites and small rural towns where it supports community efforts by financing housing development, small venture capital, and job creation.

One of the most interesting initiatives in North America is in Canada, where Calmeadow Nova Scotia has formed a partnership with the Royal Bank of Canada to provide small loans and advice on peer-group support to small entrepreneurs who have no access to credit.[9] The Royal Bank and Calmeadow have been working together since 1989, when Calmeadow received a five-year grant of C$50,000 from the bank. In 1991, the partnership launched a pilot program in the province of Nova Scotia, where unemployment is higher than in the rest of the country. In 1994, the bank provided C$500,000 in seed funds to launch the partnership's program in that province. Its main activity consists in helping community groups set up their own microfinance funds. These funds offer loans that range from C$500 to C$5,000 for new businesses or to expand existing ones. In 1995 the Royal Bank established a research fund of C$75,000 to do a feasibility study for a Calmeadow West project in Vancouver. In Nova Scotia the bank is the sole lender for the partnership's projects. It accepts the credit risk on 50 percent of each project. What makes this partnership remarkable is that it involves Canada's largest and most prestigious commercial bank. It could become an example for future partnerships between major banks and NGOs.

The Future

One interesting development that denotes the growing importance of microfinance is the Consultative Group to Assist the Poorest (CGAP). This multi-donor program with global outreach to reduce poverty through microfinance was founded in June 1995 with the participation of ten bilateral and multilateral member donors.[10] Its financial resources include a grant of US$30 million from the World Bank and $5 million in contributions from member countries and could become a major forum for the dissemination of the lessons from microfinance among its members and raise public awareness of the need for financial services for the unbankable.

Together with Grameen, the World Bank, and FINCA, CGAP was one of the main sponsors and organizers of the Microfinance Summit that met in Washington, D.C., from February 2 to 4, 1997. The summit was a gathering of more than 2,500 people from over one hundred countries. Among them were heads of state and governments, leaders of international institutions, and many celebrities. But most were practitioners of microfinance: women and men who are committed to eradicating poverty, especially that of women and children. The summit was a celebration of twenty years of collective achievements by the thousands of microfinance programs that have shown that, by banking on people, not on money, small loans can help the poor help themselves through self-employment, and give dignity and purpose to the lives of those whom the world has forgotten.

Besides taking stock of their accomplishments in making self-employment a credible tool to combat poverty, those who attended the summit signed a Declaration of Support that resolved that "We have assembled to launch a global movement to reach 100 million of the world's poorest families, especially the women of those families, with credit for self-employment and other financial and business services, by the year 2005." The occasion was used to launch a global campaign, and raise close to $22 billion by 2005 for a more than six-fold increase in the number of the world's poorest families, especially the women of those families that have access to credit for self-employment. This is many times what the leading microfinance institutions could generate in profits and clients deposits in an entire generation, let alone eight years. This means that a large share of these resources will have to come from bilateral and multilateral agencies, foundations, central banks, and financial markets. Mobilizing resources on such a scale will thus require new techniques, including guarantees from donor agencies to encourage and commercial banks to become involved in microfinance programs. There are precedents of cooperation between microfinance institutions and commercial financial markets; ACCION, BancoSol, and Grameen have already successfully tapped domestic and international markets by issuing their own debt certificates of deposit.

But, to put the summit's goal in perspective, the target of raising $2.75 billion per year, over eight years to expand microfinance represents less than 1 percent of total resource flows to developing countries in 1995, and less than 5 percent of grants and technical assistance in the same year.[11] If the Summit's annual funding goal is achieved it will change the lives of more than 60 million people, in 12.5 million households per year, with average loans of about $200 per family. This makes one wonder why so many observers at the Summit ridiculed this target as being unrealistic and unattainable.

From the selection of country studies and overview of microfinance programs in three continents presented in this book, the reader should have drawn four basic conclusions:

- Poverty is not created by the poor. It is the outcome of complex social and economic factors, which include class distinctions, gender and ethnic bias, and the socioeconomic impact of free-market policies, fiscal austerity, and cuts in programs for the needy.

- "Banking for the poor" can stave off some of the effects of economic programs and policies that push or trap people in destitution; small loans for productive activities can help reduce poverty by making people self-reliant, and empowering those who are excluded from the mainstream of society.

- Saving is always better than accumulating debts, and the most successful microfinance programs are those that encourage their members to accumulate working capital, no matter how small, by blending savings programs with their lending activities.

- Microfinance in its various incarnations has become one of the central tenets of a new paradigm of socially-oriented—and sustainable—development. It has grown into a worldwide movement that is already finding acceptance—and showing signs of success—in marginal urban areas in North America and Europe.

Notes

1. Orlando J. Sacay and Bikki K. Randhawa, *Design Issues in Rural Finance*, World Bank Discussion Paper 293, 1995, 25
2. *IFAD Microfinance Experience and Plan of Action* (Rome: IFAD, 1997), 7.
3. See, for example, Tor Jansson, *Financial Regulation and Its Significance for Microfinance in Latin America and the Caribbean* (Washington, D.C.: Inter-American Development Bank, December 1997), 1.
4. *CGAP Focus* No. 3, October 1995.
5. Michael Fletcher, *The Washington Post*, February 11, 1996.
6. FINCA *1995 Annual Report*.
7. ACCION International, *Annual Report 1994*.
8. Michelle Singletary, *The Washington Post*, May 20, 1997.
9. *Calmeadow Nova Scotia* is an off-shoot of Calmeadow, a Canadian NGO that disseminates training and business advice, and provides base financing to microentrepreneurs. Calmeadow is one of the founding shareholders of BancoSol in Bolivia.
10. Sixteen donor agencies have since joined the original founding members of CGAP.
11. In 1995 aggregate net resource flows to developing countries amounted to $231,437 million, including close to 50,000 million in grants and technical assistance. *World Debt Tables 1996*, The World Bank, Vol. I, 192.

ACRONYMS

BAAC—Bank for Agriculture and Agricultural Cooperatives

BCEAO—Banque Central des Etats d'Afrique Occidentale

BRAC—Bangladesh Rural Advancement Committee

BRI—Bank Rakyat Indonesia

CAM—Centro de Apoyo a la Microempresa

CGAP—Consultative Group to Assist the Poorest

CRS—Catholic Relief Services

FAO—Food and Agricultural Organization

FFP— Fondos Financieros Privados

FINCA—Foundation for International Community Assistance

GTZ—Gezellschaft fur Zuzammenarbeit

HIID—Harvard Institute for International Development

IADB—Inter-American Development Bank

IMF—International Monetary Fund

NAFTA—North American Free Trade Association

NEP—New Economic Policy

NGO—Non-Governmental Organization

OPEC—Organization of Petroleum Exporting Countries

ROSCA—Rotating Savings and Credit Associations

SBFI— Superintendency of Banks and Financial Institutions

SEWA—Self-Employed Women's Assocciation

UNDP—United Nations Development Program

USAID—United States Agency for International Development

WDR—World Development Report

WOCCU—World Council of Credit Unions

SELECTED BIBLIOGRAPHY

Ashe, Jeffrey, and Christopher E. Cosslet. *Credit for the Poor.* New York: UNDP, 1989.

Branch, Brian, and Christopher Baker. *Overcoming Governance Problems: What Does it Take?* Washington, D.C.: Inter-American Development Bank, March 1998.

Bornstein, David. *The Price of a Dream.* New York: Simon & Schuster, 1996.

Bouzas, Roberto et al. *Regionalism and the Global Economy: The Case of Latin America and the Caribbean.* Edited by Jan Joost Teunissen. The Hague: FONDAD, 1995.

Caufield, Catherine. *Masters of Illusion: The World Bank and the Poverty of Nations.* New York: Henry Holt and Company, 1996.

Challenges for Peace: Towards Sustainable Development in Peru. Washington D.C.: Inter-American Development Bank, 1995.

Claude, Richard Pierre, and Burns H. Weston, eds. *Human Rights in the World Community.* University of Pennsylvania Press, 1989.

Cline, William B. *International Debt Reexamined.* Washington D.C.: Institute for International Economics, 1995.

Cooper, Richard N. et al. *The Pursuit of Reform, Global Finance and the Developing Countries.* Edited by Jan Joost Teunisssen. The Hague: FONDAD, 1993.

Curran, Donald. *Tiers-Monde: Evolution et Stratégies de Développement.* Paris: Editions Eyrolles, 1990.

Dasgupta, Partha. *An Inquiry into Well-being and Destitution.* Oxford: Clarendon Press, 1993.

Declaration and Plan of Action, Microcredit Summit. February 1997.

del Pilar Tello, María. *Promesas de Progreso, Cajas Municipales de Ahorro y Crédito del Perú.* Lima: FEPMAC, 1995.

de Soto, Hernando. *The Other Path: The Invisible Revolution in the Third World.* New York: Harper & Row, 1989.

DEVELOPMENT ALTERNATIVES 5, no. 1 (Spring 1995). Bethesda, Maryland: DAI.

Feldman, Ernesto, and Juan Sommer. *Crisis Financiera y Endeudamiento Externo en la Argentina.* Buenos Aires: Centro de Economía Transnational, 1996.

Fugelsang, Andreas et al. *Participation as Process—Process as Growth.* Dhaka: Grameen Trust, 1993.

Gamarra, Eduardo. *DEMOCRACIA, REFORMAS ECONOMICAS Y GOBERNABILIDAD EN BOLIVIA.* Santiago de Chile: ECLA, United Nations, 1995.

George, Susan. *A Fate Worse than Debt: The World Financial Crisis and the Poor.* New York: Grove Press, 1988

Gibbons, David S., and Sukor Kasim. *Banking for the Poor.* Dhaka: Grameen Bank, 1991.

Globalization and Liberalization: Development in the Face of Two Powerful Currents. Geneva: UNCTAD, 1996.

Guillermoprieto, Alma. *The Heart that Bleeds, Latin America Now*. New York: Vintage Books, 1994.

Holcombe, Susan. *Managing to Empower: The Grameen Bank's Experience of Poverty Alleviation*. London: Zed Books, 1995.

Hunt, E. K., and Jesse G. Schwartz, eds. *A Critique of Economic Theory*. London: Penguin Books, 1972.

Investing in Women. International Center for Research on Women (ICRW) Policy Paper, 1995.

Kaplan, Robert D. *The Ends of the Earth*. New York: Vintage Books, 1996.

Klitgaart, Robert. *Tropical Gangsters*. New York: Basic Books, 1990.

Lever, Harold and Christopher Huhne. *Debt and Danger: The World Financial Crisis*. Pelican Books, 1987.

Lipumba, Nguyuru H. I. *Africa Beyond Adjustment*. Policy Essay 15. Washington, D.C.: Overseas Development Council, 1994.

Lonely Planet, Indonesia. Lonely Planet Publications, 1995.

Londoño, Juan Luis, and Miguel Székely. *Distributional Surprises after a Decade of Reforms: Latin America in the 1990s*. Mimeo. Washington D.C.: Inter-American Development Bank, March 1997.

North-South: A Programme for Survival: The Brandt Commission Report. London: Pan Books, 1983.

Maddison, Angus. *Two Crises: Latin America and Asia 1929–38 and 1973–83*. Paris: OECD, 1985.

Schneider, Hartman, ed. *Microfinance for the Poor?* Paris: IFAD/OECD, 1997.

Mistry, Percy S. *African Debt Revisited: Procrastination or Progress?* Edited by Jan Joost Teunissen. The Hague: FONDAD, 1991.

Morley, Samuel A. *Poverty and Inequality in Latin America*. Washington D.C.: Overseas Development Council, 1994.

Multilateral Debt, the Human Cost. Oxfam International Position Paper, 1996.

Myrdal, Gunnar. *Asian Drama: An Inquiry into the Poverty of Nations*. New York: Vintage Books, 1972 (abridged edition).

Otero, María, and Elisabeth Rhyne, eds. *The New World of Microfinance*. West Hartford: Kumarian Press, 1994.

Prayer, Cheryl. *The Debt Trap: The International Monetary Fund and the Third World*. New York: Monthly Review Press, 1974.

Poyo, Jeffrey. *A Conceptual Framework for the Regulation and Supervision of Credit Unions*. Washington, D.C.: Inter-American Development Bank, March 1998.

Radice, Hugo, ed. *International Firms and Modern Imperialism*. London: Penguin Books, 1975.

Rahman, Sidiqur et al. *From Calories to Capacity Building*. Dhaka: Grameen Bank, 1992.

Rippey, Paul. *Notes from the Interior 2* (1995). Mimeo.

Sachs, Jeffrey, ed. *Developing Country Debt*. National Bureau of Economic Research Inc., 1987.

Schama, Simon. *The Embarrassment of Riches*. New York: Alfred A. Knopf, 1988.

Shams, Khalid M. *Designing Effective Credit Delivery Systems for the Poor*. Dhaka: Grameen Bank, 1992.

———. *Raising the Productivity of the Poor*. Dhaka: Grameen Bank, 1993.

Shehabuddin, Rahnuma. *Empowering Rural Women: The Impact of Grameen Bank in Bangladesh*. Dhaka: Grameen Bank, 1992.

The Crisis of Development in Latin America. Amsterdam: CEDLA, 1991.

The Grameen Reader. Edited by Gibbons, David S. Dhaka: Grameen Bank, 1992.
The Grameen Bank: Poverty Relief in Bangladesh. Boulder: Westview Press, 1993.
The Other Side of the Story. Washington D.C.: Development Gap, 1993.
The Oxfam Poverty Report. Oxford: OXFAM, 1995.
Thorbecke, Erik, and Theodore van der Pluijm. *Rural Indonesia: Socio-economic Development in a Changing Environment.* International Fund for Agricultural Development. New York: New York University Press, 1993.
Trade and Development Report 1986 and 1995. United Nations Conference on Trade and Development. United Nations, 1986 and 1995.
United Nations, *Informe de la Comisión de la Verdad para el Salvador (UN Thruth Commission Report.* 1992–93.
Village Banking: The State of the Practice. United Nations Development Fund for Women, 1996.
Wahid, Abu N. M., ed. *Least Developed Countries 1996 Report.* United Nations Conference on Trade and Development. United Nations, 1996
Watanabe, Tatsuya. *The Ponds and the Poor: The Story of Grameen Bank's Initiative.* Dhaka: Grameen Bank, 1993.
Weeks, John. *A Critique of Neoclassical Macroeconomics.* The Macmillan Press Ltd., 1989.
Westley and Shaffer. *Credit Union Policies.* Washington D. C.: Inter-American Development Bank, March 1998.
Williamson, John. *The Progress of Policy Reform in Latin America.* Washington, D.C.: Institute for International Economics, 1990.
World Resources 1988–89. World Resources Institute. New York: Basic Books, 1988.
World Resources 1992–93. World Resources Institute. New York: Oxford University Press, 1992.
Yunus, Muhammad. *Jorimon and Other Stories: Faces of Poverty.* Dhaka: Grameen Bank, 1982.
———. *Peace is Freedom from Poverty.* Dhaka: Grameen Bank, 1991.
———. *Grameen Bank, Experiences and Reflections.* Dhaka: Grameen Bank, 1991.
———. *New Development Options Towards the 21ˢᵗ Century.* Dhaka: Grameen Bank, 1995.

World Bank Publications

All of the publications below are published by The World Bank, 18 H Street NW, Washington, D.C. 20433, except for those indicated with an asterisk.

Adjustment in Africa, Reforms, Results and the Road Ahead, 1994.
African Development Indicators, 1996.
An Inventory of Microfinance Institutions in Latin America and the Caribbean, 1997.
An Inventory of Microfinance Institutions in South Asia, 1997.
An Inventory of Microfinance Institutions in Western and West Central Africa, 1997.
Annual Reports 1994 and 1997.
Ardito Barleta, Nicolás et al. *Economic Liberalization and Stabilization Policies in Argentina, Chile and Uruguay,* 1983.
Bangladesh from Stabilization to Growth, Country Study, 1994.
Burki, Shahid Javed, and Sebastian Edwards. *Dismantling the Populist State: The Unfinished Revolution in Latin America and the Caribbean,* 1996.
Cernea, Michael M. *Non-Governmental Organizations and Local Development,* Discussion Paper 40, 1988.
Glaessner, Philip J. et al. *Poverty Alleviation and Social Investment Funds: The Latin*

American Experience. Discussion Paper 216, 1994.

Indonesia, Strategy for a Sustained Reduction in Poverty, Country Study, 1983.

Hannah, Donald P. *Indonesian Experience with Financial Sector Reform,* 1994.

Husain, Ishrat, and Ishac Diwan, eds. *Dealing with the Debt Crisis.* 1989.

Jorgensen, Steen et al. *Easing the Poor through Economic Crisis and Adjustment.* LAC Regional Studies Program, no. 3 (May 1991).

Khandker, Shahidur R. et al. *Grameen Bank, Performance and Sustainability.* Discussion Paper 306, 1995.

Leipziger, Danny, and Vinod Thomas. *The Lessons from East Asia: An Overview of Country Experience,* 1995.

Making Adjustment Work for the Poor: A Framework for Adjustment in Africa, 1990.

Pitt, Mark M., and Shahidur R. Khander, eds. *Household and Intra-household Impacts of the Grameen Bank and Similar Targeted Credit Programs in Bangladesh,* 1996.

Proceedings of the World Bank Annual Conferences on Development Economics, 1994 and 1995.

Poverty Reduction and the World Bank—Progress and Challenges in the 1990s, 1996.

Ribe, Helena et. al. *How Adjustment Programs Can Help the Poor.* Discussion Paper 71, 1990.

Smith, Gordon W., and John T. Cuddington, eds. *International Debt and the Developing Countries.* 1985.

Vanderer Webb, Anna Kathryn et al. *The Participation of Non-Governmental Organizations in Poverty Alleviation.* Discussion Paper 295, 1995.

Versluysen, Eugene L. *Financial Deregulation and the Globalization of Capital Markets.* World Development Report Working Paper, 1988.

Webster, Leila, and Peter Fidler, eds. *The Informal Sector and Microfinance Institutions in West Africa,* 1995.

World Debt Tables 1987–88, 1989–90, 1990–91, 1991–92, 1996.

*World Development Reports 1980 through 1997. Oxford: Oxford University Press.

Yaron, Jacob. *Assessing Development Finance Institutions.* Discussion Paper 174, 1992.

———. *Successful Rural Financial Institutions.* Discussion Paper 150, 1992.

INDEX

Grameen Fisheries Foundation, 87
Grameen Leasing, 87
Grameen Securities and Management, 88
Grameen Telecom, 87
Grameen Trust, 87, 216
Grameen Uddog, 87
Grameenphone, 87
Greece, ancient, 27–28, 30
Group lending, 41, 53, 153–154, 226–227, 229
GTZ (Deutsche Gesellschaft fur Technische Zuzammenarbeit), 87, 142, 162, 177, 178, 231
Guatemala, 133
Guevara, Che, 146
Guinea: African Development Foundation and, 211; baksheesh (bribes) and, 210; Crédit Mutuel de Guinée and, 203, 211, 213; Credit Rural de Guinée and, 211, 213, 217–218; debt crisis in, 210; franc zone and, 198; health care in, 4; illiteracy in, 208; income distribution in, 210; informal economy and, 210–211; kinship and, 201; life expectancy in, 208; microenterprise in, 115; microfinance in, xiii; as mineral rich, 208–210; Opportunities Industrialization Centers International and, 211; overview of, 207–208; polygamy in, 201, 208; poverty in, 208–210; PRIDE and, 59, 202, 203, 211–217; technology in, 197; as West Africa, 204n1
Guinea-Bissau, 204n1
Guzmán, Abimael, 172

Habibie, R. J., 106–107
Haiti, 105
harassment, 33
Harvard Institute for International Development (HIID), 111–112
Hasina, Sheik, 91
Hatch, John, 152
HIID. See Harvard Institute for International Development (HIID)
Hinduism, 89
HIV, 195
Honduras, 133
Hong Kong, 16, 104, 105, 126n7
Hunger. See Nutrition

Hygiene, x
Hyperinflation: in Asia, 64; effects of, 11–12; in Latin America, 11, 135, 171

IADB. See Inter-American Development Bank (IADB)
IDESI, 174
Illiteracy, 70, 195, 208. See also Education
ILO, 34
IMF (International Monetary Fund): Africa and, 197, 198; development lending and, 24n16; Indonesia and, 102, 105–106, 126, 138; intervention in developing countries, 10–11, 21–22; in Latin America generally, 134–135, 136; Mexico's peso crisis of December 1994 and, 17, 138; multinational bailouts and, 134; orthodox policies of, 135; in Peru, 170, 171–172; policy effects of, 23; Stand-by Agreement, 24n20; structural adjustment and, 9; Thailand and, 138
IMF Stand-by Agreement, 9
Impulso Credit Cooperative, 188–189
IMPUSO, 174
Inca Empire, 145
Income distribution and income statistics, 1, 11–13, 132, 137, 169, 170, 171, 210–211
India, 4–5, 20, 65
Indonesia: Asian economic miracle and, 63–64; clove monopoly of, 104, 126n8; as fast-adjusting country, 12; financial crisis of 1998 and, 18, 103–108, 122–123, 125; forest fires in, 99–100; gender gap in, 102; global economy and, 20; Green Revolution of, 111; "guided democracy" of, 102; IMF and, 102; informal sector in, 29, 32, 108–110; lessons from, 125–126; microfinance in, 64; oil industry in, 102–103; overview of, 99–100; poverty in, 107–108, 121; religion in, 101; rubber production and, 115; savings and, 44; as "tiger economy", xi–xii, 126n7; transmigration in, 101–102; unification of, 100–102; unit banking in, 99–126; working conditions in, 32; World Bank and,

90, 101, 115; Roman Catholic
Church, 49, 51, 140, 142, 227
Rippey, Paul, 215, 216
Roman Catholic Church, 49, 51, 140,
142, 227
Rome, ancient, 27–28, 30
ROSCA. *See* Rotating Savings and
Credit Associations (ROSCAs)
Rotating Savings and Credit Associa-
tions (ROSCAs), 46–47, 188, 223
Royal Bank of Canada, 234–235
Rural Credit Program, 94
Rural poverty. *See* Poverty
Russia, 33, 233
Rwanda, 196

Sachs, Jeffrey, 148, 149
Sahel, 39
Sahel Action, 202
Salinas, 17
Samaj, 72
San Salvador, 34–35
Sao Tome and Principe, 204n1
Saudi Arabia, 7
Save the Children, 50, 152, 202
Savings: Banco Solidario (BancoSol)
and, 156–157; forced savings, 44, 85,
94, 164, 213, 218; microfinance and,
43–44, 225; rural savings in Indone-
sia, 118–120; vital role of, 43–44
Savings and loans cooperatives, 52–53
SBFI. *See* Superintendency of Bank and
Financial Institutions (SBFI)
Scandinavia, 52
Schools. *See* Education
Self-employed Women's Association
Cooperative Bank (SEWA Bank), 65
Self-employment: commercial banks'
refusal to lend to microentrepreneurs,
40; costs and benefits of, 31–36;
definition of, 27–28; entry and exit
costs of, 32; hidden costs of, 32–34;
and initiative and ingenuity, 34–35;
labor market and, 36; multi-tiered
nature of informal sector, 30–32; and
organizing the informal sector, 35;
overhead for, 32; poverty and, 2, 27–
37; social geography and, 2; socioeconomic conditions and, 28–31;
structural reforms and, ix. *See also*
Informal sector; Microenterprises;
Microfinance

Semi-formal lenders: description of, 47–
48; nongovernment organizations
(NGOs), 50–51; village banks as, 48–
50
Senegal: absolute poverty in, 195; ACEP
and, 203; Crédit Mutuel and, 203;
FONGS and, 202; franc zone and,
200; health care in, 4; income
distribution in, 210; informal tier in,
31; kinship and, 201; polygamy and,
201; poverty lending in, 58; Rotating
Savings and Credit Associations
(ROSCAs) in, 47; *tontines* and, 201;
as West Africa, 204n1
Sexual apartheid. *See* Gender bias
Sharia (Koranic law), 72
Shining Path, 133, 171, 172, 186, 225
Shore Trust Bank, 234
SIDE. *See* Studies, Innovation, Develop-
ment and Experimentation Program
(SIDE)
Sierra Leone, 195, 204n1, 208, 212
SIMASKOT, 119
SIMPEDES, 119, 124
Singapore, 105, 118, 126n7
Social collateral, 53, 78, 91, 153, 226
Social programs, 51, 59, 183
South Africa, 233
South Asia: informal sector in, 28–29;
microfinance programs in, 39–40,
64–65; poverty in, 4; Self-employed
Women's Association Cooperative
Bank (SEWA Bank) and, 65. *See also*
Asia; specific countries
South Korea: financial crisis in, 18;
investment in Bangladesh, 71. *See
also* Korea
Sri Lanka, 232
Stabilization: macroeconomic stabiliza-
tion, 11–13; negative effects of, 12;
social impact of, 10–15. *See also*
specific areas and countries
Structural adjustment: deregulation and,
13–14; foreign competition and, 14;
poverty and, 6–10; roots of, 7–10;
self-employment and, ix; social debt
of, 135–136; social impact of, 5–10,
10–15; trickle down myth and, 13–
15. *See also* specific areas anb
countries
Studies, Innovation, Development and
Experimentation Program (SIDE), 87

JANE CAVE

ABOUT THE AUTHOR

Eugene Versluysen was born in Antwerp, Belgium. He lives in Washington, D.C. From 1980 to 1996 he was a financial economist at the World Bank, where he worked in treasury operations, and in financial-sector restructuring and agricultural credit in Latin America. He is now a freelance consultant on microfinance. He is one of the authors of the 1988 *World Development Report* and has published research papers on international finance and on developing-country debt restructuring. He is the author of *The Political Economy of International Finance* (St. Martin's Press, 1980). He has a Doctorate of Law from the Free University of Brussels, and an MSc. in Economics from the University of London.

Books of related interest
from Kumarian Press

The New World of Microenterprise Finance: Building Healthy Financial Institutions for the Poor
Editors: Maria Otero and Elisabeth Rhyne

This book presents some of the most innovative work in the area of microenterprise finance. It shows how viable, self-sustaining intermediaries can be created to service low income clientele, promoting private enterprise as a means of empowerment.

US$26.95 / Paper: 1-56549-030-4
US$37.00 / Cloth: 1-56549-031-2

Players and Issues in International Aid
Paula Hoy

Provides an overview of the issues surrounding development and assistance and offers multiple perspectives on the complexities of aid. Written for the student or lay person, Hoy discusses official assistance, both bilateral and multilateral, and nongovernmental assistance.

US$21.95 / Paper: 1-56549-073-8
US$45.00 / Cloth: 1-56549-072-X

Achieving Broad-Based Sustainable Development: Governance, Environment and Growth With Equity
James H. Weaver, Michael T. Rock, Kenneth Kusterer

This comprehensive and multidisciplinary work provides an excellent overview of economic development and the results of growth. The authors provide a model which looks through economic as well as social, political and environmental lenses.

US$26.95 / Paper: 1-56549-058-4
US$38.00 / Cloth: 1-56549-059-2

Creating Alternative Futures: The End of Economics
Hazel Henderson

This book has been the catalyst for many of today's debates on ways to reformulate economic theory to help industrial societies follow healthier paths toward more equitable, ecologically sustainable human development. As a renowned futurist and human ecologist, Henderson's recommendations are as valuable and as timely as ever.

US$17.95 / Paper: 1-56549-060-6

Mediating Sustainability: Growing Policy from the Grassroots
Editors: Jutta Blauert and Simon Zadek

This book explores how mediation between grass-roots and policy formation processes can and does work in practice by focusing on experiences in Latin America in promoting sustainable agriculture and rural development. The contributions to this book draw on the work of researchers, activists, farmers and policy makers through concrete evidence and appraisal.

US$25.95 Paper: 1-56549-081-9
US$55.00 Cloth: 1-56549-082-7

Kumarian Press
14 Oakwood Avenue
West Hartford, CT 06119
Phone: 800-289-2664
Fax: 860-233-6072
E-mail: kpbooks@aol.com
Web: www.kpbooks.com

 Kumarian Press is dedicated to publishing and distributing books and other media that will have a positive social and economic impact on the lives of peoples living in "Third World" conditions no matter where they live.

Kumarian Press publishes books about Global Issues and International Development, such as Peace and Conflict Resolution, Environmental Sustainability, Globalization, Nongovernmental Organizations, and Women and Gender.

To receive a complimentary catalog or to request writer's guidelines call or write:

Kumarian Press, Inc.
14 Oakwood Avenue
West Hartford, CT 06119-2127
U.S.A.

Inquiries: (860) 233-5895
Fax: (860) 233-6072
Order toll free: (800) 289-2664

e-mail: kpbooks@aol.com
Internet: www.kpbooks.com